THE REAL CONTRA WAR

THE REAL CONTRA WAR

Highlander Peasant
Resistance in Nicaragua

Timothy C. Brown

UNIVERSITY OF OKLAHOMA : NORMAN

ALSO BY TIMOTHY C. BROWN

Causes of Continuing Conflict in Nicaragua: A View from the Radical Middle (Stanford, 1995)
(ed.) *When the AK-47s Fall Silent: Revolutionaries, Guerrillas and the Dangers of Peace* (Stanford, 2000)

Published with the assistance of the National Endowment for the Humanities, a federal agency which supports the study of such fields as history, philosophy, literature, and language.

Library of Congress Cataloging-in-Publication Data

Brown, Timothy C. (Timothy Charles), 1938–
    The real Contra War : highlander peasant resistance in Nicaragua / Timothy C. Brown.
        p.   cm.
    Includes bibliographical references (p. –) and index.
    ISBN 0-8061-3252-3 (alk. paper)
    1. Nicaragua—Politics and government—1979–1990.
2. Counterrevolutions—Nicaragua.   3. Militias Populares Anti-Sandinistas (Guerrilla group).   4. Fuerza Democrâtica Nicaragèënse.   5. Counterrevolutionaries—Nicaragua.
6. Peasant uprisings—Nicaragua.   7. Insurgency—Nicaragua.
I. Title.

F1528 .F7785 2001
972.8505'3—dc21

                                                                    00-056368

The paper in this book meets the guidelines for permanence and durability of the Committee on Production Guidelines for Book Longevity of the Council on Library Resources, Inc. ∞

1 2 3 4 5 6 7 8 9 10

For Leda.
And for Enrique and all those who fell, that their
sacrifices will not have been in vain.

CONTENTS

ILLUSTRATIONS

Maps

TABLES

PREFACE

From 1987 through 1990, three group photographs adorned the walls of my office inside a vault within the American embassy in Tegucigalpa, Honduras. During those years I was Senior Liaison Officer, or SLO, to the Nicaraguan Democratic Resistance movement in the region, a career foreign service officer engaged in the decidedly undiplomatic task of overseeing in the field, as best I could, a large covert project the world knew as Nicaragua's Contra War. One photograph was of the Nine Comandantes of the 1979–90 Sandinista Revolution, the second was of the civilian directors of the Nicaraguan Resistance, and the third was of a group of comandantes of the Fuerza Democratica Nicaragüense, or FDN, the main Contra army.[1] The similarities and differences between the groups in the three photographs constantly intrigued me.

The people in the first two photographs, the Sandinistas and the Resistance civilian directors, were all what Nicaraguans call *españoles*, white Europeans, from their country's dominant elite. The comandantes were *indios* from a different world. The comandantes in the third photograph were the field commanders of an armed resistance movement against the Sandinista Revolution that began deep in Nicaragua's mountainous central highlands in mid-1979 and continued throughout the Revolution and afterward. The highlander Resistance was largely responsible for keeping the

Sandinistas from consolidating their hold on Nicaragua. Eleven years later in 1990 the Sandinista Revolution was abruptly ended at the polls by the Nicaraguan people, making it what former Sandinista Front national director Plutarco Hernández calls "history's shortest revolution."[2]

After the defeat of the Revolution in 1990, as part of an internationally brokered peace process, the Contras began to lay down their AK-47s and go home. Also as part of the negotiated process, the Organization of American States (OAS) agreed to assist with their return and reintegration into civil society, and developed a mission plan for doing so that was based on the public wartime image of the Contras: an unrepresentative army created by the American CIA under orders of President Reagan consisting of former Guardia Nacional thugs of the Somoza dictatorship the Sandinistas had overthrown. The OAS established a special office in Nicaragua to perform this mission, the Comisión Internacional de Apoyo y Verificación, known as CIAV/OAS. Several OAS officials who then went to Nicaragua to implement the mission informed me that because they initially believed in the Contra's wartime propaganda image, they were caught entirely off guard by the geography, numbers, and social origins of the real Contras when they emerged from their sanctuaries. The officials were especially impressed by the force of the FDN's combatants, its Comandos as they called themselves, who comprised more than 80 percent of all the Contra combatants. By mid-1991, the OAS office in Nicaragua had registered more than 28,000 Contra combatants, including 22,435 FDN Comandos, three times more than they had expected.[3]

The most significant revelation for American officials at this time was the social profile of the Comandos, Nicaragua's unknown Contras. Ninety-five percent of the FDN Comandos were highlander indio peasants. Seven percent were women. Nine thousand returned to just 17 peasant communities deep within Nicaragua's central mountains. In addition, more than 80,000 entirely unanticipated civilian FDN supporters who had been with them in their sanctuaries also appeared, increasing the number of Contras going home to more than 100,000. And when they arrived at their peasant communities an even larger and less expected group of Contras was there to greet them, the 400,000 to 500,000 peasants of their organized support system who had fed, housed, healed, and hid the Comandos through 11 years of war. The "Contras" turned out not to have been a small, unrepresentative American-created army but merely the armed tip of a popular peasant Resistance movement with more than half a million participants and even more sympathizers.

On the question of why American officials were caught so far off guard, a top OAS peacemaker who was still involved in 1999, Sergio Caramagna, states bluntly: "The very first lesson we learned in Nicaragua was not to bring prejudices and preconceptions to such a process. For indeed we brought our own biases and fears with us. . . . It [the highlander Resistance] was very difficult and far more complex than we had been led to believe by our only previous source of information, wartime propaganda."[4] The Comandos called the wartime propaganda image assigned to them *La Layenda Negra*, the Black Legend of the Contras. And because the OAS, along with the rest of the outside world, had believed it, the peace process initially failed and the unknown Contra War continued in the highlands for six more years, until it finally ended in 1996.[5]

This is the story of the resistance movement at the heart of the Contra War that the outside world never knew and the OAS only began to discover in 1990. I sometimes feel I have been preparing for most of my life to write it. I first came to know Nicaragua during a 1956–59 tour at the American embassy in Managua, and it was then and there I met and married my Costa Rican bride, now my wife of forty-two years, and learned idiomatic Spanish (not entirely unrelated events). From then on more than half my life has been spent dealing with Latin American affairs, including overseas tours in Paraguay, Mexico, El Salvador, and Honduras, and as desk officer for Paraguay/Uruguay and deputy coordinator for Cuba in Washington. During my ten years in the Marine Corps, twenty-seven years as a career foreign service officer (FSO) of the Department of State, and eight years studying Nicaragua, guerrilla wars have been my second major focus, including Marine service related

to insurgencies in Malaysia, Thailand, Burma, Laos, the Philip-
pines, and Indonesia, and two tours during my diplomatic career,
including one as a district senior advisor in Vietnam. Twenty-two
years on Latin America, ten on insurgencies.

When in 1987, and despite the Iran-Contra scandal, President
Reagan asked for and received from Congress $100 million in
covert lethal aid for the Contras, it came with a proviso: the secretary of state was required by Congress to take personal responsibility for the project. In response, two offices were created, one in
the State Department, the other in Central America near the main
Contra sanctuaries. I went to head up the one in Honduras, which
is how I came to spend so much time inside my vault in Tegucigalpa contemplating the three photographs. For the next three-
and-a-half years, from 1987 through 1990, I spent more time with
Contras than with Americans.

In 1992, when my twenty-seven-year diplomatic career ended,
I began working toward a Ph.D, choosing the unknown Contra
War as my dissertation subject. I wanted to do my best to minimize
the impact of my own admitted sympathies for the Comandos on
my findings. So, in addition to leaning heavily on my dissertation
committee and other knowledgeable professionals, I first attempted
to base my study primarily on published materials. But while a
review of the literature and public documents turned up a small
library of books, articles, speeches, transcripts of hearings, and
occasional papers on the Contra War, almost none described the
Comandos themselves. Then the Comandos, and some rocket-
propelled grenades (RPGs), came to my rescue.

Most of the FDN archives had disappeared, but some had
been saved. These were in the hands of their postwar veteran's
organization, the Asociacíon Cívica Resistencia Nicaragüense
(ACRN), whose president and directors I had known well during
the war. In 1992, as I began my dissertation field research, small-
scale fighting continued in Nicaragua's central mountains, and
even the former Comandos in its cities remained at risk. Just a
week before my first research visit to Managua the ACRN offices
were fired on with RPGs and automatic weapons. To protect their

surviving archives the ACRN agreed to my putting them in a safer place and gave me exclusive permission to use them in my research. They turned out to contain approximately 265,000 pages of original documents, some dating back to the very beginnings of the Resistance in 1979–81. From them I compiled data on the Comandos' social origins, birth places, dates of entry, and family backgrounds. I further obtained more than thirty thousand pages of formerly classified U.S. government documents, most originated by the Department of State, the Agency for International Development (AID), or the Central Intelligence Agency (CIA), as well as an eight-volume Costa Rican investigative archive concerning the war. I also reviewed a number of public archival collections. I was especially happy to receive among the Freedom of Information and Privacy Act (FOIA) releases many of my own reports from the SLO office in Tegucigalpa. With FOIA approval, I could now use information of which I had been aware but could not otherwise include because of its special SECRET EXDIS CONTRA classification. And yet even then the voices of the Comandos themselves remained silent. Once again they, as well as some officers of CIAV/OAS (the OAS office in Nicaragua still dealing with the reinsertion problem), came to my rescue.

From the ACRN archives I was able to develop a list of Comandos who had entered the movement during its first three years, between 1979 and 1981, and the ACRN set about locating them for me. Many had been among the 8,500 to 10,500 Comandos who had been killed during the war, many others feared for their lives, others lived deep in the mountains where fighting continued. But I was able to find more than forty who agreed to provide me with structured oral histories. Because some Comandos lived in zones still at war, CIAV/OAS officers who knew the zones accompanied me when I conducted several of the histories deep in the mountains. All were videotaped. Each explores the subject's identity, motives for becoming a Comando, combat history, opinions of other actors, and conclusions about the war. Thirty-three are listed in the bibliography by name. For the safety of the subjects, ten are not. These oral histories became a prime source of both

comparative data and individual comments. I also drew up a list
of other people with knowledge pertinent to this study, which
led to several more oral histories and more than a hundred other
less structured interviews. Again, for security, privacy, and legal
reasons, only some are listed in the bibliography.

Two features of this book may warrant explanation. One is my
treatment of noms de guerre, or pseudonyms. Revolutionaries,
guerrillas, and others engaged in clandestine enterprises usually
use pseudonyms to disguise their true identities. They also change
them occasionally. When known and when it is safe to disclose
them, real names and principal pseudonyms are both given when
first mentioned in the text. Thereafter only principal pseudonyms
are used. In some cases, only pseudonyms were available.
Pseudonyms are put in quotation marks at first mention only. The
other feature is the book's organization. For readers unfamiliar
with the subject, it is useful to learn something about Nicaragua in
general and the historical, geographic, and social contexts within
which the unknown Contra War was fought. But the main focus
of the book is the Comandos and the peasantry they represented.
If four or five chapters on context were to come first, their story
would be pushed back more than a hundred pages. So I chose to
start with the war, put short synopses of the Comandos' history,
geography, and social roles in my introduction, and leave more
detailed discussion of these topics for chapters 11–15. Thus, following a short introductory chapter, chapters 2–5 discuss the earliest
armed highland peasant Resistance groups, the Militias Populares
Anti-Sandinistas, or MILPAS, who independently took up arms in
1979–81. Chapters 6–8 then introduce exile paramilitary groups
that organized outside Nicaragua from the ranks of former soldiers
of the Somoza Guardia Nacional, the arrival on the scene of the
CIA and its Argentine surrogates in 1980–82, and the uneasy
alliance between the MILPAS and Guardia exiles that became the
FDN. Chapters 9–10 then describe the formal organization of the
Resistance movement and the key roles women played in it.
Chapters 11–13 provide discussions of the conflict's historical,
geographic and social contexts. The final chapters, 14–17, place the

war within a larger theoretical framework and discuss how it ended, its aftermath, and my conclusions. This, then, is the story of the unknown Contra War, told for the first time from the perspective of the Contras themselves.

ACKNOWLEDGMENTS

Three different groups joined with me to produce this study: former Comandos of the Nicaraguan Democratic Resistance intent on telling their stories, academics dedicated to making sure that it met their high professional standards, and my family. Without all three I would not have been able to write the book. Accounts of the Contras written by outsiders abound. Most are hostile, a handful sympathetic. My listing of these materials ran more than 135 pages, not including tens of thousands of declassified U.S. government documents. But I quickly discovered that these sources could, at best, provide only background. Only the Comandos themselves could tell their own story. My very special thanks go to those who did, especially Oscar Sobalvarro, "Comandante Rubén," who gave me invaluable and exclusive access to surviving archives, and Abel Cespedes, "Comandante Cyro," who helped me find and interview more than a hundred former Comandos in Nicaragua and Honduras. They and many others gave me hours, even days and weeks of their time. Because the war itself was still under way as I was doing the research, many risked their lives to help me. Even today, in the year 2000, many cannot be named without jeopardizing their safety. But without them I could not have completed this study. To them, my deepest admiration and thanks.

Several academic umpires and referees also provided invaluable support and advice, both professional and personal. Jose Garcia of New Mexico State University's Center for Latin American Studies (CLAS/NMSU) holds center stage, and at his side historian Ray Sadler. Other academics and friends who also deserve my warmest thanks are Walter Stephan and Larry Gregory of NMSU's psychology department, economists Jim Nordyke and Mike Ellis, and Lyn Ames of its Graduate School. To this I must add special thanks to the Hoover Institution of Stanford University, which made possible much of my research. Particular thanks go to its Deputy Director, Charles Palm, and resident scholar, Bill Ratliff, who reviewed much of this study as I was writing it.

Last—but first in my life—I must thank (and somehow make amends to!) my wife of forty-two years, Leda, my four children, and my seven grandchildren for their unstinting support through the long years that it took to complete this book. I thank them especially for putting up with my many moods, extended travels, and the uncounted "present yet absent hours" I spent in what my grandchildren labeled Abuelo Tata's "writing hole." Without their love I would never have finished. With it, I could not fail.

All the errors and mistakes in this book are purely my own, although without all those I have thanked perhaps they would never have been made public.

CHRONOLOGY

PRE-COLUMBIAN AND SPANISH COLONIAL PERIOD

2000 B.C.	Chibcha migration from South America begins.
900–1523 A.D.	Nahua conquest and Chibcha-Nahua conflicts.
1523–26	Spanish Conquest.
1523–1821	Spanish Colonial Period and Indian Wars.

PRE-SOMOZA PATRIARCHAL PERIOD, 1821–1936

1821	Independence from Spain.
1821–1950	Patriarchy-Indian Wars.

SOMOZA DYNASTY, 1936–1979

1936–56	Anastacio Somoza Garcia holds power. Assassinated in 1956.
1956–67	Luis Somoza Debayle holds power. Dies of heart attack.

1967–79   Anastacio Somoza Debayle holds power. Killed in
           ambush in Paraguay. Sandinistas claim credit.

ANTI-SOMOZA WAR PERIOD, 1958–JULY 1979

1944–58   Multiple anti-Somoza efforts by various groups.
1959–60   Cuban Revolution. Various Nicaraguan revolution-
           aries vie for Castro's support. Sandinistas succeed.
   1961   FSLN named in Havana. Its guerrilla phase begins.
   1963   Noel Guerrero, original Sandinista leader, causes
           Bocaycito disaster.
1963–77   Repeated FSLN guerrilla efforts, clandestine orga-
           nizing phase.
   1976   Carlos Fonseca Amador, FSLN leader, killed at
           Zinica in ambush.
1977–79   U.S. turns against Somoza, FSLN/Patriarchy
           united front emerges. Arms shipments to FSLN
           from Cuba via Panama begin.
1978–79   Massive arms flow from Cuba. U.S. acquiesces.
           FSLN enters large combat unit phase. Castro
           appoints Nine Comandantes in Havana.
May 1979   Preparations for Contra War by Sandinista guer-
           rillas begin inside Sandinista ranks.
July 1979 Somoza flees, Sandinistas take power. Socialist
           Revolution begins.

CONTRA WAR PERIOD, MAY 1979–1996

May 1979   First MILPAS begin to organize.
Aug. 1979 First armed clash of Contra War near El Chipote.
1979–82   Unknown MILPAS war inside Nicaragua. Guardia
           exiles still outside.
   1980   First U.S./Argentine involvement in covert aid to
           Guardia exiles.

1982   U.S./Argentine cover aid unites Legión 15 de
       Septiembre and MILPAS; combined unit becomes
       Fuerza Democratica Nicaragüense (Contras).

1988   Final cutoff of U.S. lethal aid to Contras.

1990   Coalition wins national election. Sandinista Revo-
       lution ends.

1990–96 Conservative-Sandinista co-government. Re-Contra
       silent war.

1996   Liberals win national election. Contras legitimized.

THE REAL CONTRA WAR

CHAPTER ONE

INTRODUCTION

"A Whole Bunch of Really Pissed-off Peasants"

Iran-Contra, Oliver North, Congressional hearings, campus demonstrations, Contras as archvillains in movies and novels: Nicaragua's Contra War was at the center of a political fire storm second perhaps only to Vietnam in the passions it generated. At the height of the controversy, the Contras were regularly maligned as being no more than a mercenary gang of former Guardia soldier thugs of Nicaragua's odious Somoza dictatorship, hired by the Central Intelligence Agency (CIA) under orders from reactionary American President Ronald Reagan to fight the popular Sandinista Revolution. In reality, more than 80 percent of the Contras were highland peasants and the remainder were tribal Indians or Black Creoles trying to defend themselves against what they saw as an attempt to destroy their ways of life.

In public, President Ronald Reagan called the Contras Freedom Fighters, but in private, even Reagan and his insiders apparently shared the darker vision of the Contras. Even though the CIA spent about $250 million for covert military aid to the Contras and worked with them daily for almost a decade, it now seems evident that they never really understood who the Contras were. As a result, President Reagan, CIA Director William Casey, and the U.S. Congress also got it wrong. The media and academics did no better.

Who were the "real Contras"? To begin with, they called themselves Comandos, not Contras, which was a propaganda pejorative coined by their enemies. The largest "Contra army"—there were five—was led primarily by former anti-Somoza Sandinistas, not former Somoza Guardia. Their war began in 1979 as a peasant uprising, not in 1982 as a Reagan initiative. They initially organized themselves under the name of MILPAS, for Militias Populares Anti-Sandinistas. For the first three years they fought with no outside help or interference. It was not until 1982, when the United States sponsored an alliance between the MILPAS and exiled former Somoza Guardia, that armed opposition to the Sandinistas came to world attention. The alliance was called the Fuerza Democratica Nicaragüense, or FDN. It was not a Guardia-only movement, but an uneasy alliance between a large MILPAS army of peasants and a small Guardia staff.

Two recent books by insiders demonstrate that even the best informed and most sympathetic Reaganites still do not understand the Contras. One of these books, *A Twilight Struggle,* is by Robert Kagan, a Reagan point man in the State Department on the Contras, speech writer for Secretary of State George Schultz, and deputy to the assistant secretary for Latin America. Kagan says that as part of his job he "helped carry out U.S. policy towards Nicaragua and, in particular, American support for the armed Nicaraguan Resistance [the Contras]." According to Kagan, the earliest Nicaraguans to take up arms against the Sandinista Revolution were a small number of former Somoza Guardia: "bands of marauders, fighting their own private wars in the northern countryside of Nicaragua . . . foraging and cattle rustling, fighting only to stay alive and, on occasion, for revenge." He states further that "as late as February of 1981, clashes between opponents and the Sandinistas had taken violent form only on the Atlantic Coast."[1]

A Spy for All Seasons, by Duane Clarridge, dates the beginnings of the Contra War even later, to November 1981. Clarridge, the CIA's deputy director for operations (DDO) for Latin America from 1981 through 1984, states categorically that before then the only armed men opposing the Sandinistas were "five hundred rag-tag troopers along the Nicaragua-Honduras border . . . remnants of the Nicaraguan National Guard" who were receiving some help from Argentina. As required by law, and drawing on this CIA analysis, Reagan's CIA director William Casey in much the same words formally informed the Senate Select Committee on Intelligence (SSCI) that the CIA planned to initiate a covert project to organize these rag-tag troopers into a "500-man force as a carefully limited group whose target was the Cuban support structure in Nicaragua." Clarridge quotes President Reagan as later calling the Contra army that Casey had then produced the CIA's "vandals."[2]

Kagan, Clarridge, Casey, and Reagan had the very best information available to the U.S. government, and their comments presumably reflect what they thought were the facts. Nevertheless, they were wrong. The portrait they painted coincided much more closely with the Left's wartime propaganda image of the Contras than with the truth. This darker image nonetheless became the conventional wisdom on the Contras, even according to Reaganites.

No one ever asked if the Black Legend was true; perhaps everyone from Reagan and his staff to the most learned academics was firmly convinced that they already knew the answer. Had everyone been less certain, someone just might have asked the Contra Comandos themselves who they were, and when, where, and why they had started fighting. Had they done so, they would have heard answers from the fighters that differed vastly from the myths.[3] Perhaps then the image of the Contras would have changed from one of either devils or angels, to one more human, of simple peasant farmers trying to protect their tiny farms and families from outsiders they saw as trying to "revolutionize" them against their will. But no one asked, so the war and the accompanying political vitriol boiled for more than a decade, with both groups in equal ignorance.

This study was undertaken to try to fill the void left by failure during the Contra War to ask the right questions of the right people. Albeit belatedly, I tried to answer four questions: Who were the first Comandos? Where were they from? When did their war start? Why did they rebel? At first the task seemed straightforward: contact as many veteran Comandos as possible, especially founding members, and ask them these questions. Then, as a cross-check, find non-Comandos with personal knowledge of the period and ask them the same questions. Finally, review their answers against existing records,[4] look at the limited literature on the earliest Contra period, consider other contemporary records,[5] derive some conclusions from this evidence, and write up the results. This approach, seemingly simple and direct, proved to be neither.

One of the first Comandos with whom I spoke was a legendary guerrilla fighter, a very old man whom I knew only by his nom de guerre, "Abuelito," Great-Grandfather. A peasant from Nicaragua's mountainous north, Abuelito as a young man had joined Gen. Augusto César Sandino's rebel army to fight against the U.S. Marines. Years later he again joined the Sandinistas to fight Somoza. In 1979, he joined the Contras. Abuelito's answer would have startled Ronald Reagan and his point men:

> Nosotros? Guardia? No'ombre! No somos mas que un aterro de campesinos bien encachimba'os! (Us, Guardia? No way! All we are is a whole bunch of *really* pissed-off peasants!)[6]

General Sandino's last Segovian highland campaigns began in 1918 and ended in 1933. By 1979 his surviving soldiers were getting on in age, so few joined the Contras. But the younger peasants who did join them were the children and grandchildren of the same peasantry that had made up almost all of Sandino's army. Without the support of these people—the forefathers of the Contras—Sandino would probably have been little more than a minor historical footnote in an obscure episode. With them he had an army and a popular support base.

In addition to Abuelito, I located one other former Sandino soldier and Contra who turned out to have been exceptionally close to Sandino himself. This was his former chief bodyguard, Alejandro Pérez Bustamante. "Don Alejandro," as he is affectionately called, was nearing his eighties when the MILPAS war started and could not become a Comando, but he did head up a local *correo* network. Such networks, along with clandestine support committees, formed the massive support base that from the beginning sustained the MILPAS in the field. The correos were their extended eyes and ears and link to the clandestine committees in local peasant communities. They collected food, supplies, and other help from sympathizers and carried these items to the MILPAS. (Correos are discussed in greater detail in chapter 9).

A number of peasant comarca leaders headed up such networks. Don Alejandro, who became an active Contra supporter after he was arrested and mistreated and after his wife was killed by the Sandinistas in 1980, was one of them. From 1918 to 1923, during Sandino's first Segovian campaign, he was personal bodyguard to Sandino, after whom the Sandinista Front was named. During my oral history interview with him, Don Alejandro insisted that "if Sandino had been alive during the Sandinista's Revolution, he would have been a Contra."[7]

By the time Casey's five hundred "rag-tag" former Guardia troopers finally arrived on the field of battle in mid-1982,[8] Abuelito and thousands of peasants like him had been at war for three years, and dozens, if not hundreds, had died.[9] From 1982 on, former Guardia, later defectors from Sandinista ranks, tribal Indians, and south Atlantic coast peasants did join the rebellion, and all played important roles. But because these later participants were far more accessible, visible and articulate than the peasants, their presence masked, even from the CIA, and certainly from Kagan and Clarridge, the underlying reality of who the "Contras" really were. Neither Reagan nor the rest of the world ever learned at the time that from their first stirring in May of 1979, until they laid down their arms in 1990, more than 96 percent of the troopers and combat leaders of Nicaragua's largest Contra army were simple mountain people: illiterate, unsophisticated, unworldly, perhaps, but also free, extremely attached to their land, homes, and families, and fiercely independent. Abuelito, not Casey, the director of the world's most powerful intelligence organization, best knew who the real "Contras" were. He also best understood that theirs was not the externally generated war that the world, Reagan, academia, and even Casey's CIA thought it had organized. They were just *"really* pissed-off peasants."

Yet even Abuelito understated the case. As this study progressed, it became clear that the Comandos had merely been the armed tip of a much larger highland peasant movement they called La Resistencia. The highland war of 1979–90 was not *only* a local conflict fought by angry peasants. It was the armed manifestation of a much larger regional rebellion by a previously marginalized, faceless, yet historically, geographically, and ethnically homogeneous populace that comprised between 37 and 52 percent of Nicaragua's entire population. This hidden reality became clear only after the geographically highly concentrated nature of the war became apparent. Armed resistance efforts from the beginning were found to be centered in Nicaragua's Segovian highlands, as were the birthplaces and historical origins of the Comandos. Also highly concentrated were the size, form, and peasant origins of the popular movement that fed, clothed, and housed them, guided their units, supported their recruiting efforts and political activities, and kept them exceedingly well informed on their enemy's movements.

The discovery that the Comandos had merely represented a much larger populace in rebellion caused me to look in much greater depth at the Segovian highlanders. They proved to be a homogeneous group with a shared history, pre-Columbian roots, and a centuries-old tradition of violent resistance to outsider challenges that sets them apart from other Nicaraguans. In fact, their history can be traced back more than four thousand years.

Before the Spanish arrived, Nicaragua was home to two very different Indian peoples. The Pacific lowlands, heavily populated by sixteenth-century standards, were settled by Nahua-Mexica Indians who were the descendants of Nicaragua's first conquistadores, an Indian group that, beginning in the ninth century, had descended from the area of present-day Puebla, Mexico, into Central America and conquered the Pacific littoral all the way from Soconusco in present-day Chiapas, Mexico, to the Gulf of Nicoya in Costa Rica. Nahua societies were hierarchically organized with well-defined and rigid class structures. Their main settlements, with names like Managua, Imabíte, and Jalteba, took the form of city-states. The Nicaraguan Nahua were a distant but integral part of the Aztec empire, to which they were linked historically, culturally, and commercially. Their most valuable export was cacao beans, which served the empire as both a medium of exchange and a sumptuary item to be consumed only by members of the nobility. These were carried to the empire's capital, Tenochtitlan, present-day Mexico City, on the backs of human porters, or tamemes.

Nicaragua's central highlands were also heavily populated but by a very different people. The highlanders were Chibchan Indians of South American origin who had been slowly drifting into Central America since before 2000 B.C. Unlike the Nahuas, they did not live in cities or even villages but rather on individual farms. The Chibchas also had no central government and apparently liked it that way, coming together under temporary war leaders only when threatened from the outside. Both Nicaragua's Nahuas and its Chibchas were heavily populated by sixteenth-century standards. Managua, for example, appears to have been larger than most contemporary Spanish cities and second in the New World in size only to Tenochtitlan. Given their levels of technology, the size of both groups was near the optimal carrying capacity of the lands they occupied. The Nahuas and Chibchas were also constantly at war against one another, the Nahuas pushing outwardly into Chibchan territory, the Chibchas reacting.

The Spanish arrived in Nicaragua in 1523 and by 1526 had conquered the Pacific lowland Nahua. Within two decades, slaving and other forms of exploitation had reduced the Nahua population from more than one million to about 27,000. Those who survived became the base Indian population of Spanish colonial Nicaragua. In the highlands things went very differently. The Spanish did not immediately conquer the highlands and as a result most of the region's 350,000 to 400,000 Chibchas survived. For the next three centuries, until Nicaragua's independence in 1821, Spanish colonial Nicaragua was divided between the Spanish Pacific and Indian highlands, with Indian wars occurring regularly in the highlands. Over the centuries and under constant pressure from the outside, the highland Chibchas did slowly convert to Catholicism and lose their native language. But even as they were being transmuted under pressure from Indians into *indios*, the highlanders continued to violently resist Pacific lowlander domination.

The last widely recognized highland Indian war took place in Matagalpa in the 1920s. But if the geography and history of the region, and the Comandos' self-identification as indios (discussed further in chapters 11–13) are taken into account, Nicaragua's unknown Contra war should probably be added to the list. Map 1 and table 1 illustrate my reasons for reaching this rather unexpected conclusion. Map 1 shows the following: (1) where Indian wars took place from 1526 through the 1950s, (2) where the first Contra groups emerged in 1979–81, and (3) the locations of the seventeen peasant communities to which 8,977 FDN Comandos returned in 1990–91. Table 1 lists the number of Comandos who returned to each of them. Maps 2–9, and tables 3–7, which appear in later chapters, further reinforce these findings. The Sandinistas and their sympathizers may have viewed the Comandos as useful counterrevolutionary foils, the Americans may have seen them as convenient surrogates in a late cold-war skirmish, and civilian politicians may have thought of them as useful stepping stones to power. But the peasants of Nicaragua's highlands saw them as their shield against yet one more in a thousand-year-old string of attempts at subjugation by outsiders. The highlander peasants were almost entirely illiterate and had long since been robbed of their own history. But to them the conflict the outside world called the Contra War was a struggle to defend their embattled identity. Although they did not speak in such modern academic terms, the responses of the Comandos to my interview questions made the same point in even more poignant terms.

TABLE 1

FDN Returnees: Seventeen Top Locales

Rio Blanco	1,009
Waslala	976
Jinotega	889
Wiwilí	871
Santo Domingo	640
Matagalpa	589
San José de Bocay	568
El Cuá Bocay	504
Quilalí	463
Santa María de Pantasma	445
San Juan del Rio Coco	336
Yalí	259
Chontales	452
Juigalpa	246
Villa Sandino	155
Rancho Grande	136
Santo Tomas	119
TOTAL	8,977

SOURCE: CIAV/OAS, *Numero de Desmovilizados por Lugar de Nacimiento,* Managua, Computer run, 1993.

The peasant Comandos made it clear to me that they saw themselves and the peasantry from which they had emerged as different from others in their country. They also saw themselves in "us-versus-them" terms and their war as not only a battle against a revolution, but also a peasant fight against urban Pacific lowland *españoles,* or Spaniards. Of forty-four Comandos formally interviewed, all but one identified himself or herself as *indio.* This strongly suggests that the highland war had an ethnic dimension and that the Comandos had consciously placed themselves on the Indian side of Nicaragua's principal ethnic divide.[10]

Map 1. Comparison of the Nicaraguan highlands (Segovian and adjacent), the Pre-Columbian division of highland Chichban Indians to the east and Pacific coastal Nahua-Mexica to the west, the 1523–1920s Indian wars, and the 17 locales to which almost 9,000 Comandos returned most frequently in 1990–91.

CHAPTER TWO

THE MILPAS WAR, 1979–1982

When the last Somoza, Anastacio Somoza Debayle, fled Nicaragua in July 1979, the most radical of the leaders of the Frente Sandinista de Liberación Nacional, Sandinista National Liberation Front or FSLN, who had led the effort to overthrow him, took power almost immediately and launched a socialist revolution. Even before they began, however, an incipient revolt against their plans to revolutionize Nicaragua had begun to brew among guerrillas of a Sandinista unit made up of Segovian highlander peasants, known as the Militias Populares Anti-Somocistas (People's Anti-Somoza Militias, or MILPA).[1] The MILPA battalion was part of the Sandinistas' northern Carlos Fonseca Front.[2] (Why they rebeled so early is explained in Chapter 3.)

Only days after they took power, the radical Sandinistas began sending political cadre from Nicaragua's Pacific cities into the highlands to implement their new programs. Almost as quickly, the highland peasants began to resist. It is not clear exactly when or how they first linked up with the already rebellious anti-Somoza Milpistas, but within weeks peasants in several rural highland comarcas[3] joined efforts with Milpistas to organize an armed resistance movement. According to involved Milpista Comandos, such cooperation resulted in the earliest comarca-based small guerrilla groups in August 1979.[4] Each was autonomous and, in the beginning, usually unaware of the existence of other groups. Even so, and despite their lack of central organization, several of them chose to call themselves the Militias Populares Anti-Sandinistas (People's Anti-Sandinista Militias, or MILPAS) deliberately, in order to indicate continuity with their earlier anti-Somoza incarnation. MILPAS combatants were still called Milpistas.

The first serious battle of the Contra War was fought on the slopes of El Chipote in November 1979. Seventy peasant rebels attacked a Sandinista military camp northeast of the small Nicaraguan mountain town of Quilalí. On the slopes of this legendary mountain, deep in the Segovian highlands, Augusto César Sandino had stationed his main camp during his 1927–32 fight against the United States Marines.[5] Five of the attackers were killed, and a sixth wounded.[6] (Two who died went by the noms de guerre of "Chacal" and "Rudino." The names of the other three have been lost to history.[7] A sixth peasant, "Cáliz," was wounded. The story of the battle was recounted to me by Cáliz's half-brother, "Pryor.")[8] By then a number of MILPAS groups, each with from forty to eighty Milpista guerrillas, had become active in comarcas on Nicaragua's agricultural frontier. This lay along the Coco River and its tributaries, the Murra, Pantasma, Chachagua, and El Cuá Rivers. The groups were established, in particular, near the riverside towns of Quilalí, Wiwilí, El Cuá, Las Praderas, and nearby villages. A few were also active along the Bocay River.[9] All these places are in the heart of Nicaragua's highlands (see map 2), and are primarily populated by peasants.

One of these guerrilla groups was led by "Gerónimo,"[10] a peasant from a comarca in Jinotega near Santa María de Pantasma just east of Las Praderas. Gerónimo was a veteran guerrilla who had fought for several years as an anti-Somoza Milpista under legendary Sandinista MILPA commander Germán Pomares Ordoñez, "El Danto."[11] By November 1979, Gerónimo's new MILPAS group had about seventy combatants, thirty-five of whom were working in teams of two or three near Jinotegan areas known as Planos de Bilán, La Pita del Carmen, Aguas Calientes, and La Zompopera.[12]

Map 2. The earliest MILPAS operating areas in 1979, from El Chipote south through Quilalí to Las Praderas.

The teams cooperated with the peasants, organizing correos and clandestine comarca committees in anticipation of the coming war.[13]

Pryor's half-brother Cáliz was with one of the teams and told the following story. A number of peasant comarca *caciques* (community chiefs)[14] complained to Gerónimo's teams about a new Sandinista cooperative farm, a form of collective, being developed nearby on the slopes of El Chipote.[15] The Sandinistas were creating

the cooperative out of ten small *fincas* (farms) that they had seized
and were turning it into what the campesinos called an "aldea
armada," or armed hamlet. The campesinos feared that if the
Sandinistas succeeded, they would be encouraged to seize their
fincas as well, in order to create even more cooperatives. Because
the Milpistas also wanted to stop the Sandinistas from establishing themselves in the rural highland comarcas and to push them
out of the mountains, they were receptive to the complaints.
Gerónimo and his Milpistas agreed to attack a military base being
built to protect the new cooperative, which was garrisoned by
about thirty-five soldiers of the Sandinista's Nuevo Ejército (New
Army)[16] and by some 160 militiamen.[17]

From a military perspective, Gerónimo's attack did not go especially well. Five of his Milpistas were killed; his group captured
only one weapon; and they did not inflict any known casualties on
the Sandinistas. But from a political point of view it was a success,
and that was more important; the peasants were pleased and their
support for Gerónimo's group increased,[18] and the Sandinistas'
efforts to establish a viable cooperative on the slopes of El Chipote
were seriously delayed. The attack also advanced the Milpistas'
objective of stopping the consolidation of the Sandinista Revolution in the highlands.

Another former anti-Somoza Milpista, "Tigre," described two
other early MILPAS clashes with Sandinista military units.[19] In
early January 1980, he and three comrades were ambushed near a
settlement known as La Morena near La Chachagua. Like Cáliz,
they had been working as a team in nearby comarcas and helping
organize systems of correos and clandestine comarca committees.
The campesinos had given them a few hunting weapons that they
hoped to use to capture superior weapons from Sandinistas. But
before they could do so, they themselves were attacked by a Sandinista patrol one night, as they slept in the hut of some friendly
campesinos. In the ensuing skirmish one of the Milpistas, "Olla
Fuerte," was killed,[20] and a Sandinista soldier was wounded. Tigre
escaped by dressing in women's clothes and running through the
darkness into a nearby woods while screaming in a falsetto voice

that he hoped sounded female.[21] He was also involved in a skirmish in October 1980, near San Antonio La Cuchilla, while with another small group of Milpistas that included "El Norteño," "Gato Brunés," "Silvio Picado," "Pocoyo," and "Jimmy Leo."[22] The group was ambushed by a Sandinista patrol while going to pick up some hunting weapons from sympathetic campesinos. Another Milpista, "La Sorpresa," was killed.

Several Comandos said that during 1979 and 1980, the Sandinistas captured and executed a number of Milpistas, including a member of the extensive Galeano clan, in December 1979.[23] Another, Richard Zelaya, suffered the same fate in January 1980. A half-brother of Zelaya, Denis Meza, was reported missing in action and presumably executed that June.[24] Another well-known Milpista, the first "Rigoberto," is said to have been executed by the Sandinistas after he was captured in a clash in September 1980.[25] Another prominent fellow Milpista, Tirso Moreno, promptly adopted his nom de guerre in tribute.[26]

In addition to those killed in battle or executed after they were captured, a few Milpistas were killed or executed by their own companions. Tigre recalled that one known as "Caturra" died in late 1980, victim of a Milpista ambush. A peasant from Wiwilí, Caturra had been with El Danto during the war against Somoza. In 1979, he had a serious falling out with the leader of his MILPAS group, Irene Calderón,[27] and he was killed shortly thereafter in an ambush led by Calderón, while bringing back ammunition that Calderón had sent him to buy in Honduras. Tigre was not sure whether Caturra's death was deliberate or a matter of "friendly fire."[28]

Oscar Sobalvarro, whose original nom de guerre was "Culebra," was one of the earliest Milpista leaders, eventually rising up the ranks to become the FDN's last overall commander. He later changed his nom de guerre to "Rubén," which is how I knew him. During one of numerous conversations we held, he described the circumstances of another case in more certain terms than had Tigre regarding the case of Caturra. A former Guardia, Antonio Aráuz, joined Rubén's group in late 1980 but could not be controlled.[29] Rubén and his peasant Milpistas were fully aware that they were there as representatives of the comarcas, not as individuals. They knew that they were dependent on the campesinos for their survival and success as guerrillas, and many compesinos were, in any case, personal friends or family members. They were therefore extremely sensitive to local feelings and sensitivities. Aráuz was not so restrained and was reprimanded several times for misconduct but would not stop behaving unacceptably. His final infraction occurred only a few weeks after he joined the group, when he raped a schoolteacher. Rubén's group, appalled, held a field trial, found Aráuz guilty of rape, shot him, and buried his body in the mountains.[30]

Rubén commented that during this early period, when possible, the Milpistas preferred to avoid combat and even tried to avoid inflicting unnecessary casualties on the Sandinistas. This was difficult during skirmishes, but possible in casual contacts. In June 1980, his group captured two State Security soldiers near the settlement of Agua Fresca. They turned out to be young students from the Pacific Coast who were going to visit some girls in the nearby hills. Much to the troopers' surprise, Rubén's group took their weapons but did them no harm. Instead, after subjecting them to a harangue, they sent the soldiers back to their base with a message. "We're not Guardia, just very angry peasants. If you leave us alone, we won't fight you."[31]

At first, although sometimes aware of other groups, each MILPAS group operated more or less autonomously within its defined territory and in cooperation only with its home comarcas. But as the rebellion spread, and the number of MILPAS groups multiplied and became more active, a few began to coordinate their efforts. At this point, the MILPAS groups stopped avoiding direct military action. This became clear even to outside observers when, on 23 July 1980, several MILPAS groups emerged from their mountain sanctuaries and, in a planned joint attack, captured Quilalí.

Cuba's Fidel Castro, in Nicaragua at the time to help celebrate the first anniversary of the Sandinista revolution, was a mere fifty miles away, giving a speech in another mountain town, Estelí.[32]

Perhaps in part because of Castro's proximity, Sandinista State Security chief Lenin Cerna rushed to the region, and the army launched helicopter patrols and infantry sweeps in search of the Milpista attackers.[33] The Sandinistas also acted against one of their own units that had mutinied and refused to fight when the Milpistas attacked. They arrested the police commander of Quilalí, who had abandoned his post under fire and led away most of the town's best-armed troops, leaving the city defenseless. Eighteen other Sandinistas were placed under investigation.[34] Apparently to blunt rampant rumors, the Sandinistas also found it necessary to make a nationwide announcement that they still controlled northern Nicaragua.[35] The Sandinistas blamed the Quilalí attack and other guerrilla actions then taking place in the highlands on former Guardia, although no Guardia had yet taken part in the combat. Following that one newsworthy episode, the outside world's attention turned quickly to other events. Inside Nicaragua, however, the reality of serious armed highlander resistance to the Sandinista Revolution had been driven home.

CHAPTER THREE

DIMAS, FATHER OF THE CONTRAS

The MILPAS attack on Quilalí had been planned and led by the former deputy commander of the anti-Somoza MILPA, Pedro Joaquín González Chamorro, whose nom de guerre was "Dimas." Although Dimas had fought against the Somoza dictatorship from 1961 to 1979, for almost eighteen years, by July 1980 he had been at war against his former Sandinista comrades-in-arms for over a year. Dimas told those who asked that he was fighting because he was convinced that the Sandinistas, having first betrayed his old commander El Danto, were also betraying Nicaragua.[1]

González kept Dimas as his nom de guerre when he rebelled. Dimas was killed, almost certainly under the orders of his erstwhile Sandinista comrades-in-arms, in August 1981. I pieced together his story from several sources, including from interviews with people who had been close to him during both his wars. Among those I interviewed were two senior Sandinista commanders of the initial 1959–79 phase of the Sandinista revolution, Plutarco Hernández and Alejandro Martínez, who had both also known well Dimas's commanding officer, Germán Pomares Ordoñez, "El Danto" (discussed below). I was also able to locate Dimas's two wives. His lawful wife was not willing to be interviewed, but his common-law wife Marina, whom I found in Quilalí, was especially cooperative. She even provided two photographs of Dimas that are included in the photo gallery. Several Comandos who had served under him during both conflicts also provided me with information. I reconstructed his story from their comments and a meager handful of published accounts.

Born in the town of Sébaco but raised in Quilalí, Dimas was the most prominent highlander among the Sandinistas' guerrilla field commanders during the war against Somoza.[2] He had joined the struggle against the dynasty in 1961. From 1972 through 1979 he commanded a guerrilla column and was serving as principal deputy to the MILPA batallion's well-known guerrilla commander, Sandinista leader Germán Pomares, El Danto, when El Danto was killed by a bullet fired from within the ranks of his own unit during an attack on Jinotega in May 1979.[3]

EL DANTO

El Danto himself was a fascinating, near-legendary figure. Born and raised in the Pacific lowland Department of Chinandega, he was a farmworker with little formal education.[4] Nevertheless, he demonstrated early on the leadership qualities that were to make him an admired and feared guerrilla leader by helping found, in opposition to the Somoza government, a branch of the Juventud Conservadora (Conservative Youth) movement on the Hacienda El Puertón where he worked. Although he had been an active opponent of the Somoza regime for several years, El Danto's first attempt to become an armed anti-Somoza fighter came in April 1958 when he and four companions went to Managua, intent on joining a group then planning to go to Costa Rica to prepare an armed attack against the Somozas. On that occasion he and his companions were rejected because of their peasant origins. In retrospect, their rejection on these grounds proved symbolic.[5]

El Danto's first paramilitary experience came in 1960, when he received some training in the use of military weapons, including the .45 caliber pistol, M-1 Garand rifle, and Thompson submachine gun.[6] By July 1961, he had been recruited by a Conservative rebel leader, Cristobal Guido, to join another group then leaving Nicaragua to receive professional guerrilla warfare training. El Danto made the first of many trips to Cuba.[7] Once in Cuba, Castro's irregular warfare experts trained and equipped El Danto's group in preparation for their return to Nicaragua as guerrillas. El Danto also visited other countries that were supporting attempts to overthrow the Somoza regime.[8]

From 1961 until his death in 1979, El Dantò was an active anti-Somoza guerrilla, eventually advancing to become one of the Sandinista Front's national directors and a senior field commander. In 1969, he was with the Sandinista commando led by then-FSLN Director Plutarco Hernández that briefly freed FSLN founder Carlos Fonseca from a Costa Rican jail in Alajuela, just outside the capital of San José.[9] Unlike Fonseca or the others in the team, who were captured almost immediately, El Danto escaped capture by the Costa Ricans. Between 1969 and 1976, however, he was arrested at least twice inside Nicaragua for his revolutionary activities but released on both occasions. Two Guardia Nacional colonels who spoke extensively with him while he twice was in custody during the 1960s described El Danto as being very charismatic, able to be charming when he wanted to, and a natural leader.[10] Hernández and Martínez, and the former Sandinista comrades-in-arms,[11] characterized him using many of the same words but added that he could also be cold-blooded when he believed that it was necessary and also very independent-minded. Hernández noted that, given his roots within the Conservative Youth movement, his Marxist comrades were concerned about the latter tendency.[12]

According to a former Comando who was himself present as a MILPA officer, in early May 1979 the FSLN political cadre began telling their officers at meetings in the Segovian mountains that the Front, convinced Somoza would soon fall, had developed a comprehensive plan of how it would rule once it had seized power. What they described was a Marxist revolution.[13] He and other former Comandos, who as MILPA officers had also been present at the meetings, said that El Danto had become incensed and railed loudly and forcefully against the Sandinistas' plans. He argued that he and his Milpistas had fought hard and long for a Costa Rican–style democracy, not a socialist revolution, in Nicaragua. A few of his Milpista comrades tried to shut him up because they knew the Marxist Sandinistas and were afraid for his safety, but he would not stop.[14]

About three weeks later, on 24 May, El Danto was killed during an attack on the highland town of Jinotega. Initial reports claimed that he had been shot by a Guardia sniper firing from the tower of the town's cathedral. But the place where he fell, which is now marked by a small red metal monument, cannot be seen from the cathedral, and everyone familiar with Jinotega knew it.[15] A Sandinista correo, active in Jinotega at the time under cover as a Red Cross volunteer, was with El Danto five minutes before he was shot and said that when he visited, no Guardia were anywhere nearby.[16] A posthumous note attached to El Danto's Sandinista-authorized posthumous "autobiography" says simply that he was killed by "una bala averiada," a stray bullet, fired from within his own ranks, making his a "death by friendly fire."[17] But three of El Danto's closest comrades challenged this version. Sandinista field commander Martínez, or "Comandante Martinez," then a column commander in southern Nicaragua, was told within days by a Milpista en route to FSLN army headquarters in southern Costa Rica that it was common knowledge that El Danto had been killed under orders from the Sandinista leadership. Hernández, then Martinez's immediate commander and close to El Danto, heard and believed the same story, as did a top Mexican Marxist liaison agent in Mexico City, José Ovídió "Pepe" Puente León.[18]

More important, El Danto's Milpista troops seem to have fully agreed that the bullet that killed their commander was fired from within the Sandinistas' own ranks. They did not believe it was a case of "friendly fire." They believed instead that his erstwhile Sandinista comrades had killed him deliberately. Whether or not they were right, the actions that they then took based on that belief started the Contra War.

Dimas continued on as a senior Sandinista combat commander. He was, however, convinced the Sandinistas had murdered El

Danto to remove him as a challenge to the impending Sandinista Revolution. As a result, by July, when he helped capture the town of Ocotal just before Somoza fled, he was already two months into preparing for a new armed struggle against that revolution. He too had been shocked by the Sandinistas' plans to launch a Marxist revolution. Unlike El Danto, Dimas had kept his opinion secret from his Sandinista superiors.[19] He did, however, begin in May 1979 to carefully recruit like-minded Milpista comrades, explaining to his common-law wife Marina that "Germán Pomares's [El Danto's] ideology was not the ideology of the Sandinistas. When Pomares fell is when they began to twist everything into a different form." He also told Marina that it was the death of El Danto more than anything else, that led him to turn against his erstwhile comrades-in-arms.[20] Most of Dimas's fellow Milpistas were also angered by the Sandinistas' revolutionary plans and outraged by the killing. They quietly rallied to Dimas's side even before Somoza fell.

THOSE AROUND DIMAS

Marina

[In Quilalí] it was the Sandinistas who created the MILPAS. In the beginning, everyone in Quilalí was pro-Sandinista. A few important Sandinistas, but no Guardias, were even from here. But they turned the people against them by their own actions.

—MARINA[21]

The story of Marina is instructive. A campesina woman raised in the mountains near Quilalí in the hamlet of El Yocíte, she moved to Quilalí while a young teenager, soon married, and had two children.[22] During the war against Somoza, she served as a correo for the Sandinistas' Carlos Fonseca Front, taking goods and information to El Danto, Dimas, and others in the nearby mountains. Her first husband, from whom she was separated and who had custody of their two children, was drafted into the Guardia Nacional toward the end of the war and became a truck driver for about six months. In early August 1979, shortly after Somoza fell, the Sandinistas detained him with their two children. While they were in custody, State Security agents beat all three to death with baseball bats.[23]

Apparently because of her first husband's Guardia service, and despite her own service with the Front, the Sandinistas also detained Marina and severely abused her.[24] When asked if they had tortured or raped her, Marina became extremely agitated and would only say that since her detention she had suffered constant nightmares and nervous attacks, as well as occasional memory loss. She was released after a few days and promptly contacted Dimas. She once again became a correo for him but this time as an anti-Sandinista, and was later to have his daughter. Their teenaged daughter stood quietly beside her in 1994 as Marina was interviewed for this study.

After Dimas was killed in 1981 (his death is described below), Marina moved to the highland town of San José de Bocay and became a *jefa de correos,* or chief of an intelligence and support network, serving the MILPAS group of "Tigrillo" (introduced in chapter 5), and was responsible for that very dangerous work over a wide area.[25] She remained an active correo chief for the rest of the war. The killing of her two children and first husband by the Sandinistas, her own detention, mistreatment, and a powerful sense of betrayal, as well as her personal closeness to Dimas gave her more than enough reasons to join the MILPAS and to remain a highland Resistance activist.

Marina's account illuminates the reasons for highland resistance to the government. Soon after the Revolution began, Sandinista security forces fanned out into the mountains where they quickly began seizing the campesinos' personal goods, and detaining, torturing, even killing, without trial, anyone who resisted. They charged that all resistance to their actions was "counter-revolutionary activity." Reports of rapes of peasant women were common, and life in the deepest mountains where most of the campesinos lived became unbearable. Almost all the earliest anti-Sandinista rebels were peasants. They told Marina that as long as they remained within reach of Sandinista security forces, they lived in constant fear of being beaten, arrested, or killed for resisting "seizure" of their meager personal properties "in the name of the Revolution" or for "failing to report the presence of counterrevolutionaries," even if they knew of no such activities. They joined the MILPAS in anger and self-defense.

As a correo, Marina lived under cover in the region's towns. She saw people accused of being counterrevolutionaries killed by being dragged alive through the streets of Quilalí behind Sandinista army trucks. She remembered two occasions when the people of Quilalí, herself included, were forced to watch as accused Contras were burned alive atop pyres behind the town's church. These horrors still figure in her nightmares. Once she saw the body of an accused Contra that had been laid out in a town square for public display. He had been tortured by having the skin peeled strip by strip from his face before being killed, a method that harkened back to Indian warfare before and during the Spanish Conquest. She believed such atrocities were the primary reason that the people in her region turned against the Revolution.

Marina confirmed that after the fall of Somoza, the Sandinistas made Dimas military commander of Estelí.[26] He was later transferred to Ocotal and then to their home town of Quilalí.[27] Beginning in May 1979, he played a double game, secretly organizing his new anti-Sandinista MILPAS guerrilla group. By late July several comarca chiefs who had cooperated with his MILPA against Somoza had contacted him. They asked that he work with them to coordinate networks of correos, clandestine comarca committees, and popular base supporters. Dimas was especially attentive to this clandestine organizational process because he understood that strong and secure local support networks, good intelligence, and a secure logistical system were critical to a successful guerrilla effort. Several of Dimas's Milpistas described how they came to join him.[28]

Pirata

Pirata, a former Milpista, was unusually sensitive to his ethnic roots and described himself and his entire comarca as "indios puros," pure Indians.[29] He became aware of the anti-Sandinista guerrilla movement almost as soon as the Revolution began but, although disturbed by the course of the Revolution, did not immediately join the Resistance. A first cousin, "El Cadéjo,"[26] had been with Omar Cabezas during the war against Somoza and was then still in the Sandinista army. But when this cousin contacted Pirata in September 1979 to say he was so disillusioned with the Revolution that he was going to join the rebels, Pirata also acted. By November he was a correo for Dimas. His cousin, an experienced guerrilla with Omar Cabezas, immediately became a Milpista combatant.

During his time as a correo, Pirata regularly visited the MILPAS camps and observed that almost all those with Dimas had served under El Danto as Milpista fighters during the war against Somoza. Of the twelve guerrillas at Dimas's main camp on Pirata's first visit, several went on to become important Resistance comandantes. This group included "Coral," "Douglas," "La Iguana," "Mono," and "Gallo."[30]

Oscar Kilo

"Oscar Kilo" joined Dimas in late 1979 as a Milpista.[31] His father was a small farmer who eked out a marginal livelihood from about fifteen acres of land near the remote Segovian mountain town of Wiwilí, and Oscar Kilo had continued to work on his father's finca during the war against Somoza. His family began having problems with the Sandinistas in August 1979, within weeks of the start of the Revolution.

Oscar Kilo vividly recalled the actions and attitudes of the State Security forces and political cadre who arrived in his area almost immediately after the fall of Somoza to implement the Sandinistas' revolutionary plans. Virtually without exception, they were arrogant and abusive outsiders from the Pacific lowlands who clearly looked down on the highland peasants as unlettered indios. They quickly took up stealing domestic animals and personal property in the guise of "loans to the Revolution." Some of the property the Sandinistas stole belonged to his family, but when Oscar Kilo's father objected, the Sandinistas labeled him a "counterrevolutionary" and began taking reprisals.[32]

In September 1979, Oscar Kilo was kicked to the ground and severely beaten by a Sandinista officer who overheard him criticizing the Sandinistas' actions. His father was arrested. At the age of twenty, in fear of what the Sandinistas might do to him next, Oscar Kilo fled deep into the mountains. When he arrived at Dimas's camp, the commander had with him over a dozen guerrillas. Within weeks, more frightened campesinos flocked to join them, and the group had grown to between twenty and thirty.[33] Most were armed with hunting weapons, .22 caliber rifles, or shotguns. Oscar Kilo himself had only a machete.

By November Oscar Kilo was helping a correo named David Valenzuela smuggle arms and supplies to the group. The anti-Sandinistas were being fed and protected by local campesinos who were as angry as Oscar Kilo's family at the Sandinistas. Beyond seizures of private property and physical violence, the Sandinistas were manifesting disrespect for the traditional Catholic Church. This included desecrating churches and quartering of troops in chapels, as well as constant verbal insults directed at traditional religious practices. These provocative acts added fuel to the growing fires of rebellion.

Oscar Kilo remembered Dimas himself as a short, hirsute, bearded commander with one eye noticeably smaller than the other. Friendly and charismatic, Dimas called almost all the men hermanito, or little brother.[34] A former Sandinista comrade who for fifteen years fought side by side in the mountains with Dimas added that he was also an excellent field commander.[35]

Rubén had his own MILPAS group and was not one of Dimas's Milpistas. But he knew personally almost all the Comandos who had been with him and confirmed that both Dimas and his Milpistas were highlanders who had served under El Danto.[36]

Hombrito

Mejor irme donde me gustaba (y) el Sandinismo no me gusto desde el principio.

(It was better to go where I liked [and] from the beginning I didn't like Sandinismo.)

—HOMBRITO

"Hombrito" (Little Man) was another highlander Comando who joined Dimas in 1979.[37] His was a family of peasant farmers who made their living working a tiny plot near the Honduran border. His father was a very indio campesino from Las Trojes, Honduras, who had married a mostly india mestiza Nicaraguan woman and moved to Nicaragua while still a youth. They raised bananas, beans, and some corn, mostly for home consumption, and had a few head of cattle. They sold their modest surpluses in a nearby market town to buy what they could not produce.

In August 1979 the Sandinistas began pressuring Hombrito to join one of their new Committees for the Defense of Sandinismo (CDS).[38] He considered them, however, little more than nests of police informers and resisted. As a consequence, he was denounced as a "counterrevolutionary Somocista," and threatened with reprisals. As his situation became increasingly difficult, he began to look for a way to fight back. By October he had become an active correo supporting Dimas. But the Sandinistas quickly became suspicious, and he had to flee into hiding in the mountains by November. Early in 1980, after a short period of testing and preparation, he became a combatant.[39]

Hombrito remembered that most of Dimas's group, almost eighty Milpistas strong when he joined them, were former anti-Somoza guerrillas who had been with El Danto. Those like himself who had not fought had also been pro-Sandinista during the uprising. Most carried only hunting weapons and were dressed in ragtag civilian clothes. The most sophisticated weapons he saw were three M-1 rifles.[40] Those around Dimas included members of three family clans, the Mezas, Rugamas, and Galeanos. (The Galeano clan is described in chapter 4.) The former anti-Somoza Milpistas told Hombrito that the Sandinistas had deceived them about their real intentions during the war against Somoza. These campesinos had then been angered by the killing of their leader. The Sandinistas had promised that after Somoza fell, Nicaragua would become a Costa Rican–style democracy, but they had been preparing all along, in secret, to stage a Marxist revolution.

The peasants who had rallied to Dimas, like Dimas himself, said they joined the Resistance mostly because they were angry at the conduct of the Sandinistas' security forces and new laws that forced them to sell their surpluses to the state at low prices and then buy what they needed from the state at high prices. This system put them in a double bind, simultaneously terrorized and rapidly pauperized, and they could see no way to escape. If they went along with the Sandinistas' demands, they would be ruined and unable to support their families. If they resisted, they were labeled "Somocistas" and "counterrevolutionaries"; their already meager personal goods were confiscated, their farms endangered, and their families still threatened with starvation. Either way, they were unable to survive as independent farmers. This group was especially embittered by the only alternative offered them: to join new agricultural cooperatives, because they saw these as nothing more than the Revolution's way of taking their land and destroying their independence. Another Sandinista practice generated further resistence. Local students were being taken away to Nicaragua's Pacific coast cities for ideological indoctrination that often turned them against their own families. This was especially tragic for the family-centered peasants of the highlands.

Name Withheld

*Cuando los Sandinistas entraron todo el mundo les quierían,
pero no aprovecharon de esto. Ellos traicionaron el amor que
el pueblo les tenía. Los hacían hacer lo que el pueblo no estaba
acostumbrado hacer, y se reventó. (When the Sandinistas
came to power, everyone loved them, but they didn't take
advantage of their popularity. They betrayed the love the
people had for them. Instead they forced them to do what they
were not accustomed to doing, and the people exploded).*

*El que toca el estomago de un pueblo tiene que encachim-
barlo. (He who makes a people hungry also inevitably pisses
them off.)*

—NAME WITHHELD[41]

A Comando I interviewed, who asked that neither his real name
nor nom de guerre be mentioned, was the son of a peasant
campesino family from the Department of Madriz and had been a
member of the tiny group that had joined Dimas by September
1979. He had not fought on either side during the war against
Somoza, but one of his older brothers had been in the Guardia
Nacional. He was markedly indio in appearance and described his
home comarca as being almost pure Indian.

Shortly after the Revolution began, the Sandinistas established
an army post and a political action center near his family's farm. At
that time they began pressuring members of his family to join various revolutionary organizations and to participate in political
activities. When they resisted, two of his brothers were arrested,
including the one who had been an enlisted man in the Guardia.
The Sandinistas threatened to confiscate the family farm, and one
night their home was machine-gunned.[42]

When this Comando and his brothers came under intense pressure in early 1980 to join the new Sandinista Militia, their family
sent them instead to join Dimas. In doing so, they became part of

the growing stream of campesinos traveling to the mountains to join the MILPAS. By mid-1980, most of his family, including three other brothers and some nephews, cousins, and uncles, had also fled to join the growing rebellion. Their farms were seized.

The Comando's comments on why the highlanders rebelled emphasized the Sandinistas' extensive use of coercion and force. They regularly employed threats, detentions, beatings, and killings. He also emphasized the destructive impact of the Sandinistas' agrarian policies on the peasants' ability to survive as independent farmers and the decidedly unwelcome pressures to join the new CDS and militias. He believed that these measures together had jeopardized the peasants' very ability to survive, and they had reacted accordingly.

THE GROWTH OF DIMAS'S GROUP

Dimas's group was the most prominent of the early MILPAS groups. Led by a very experienced former senior Sandinista guerrilla commander and made up largely of veteran anti-Somoza Milpista guerrillas, its roots lay deep in the anti-Somoza Sandinista guerrilla movement itself. The rebellion leading up to their revolt dated all the way back to May 1979, when they were still fighting against Somoza. Later estimates of the numbers of correos, committee members, and base supporters it would have taken to support his group in the field suggest that by the end of 1979 Dimas's MILPAS would have had at least 400–600 correos, clandestine committee members, and peasant comarca popular-base supporters. This estimate may be low.[43] By then the group had captured or been given some military small arms by militiamen but was still mostly armed with hunting weapons, .22 caliber rifles, shotguns, pistols, or machetes, which they had either brought to the war themselves or been given by sympathetic peasants.

By early 1980, Dimas's group had almost tripled in size and would have had perhaps two to three thousand correos, comarca committee members, and active supporters. Unarmed correos such as Marina, Hombrito, and Oscar Kilo, working as intelligence and logistics runners, were bringing them intelligence information, ammunition, and supplies unavailable in the mountains such as rubber boots,[44] medicines, and candles. The peasants who were living deeper in the mountains, where the MILPAS had their base of operations, were providing them with food and protection from detection or surprise attacks by keeping them informed of Sandinista movements.

ACTIVITIES

During 1979 and early 1980, Dimas's MILPAS group concentrated on establishing a strong base of support within the comarcas. Security and food availability concerns led the Milpistas normally to camp in widely dispersed small groups. Many moved about in areas near their homes. Those who stayed permanently in the mountains were poorly dressed in raggedy civilian clothing, were short on decent shelter, usually avoided contact with Sandinista patrols, and generally did not engage in offensive operations.

By mid-1980 Dimas's MILPAS and other nearby groups had become acquainted with one another, had grown considerably, and felt strong enough to stage a major attack. It was then that Dimas, Irene Calderón, and a third MILPAS leader known as "Fabian" agreed to make the attack on Quilalí (mentioned in chapter 2). They timed their attack to coincide with the first anniversary of the Sandinista Revolution. Their planning was greatly simplified by Dimas's detailed knowledge of the town and its defenses. On 23 July, four days after the Revolution's 19 July anniversary, seventy to eighty of Dimas's Milpistas attacked and occupied Quilalí. The two other MILPAS groups made simultaneous diversionary attacks. Fabian, another former anti-Somoza Milpista from near Quilalí, hit the hamlet of La Jícara with an eight-man unit. Irene Calderón, with twenty men, attacked La Chachagua.[45] Hombrito, a participant, recalled that the attack on Quilalí went smoothly and led to the recovery of a fair amount of arms and ammunition. The

Map 3. Dimas's (Pedro Joaquín González's) MILPAS areas of operation, 1979–81.

mutiny by Quilalí's defenders that was described earlier suggests Dimas may have had inside help.

The Sandinistas responded sharply to the MILPAS challenge and, following the attack on Quilalí, Dimas broke his force into small detachments. Most went back to the nearby mountains,[46] but one was sent to Honduras in search of support and to buy ammunition.[47] Before the attack, Sandinista pursuit of the MILPAS had been rather desultory. But after the MILPAS had occupied Quilalí, the Sandinistas became notably more determined, sending in larger units and using helicopters for the first time.[48] At least a platoon of Sandinista soldiers and several of their helicopters reportedly pursued the detachment across the Honduran border, triggering protests from the Honduran government and the public.[49] Dimas's MILPAS was forced to range across a large area, especially up and down the course of the Coco River.[50]

Several Milpistas who had been involved in the attack had indelible memories of this sudden pursuit, the strength and ferocity of the Sandinista response, and their reactions to the first use against them of such advanced military systems as helicopter gun ships and massed rocket fire. Some Milpistas cited this experience as the one that convinced them they would either have to find external help or accept defeat.

Despite these more vigorous Sandinista actions, or perhaps in part because of them, the highlander rebellion continued to grow rapidly. A year later, in August 1981, Dimas was killed at San Bartolo just outside Quilalí, and the Milpistas who had been with him joined other groups.[51] But by then the armed conflict that was later to become known as the Contra War had been under way for over two years.

THE DEATH OF DIMAS

A booklet on the Sandinista Militia describes one version of Dimas's death:

> The Militias, operating together with the EPS [Ejército Popular Sandinista, Sandinista People's Army] and MININT [Ministry of the Interior] had been engaged in major operations in the mountains, disrupting and annihilating gangs of counterrevolutionaries, criminals, and thieves. One of the gangs that was murdering and pillaging in the region between Wiwilí, Quilalí, and other communities was that of

"Dimas," which had been terrorizing all the campesinos in the area.

"Dimas" and his gang launched a cowardly attack from Honduran territory against a native dugout canoe, killing three persons and wounding many others. "Dimas" was tied in with Somocistas in Honduras and with other groups of terrorists who had a vast plan of counter-revolution against our people.

In July 1980 they had attacked the town of Quilalí where they killed four persons who fell beneath the bullets of the counterrevolutionary murderers.

The counterrevolutionary "Dimas" had established contact with officers of the former Guardia Nacional and other anti-social elements in Honduras and El Salvador who provided economic help and military supplies so that he could continue his campaign of crimes and felonies. [An accompanying sketch shows Dimas accepting M-16 rifles from Miami.]

He was chased night and day by the indefatigable patrols of the Militias who knew the region tree by tree, together with EPS and forces of the General Directorate [of State Security].

On Thursday September 19 the gang was located near Quilalí, Nueva Segovia, and an operation was mounted against them. When the gang found itself under attack, it opened fire. The gang put up fierce resistance and increased its fire from protected positions behind large boulders.

The Territorial Militias, determined in their struggle against the criminals who had murdered so many of their brother workers, and armed with BZ-M52s, opened fire beneath the banner of "Patria o Muerte" [My Country or Death].

"Dimas" died in combat along with many of his followers. The rest of his gang escaped to Honduras. The death of "Dimas" and so many of his lieutenants destroyed the vast counterrevolutionary plot, known as the "October Plan" which had sought to bring together all the groups of Somocistas and criminal assailants.[52]

This version of Dimas's death varies significantly from others. Nevertheless, it warrants extensive quotation because, although it makes no mention of his eighteen years as an anti-Somoza guerrilla commander, it does confirm most of the Comandos' comments on the who, when, and where of the origins of the MILPAS movement.

Other accounts of Dimas's death, including later Sandinista versions, concur that, in fact, neither Militia, EPS, nor State Security, save possibly the Ministry of the Interior's covert operations section, were involved. According to these accounts, he was assassinated in August 1981 by a close friend or cousin, Mamerto Herrera, a veteran Sandinista who had first helped recruit him into the movement in 1961.[53] Oscar Kilo remembered that Herrera visited Dimas at his mountain camp on numerous occasions and that Dimas always called him *compadre* and treated him with particular affection. As it turned out, by pretending to support his war against the Revolution, Herrera had simply been retaining Dimas's trust. On the fateful day, Herrera engaged Dimas in a drinking bout, and then killed him while he was drunk.[54] No other Milpistas died with him. Shortly after his death, Dimas's Milpistas dispersed to join other MILPAS groups. All stayed with the Resistance. More than half died in the war that followed.[55]

CHAPTER FOUR

THE MILPAS OF IRENE CALDERÓN

While Dimas's group became the best known of the 1979–80 MILPAS rebel groups, a second if less well known MILPAS group was of comparable importance. It was led by Irene Calderón, the leader of one of the MILPAS groups that later joined Dimas in the July 1980 attack on Quilalí. He had also been with El Danto earlier as a member of the Sandinista MILPA battalion and had fought against Somoza's forces for several years.[1] He was among the earliest Milpistas to turn against the Sandinista Revolution.

"Bruce Lee," who fought with Calderón, remembered that when they first met in October 1979, Calderón had been in the Segovian mountains for about three months with four other former anti-Somoza guerrillas. This would date the birth of Calderón's MILPAS in July, the month Somoza fell. In early August 1979, Calderón's group attacked a new Militia camp near San José de Bocay, beside the Bocay River to the west of the Coco River basin, and captured a few military weapons and some munitions, an attack they had planned even before they went into the mountains. Although not large enough to be called a battle—that distinction belongs to Gerónimo's November 1979 attack on the new cooperative at El Chipote discussed in chapter 2—this is

Map 4. Irene Calderón's MILPAS areas of operation, 1979–82.

the earliest MILPAS raid on a Sandinista military target mentioned by the Comandos I interviewed. (Map 4 shows Calderón's
area of operation.) From San José de Bocay, Calderón moved
westward across the mountains, to near Quilalí. Although
Calderón survived the war, he chose not to be interviewed, so a
profile of his MILPAS group was developed from other sources.
One was Bruce Lee.

BRUCE LEE

A campesino from San Sebastian de Yalí, Bruce Lee fought against the Somoza dynasty as a guerrilla with El Danto. He remembered clearly how his own guerrilla career had started. On 3 May 1977, then just sixteen years old, he had expressed some anti-Somoza sentiments too loudly during a religious procession and was clubbed to the ground by a passing Guardia officer. He promptly fled into the nearby mountains to join the Sandinistas, who first sent him to their clandestine training base in Pantasma, near the Jinotegan settlement of Las Praderas, and then assigned him to a unit called Los Yacob, part of the Sandinistas' larger Picado Column.

Bruce Lee was an enthusiastic young recruit and was especially pleased when the Sandinistas initially promised him that, following their victory, they planned to set up a Costa Rican–style democracy that would be much more prosperous than Somoza's Nicaragua. In May 1979, after he had been with them two years, he was very angry when they acknowledged that, far from setting up a Costa Rican–style democracy, they intended to stage a Cuban–style revolution. He was particularly incensed when Sandinista cadre he knew told him that, as part of their revolution, they planned to break up Nicaragua's traditional social structure by taking children from their homes to receive ideological indoctrination. They explained that the children would then be sent back to begin establishing a new social order. Bruce Lee was deeply shocked by this deliberate attack on Nicaragua's traditional family structure. But he also knew that the Sandinistas would punish him if he expressed his opinion, so he kept quiet.

Despite his secret anger, Bruce Lee stayed in the Sandinista Nuevo Ejército (New Army) after Somoza fell, assigned to a unit near Lake Apanás, just north of the town of Jinotega. While a soldier, he was even more shocked than he had been as a civilian by what he saw fellow Sandinista soldiers do to campesinos "in the name of the Revolution," especially the widespread "seizures" of private goods and property and the harassment and detention of any who dared to protest.[2] Bruce Lee began to clash openly with the Sandinista cadre over him. In September 1979, angered by his criticism, a Sandinista officer took a shot at him. He missed. But soon after, several friends warned him he was going to be arrested for his counterrevolutionary attitude. Before this could happen, he fled into the mountains.

In hiding, angry, and feeling betrayed and thoroughly disillusioned, Bruce Lee found a temporary job near El Cuá Bocay. There, he soon heard about a group of Milpistas in the nearby mountains, organized under Calderón, an experienced guerrilla leader he had known during the war against Somoza. In October, fearing that Sandinista State security was closing in on him, he fled even deeper into the mountains to join Calderón's MILPAS. When he arrived, there were only four Milpistas at the camp, including Calderón's girlfriend. Calderón told Bruce Lee that he had been in the mountains since July and that others in his group were not then at the camp. He said he was also in touch with another nearby MILPAS group led by Dimas, whom Bruce Lee also knew from his years as an anti-Somoza Milpista. Calderón was short of firearms but had a few hunting weapons that had been given to them by a sympathizer.[3] During the several months that Bruce Lee stayed with the group, it grew to about sixty combatants.

TIGRE

Alli estuvo Sandino; alli estuvo Pomares [El Danto]; alli tambien estuvo Dimas. [Wiwilí] es una zona de guerrillas.

(Sandino was there; Pomares was there; Dimas was there. [Wiwilí] is guerrilla country).

—TIGRE

"Tigre" served as a correo for Calderón's MILPAS.[4] Born in Somoto, he was raised near the Segovian mountain town of Wiwilí

on his family's fifteen-manzana (twenty-five acre) tobacco farm.[5]
He was in high school when Somoza fell and did not fight in that
war. But he did meet both Calderón and Dimas during the war
against Somoza. He learned soon after the Sandinistas took power
that both had gone back into the mountains to form new MILPAS
guerrilla groups.

Tigre's family's farm was quite small, and his father had never
been politically involved. Nonetheless, in September 1979, the
Sandinistas tried to seize it, claiming that his father had allowed
Guardia to visit the farm to pick fruit from the family's trees and
that this proved he was a Somocista. Tigre believed that the real
reason for the attempted seizure was that his father raised excellent
tobacco, an especially lucrative cash crop, and the Sandinistas
wanted to get their hands on his father's profits.

Tigre's family was able to block the Sandinistas' first attempt to
seize their farm by mobilizing neighbors to help them, but the
Sandinistas persisted, and shortly thereafter they seized his father's
farm permanently in the name of the Revolution and arrested
Tigre. The officer who arrested him threatened Tigre with execution for his counterrevolutionary attitude. He was blindfolded and
a pistol was put to his temple. After a slow countdown, the officer
fired a second pistol into the ground at his feet. Apparently satisfied that he had terrorized Tigre sufficiently, the officer freed him
after warning him never to mention the threatened execution to
anyone.

Tigre was outraged, not intimidated, and began looking for a
way to avenge himself. In early 1980, he became a correo for
Calderón. After a few months, aware of what their son was doing
and worried about his safety, Tigre's family insisted that he go
away to school in Managua, which he did. Despite the distance, he
continued to help Calderón whenever he could, especially during
visits home.

In 1981 the Sandinistas came to his high school in Managua and
asked for volunteers to help root out "a small group of about
seventy counterrevolutionaries who were in the mountains." Tigre
could not understand why the Sandinistas "were sending [high

school students] when they had plenty of men in their army." He also knew that by then there were actually well over a thousand guerrillas in various MILPAS groups the mountains, not seventy, and that almost all were former Sandinistas, not Guardia. Some of Tigre's high school acquaintances volunteered, and he remembered later attending several of their funerals. None had received decent military training, and seven were killed during one engagement alone. A short while later, Tigre, still an occasional correo for Calderón, started to worry about his own security and left to join the MILPAS in the mountains. This time, when he arrived, Calderón had more than a hundred Milpistas with him, almost all of whom were former Sandinistas.

Tigre cited several reasons why the rebellion had gathered so many early adherents. He pointed first to the arms sweeps staged by the Sandinistas in the highlands, including one in May 1979, even before Somoza fell, that had generated considerable fear and anger among the peasants. The sweeps had also put them on guard that worse was probably to come. He commented that "even Somoza had not felt the need to disarm the highland peasants." The sweeps convinced many campesinos that they were going to be special targets of revolutionary zeal. Seeing the soldiers coming from afar, many had hidden their best weapons, which they later gave to the MILPAS. Tigre next mentioned Sandinista agrarian policies. The Sandinistas touted their seizures of farms as aimed only at Somocistas. But in reality, they confiscated the lands of many non-Somocistas as well through the simple device of labeling anyone whose property they wanted a Somocista counterrevolutionary, whether or not they were. Because there was no judicial process and no avenue of appeal, confiscations were normally final.

Tigre, who had firsthand experience with the Sandinista Army both in Managua and in the highlands during the early years of the war, drew some interesting contrasts. In general, the Sandinista soldiers conducted themselves relatively well in the cities and towns of the Pacific. In the highlands, however, their behavior was vastly different. This was especially obvious at road blocks or during other security operations, and even at such events as country dances or social gatherings. On these occasions, armed Sandinista soldiers, mostly young men from Pacific lowland cities, tried to intimidate the highlander men and take advantage of the peasant girls. The Ministry of the Interior's State Security forces were the worst. They were especially brutal and engaged in systematic, not only episodic, intimidation and coercion. Tigre noted as a third reason for the early resentment that Cuban and other foreign advisors became highly visible in the highlands very early on and "acted as though they were actually in charge."[6]

LA CHAPARRA

Another former Comando who remembered Calderón's group well was female Comando Elisa María Galeano Cornejo, "La Chaparra," slang for Shorty, and a member of the extensive Galeano clan.[7] She became a correo for Calderón in early 1980.[8] At the same time, she infiltrated the Sandinista army garrison in Quilalí as a cook. While working inside the Sandinista base, she was able to steal some 1,200 rounds of ammunition, which she gave to Calderón, and to collect about fifteen thousand Nicaraguan Cordobas (about two thousand U.S. dollars at the time) from sympathizers, which she used to buy boots for his Milpistas. She also became a member of the Sandinistas' People's Militias and used her access to steal weapons for those she referred to as "chilotes," a popular term for Milpista.[9] La Chaparra recalled that by the autumn of 1980, about thirty guerrillas had joined Calderón, all campesinos from the nearby countryside, including a number of her brothers, sisters or cousins. She listed many of them by their noms de guerre: "Tiro al Blanco,"* "Pajaro," "El Cacao," "Julio," "Sergio," "Johnny,"* "David,"* "El Negro," "Yorli," "Irma,"* "G-3," "Juan Viejo," "El Bufalo," "Salto," and "Evelor" (asterisks indicate her siblings). Most were from Jinotega or Nueva Segovia.[10]

La Chaparra joined the rebellion for personal reasons. Because her family refused to allow Literacy Brigade personnel (urban

Sandinista youth ostensibly dedicated to teaching reading and writing but also serving as ideological cadre) to be quartered in their home, they were branded as Somocistas, and her father and older brother "Franklyn"[11] were jailed and mistreated. An entire family of relatives, the Polancos, were similarly labeled and then chopped to death with machetes by a Sandinista mob. Two uncles were also killed.[12]

Other Participants

Several Milpistas who had been with Dimas and had personal knowledge of Calderón's group also commented on it. Oscar Kilo remembers that at various times Calderón's MILPAS operated near the small hamlets of La Chachagua, Puna, and Wamblán.[13] "Dimas Tigrillo," a brother of Tigrillo, one of many Comandos who later took the name of Dimas, met Calderón in early 1980, just after his MILPAS had clashed with a Sandinista force. He too confirmed that Calderón had been with El Danto and also remembered that the group was made up of former Sandinista guerrillas and campesinos, had an independent system of collaborators, and was growing rapidly.[14] "Jimmy Leo" remembered that once Calderón's group had grown to about eighteen Milpistas, it moved westward to be nearer the homes of its members in regions around La Zompopera, Kilambé, Plan de Grama, and Planos de Bilán, near Quilalí and Wiwilí.[15] He said that Calderón's men were almost all former Sandinista guerrillas who had fought under Germán Pomares, "El Danto." Bruce Lee estimated that Calderón had close to sixty guerrillas by the end of 1980.[16] In addition to guerillas, the organization would have had fifteen to twenty times that number of correos and clandestine comarca committee members. All together, Calderón's comarca support organization probably numbered over a thousand, only slightly smaller than that of Dimas.

Calderón remained an active Milpista until early 1982. But when a MILPAS-Guardia alliance emerged (see chapter 8), Calderón was angered that he was not accepted as the principal leader of the

Milpistas who joined it. That distinction went to another MILPAS leader, Tigrillo, who is discussed in the next chapter. Calderón stayed with the alliance for a while, but disappeared from the scene in early 1984.[17]

Several versions of what happened to him circulated. Some former Comandos believed Calderón had returned from Honduras to Nicaragua independently, accompanied by a few of his men, only to be killed in an unreported ambush. Others thought he defected to the Sandinistas. Still others said that whether he had defected or been captured, Calderón was then recruited by the Sandinistas as a guide. Subsequently, according to this version, he led a Sandinista army unit into an ambush in which it lost a large number of men, after which he disappeared. In 1992, well after the war had ended and other prisoners had been freed, Calderón emerged from a Sandinista prison where he had been held incommunicado for eight years. In 1998 he was living quietly in a small Nicaraguan town and remained in touch with a handful of his former Milpista comrades, but an interview could not be arranged.

OTHER MILPAS GROUPS

Dimas and Calderón were not the only two anti-Somoza combatants among El Danto's Sandinista Milpistas to have secretly rebelled against the Sandinistas' even before Somoza fell. And, unlike in the case of Calderón, who was reluctant to speak to me, I was able to obtain oral histories from several of the more prominent among these combatants, including Calderón's later rival for leadership of the MILPAS, Tigrillo. Two others proved to be representative of a second phenomenon, the participation of entire clans in the highlander Resistance movement.

THE GROUP OF TIGRILLO

Tigrillo (Wildcat) and his younger brother Dimas Tigrillo were among dozens of members of the highland Baldivia clan who were first anti-Somoza and then anti-Sandinista Milpistas.[1] Operating from a rural comarca near La Concordia, the two brothers had been guerrilla commanders with the Sandinistas during the war against Somoza. Tigrillo went on to lead a small unit with El Danto. Dimas Tigrillo started with Edén Pastora in 1977, before transferring north to join the Blanca Aráuz de Sandino Column, where he too led a small unit for El Danto. Both became officers of the Sandinista army after the fall of Somoza. At the same time both were secretly dismayed when in May 1979 the Sandinistas announced that the fall of Somoza was to be followed by a Cuban-style revolution and the killing of their leader.[2]

As had Dimas, Calderón, and others, the Baldivia brothers began in May 1979, even as they fought to overthrow Somoza, to prepare to fight later against the impending Sandinista Revolution. They were even more cautious than Dimas but followed essentially the same path to rebellion. For six months after the fall of Somoza they served as Sandinista army officers while simultaneously hiding arms and ammunition in preparation for their own rebellion. By February 1980, they were ready, and they went into the mountains, taking with them M-1 rifles, .38 caliber pistols, and ammunition that they had been secretly stashing away.[3] A MILPAS group quickly began to coalesce around them. By July 1980, they felt strong enough to join Dimas for the attack on Quilalí. Pursued by the Sandinista army following the attack, they moved their group to the region of Kilambé, a very mountainous area about thirty miles to the east.

By late 1980, Tigrillo's force had grown considerably. Dimas Tigrillo remembers that by then they had about eighty combatants. Two were former Guardia, but even they were first and foremost peasants from the Quilalí/Wiwilí region.[4] All except the two Guardia had fought against the Somoza regime as Sandinistas, most as guerrillas with El Danto's force. Many were either Baldivias or Galeanos. As with Dimas and Irene Calderón, Tigrillo's group developed its own independent networks of correos and other supporters. Johnny, one of the Galeanos with Tigrillo, recalled that these included quite a few supposedly Sandinista activists, including at least two members of the intelligence services of the new Sandinista army. He also confirmed that Marina was one of Tigrillo's correos.[5]

Jimmy Leo, who was first a Sandinista and then a Milpista with Tigrillo, remembered how he began his own war as a Milpista: "El mismo Frente provocó nuestros resentimientos con sus reprisalias, golpes, asesinatos, robos, y amenazas. [It was the (Sandinista) Front itself that provoked our resentment, with reprisals, beatings, assassinations, thefts, and threats.]"[6] Having attended high school for three years, he was one of the most educated of the Milpistas. He had a mestizo father and an india mother, and before the Revolution the family lived in Los Planos de Bilán in the Jinotegan mountains north of Las Praderas and Santa María de Pantasma.

Jimmy Leo became a Sandinista in 1977 when his older brother was charged by local Somoza officials with being a Sandinista and was beaten by a Guardia Nacional colonel. Jimmy Leo joined the Sandinistas out of resentment, serving them as a correo until early 1978, when he went into the mountains to join Dimas Tigrillo's Blanca Aráuz de Sandino Column. Perhaps because he had an unusually good education by regional standards, he rose quickly to command a column of his own. One of his most memorable tasks was helping establish the Sandinistas' clandestine training base at Pantasma, just south of his Planos de Bilán home.

After Somoza fell, Jimmy Leo, satisfied with what he had done, returned to his family's farm. But neither his prior service as a Sandinista Front guerrilla nor the militant anti-Somocismo of his family protected them. Within weeks the Sandinistas threatened to confiscate his family's farm, and he clashed openly at several mass meetings with former Sandinista comrades-in-arms over the path the Revolution was taking. His paternal grandfather "Pechón" Altamirano, who was openly critical of the Revolution, was detained by the Sandinistas, beaten, and then hanged. Jimmy Leo recalled other campesinos who he believed were innocent of anything other than criticizing the Revolution's programs and who were also killed in the fall of 1979 by the Sandinistas. They included several of his close friends.[7]

Jimmy Leo remembered in vivid detail the Sandinistas' arms sweeps in May, July, and August of 1979, and other actions that alarmed the campesinos, who became both frightened and angry. In the peasant way they kept their anger and resentments to themselves, especially after they saw how anyone who protested openly was silenced by accusations, labeled as counterrevolutionary, threatened, sometimes detained, often beaten, and occasionally killed. This is typical of how highland peasants respond to threats and pressures. They smile and pretend to accept what is being forced on them but begin secretly to seethe with anger and look for ways to avenge themselves, from silent go-slow tactics, to petty acts of sabotage such as cutting fences or killing livestock, to violent revenge whenever they have the chance. By September 1979 the Sandinistas had thoroughly alienated almost all the campesinos of Planos de Bilán, and most began seeking revenge by helping the MILPAS in the nearby mountains and by sending their sons to join their ranks.

Shortly after the Sandinistas hanged his grandfather, Jimmy Leo and a handful of other youths from Planos de Bilán joined Tigrillo, and Sandinista reprisals against the peasants of their comarca began in earnest. His parents' small farm was confiscated. This pushed even the few fence-sitting peasants into rebellion. By the end of 1981, some 480 campesinos from Planos de Bilán, half its population, had fled. Almost all of its young men and many of its young women, about 220 in all, became Milpista combatants.

Jimmy Leo recalled that for the first few months he was with them, Tigrillo's group concentrated on polishing its relations with the peasant popular support base. These people were vital because they provided the group with early warnings of Sandinista movements and with other intelligence information, as well as food, medicines, and other goods not available in the mountains. The challenge of solidifying this support, however, was purely organizational. The Sandinistas were the MILPAS' best allies because their actions made proselytizing all but unnecessary; they had already convinced the peasants they would have to fight. For the peasants the only remaining question was how.

The Sandinistas' labeling of the MILPAS as merely gangs of former Guardia apparently convinced outsiders ignorant of the highlanders' participation and of Nicaragua's historical divisions. But the propaganda campaign backfired in the mountains, where even those rare peasants who did not know some Milpistas personally knew who they were. Jimmy Leo commented, "If we had been Guardia, we would not have had so much success. We were successful because we were from the mountains ourselves, from the same region, and the campesinos knew it."[8] Because the Sandinistas' claims were so far off the mark, their credibility among the highlanders went into free fall, and the rebellion spread rapidly.[9]

EL GRUPO PIRATA

Las ciudades hicieron bien. Pero para los campesinos en las montañas, la llegada de la Revolución era una Via Crucis, un Calvario.

(The cities did well. But for the peasants in the mountains the arrival of the Revolution was a Stations of the Cross, a Calvary).

—PIRATA[10]

"Pirata" is from a peasant family. His father raised corn and beans for home consumption on a thirty-acre plot near Wiwilí. The family was poor but usually managed to produce a small surplus to buy things they could not make for themselves, such as sewing needles, cloth, or kerosene. Pirata and his seven brothers, all of whom were to become Comandos, helped their father work the farm, living together in an isolated dirt-floored house built of wood that they had hewed by hand from local trees. Pirata proudly described himself and his entire family not just as "indios," but as "indios puros," pure Indians, and commented that his paternal grandfather actually spoke "more Indian than Spanish."[11] His fellow *comarqueños*, or comarca neighbors, were suspicious of all outsiders, even peasants from nearby communities. He mentioned with evident pride that his community's most prestigious family was known as the Walakitans,[12] from a lineage of tall dark-skinned people from which came the community's hereditary cacique, or chief. They were always addressed formally as *usted*, never with the informal *vos*.[13]

When the Revolution began, Pirata became a member of both a local CDS and a new Militia battalion.[14] The Sandinistas considered him a loyal supporter and offered him military training in Cuba. They may have been pleased with him, but he was not pleased with them. He had been pressured into joining the CDS and Militia and was unhappy in both. He was also displeased with Sandinista criticisms of the traditional Catholic Church, with the way their rural programs were destroying the independence of the campesinos, and with the way that the Sandinistas intimidated anyone who opposed them and by doing so made everyone afraid to speak out honestly. He was even more disturbed because the Sandinista cadre were all outsiders from the Pacific lowlands, openly contemptuous of the highlander indio campesinos and obviously bent on changing their traditional customs and habits, by force if necessary.[15]

By November 1979, Pirata had had enough.[16] He had known Dimas as a Sandinista commander and knew that he was organizing a new insurgent group, so he made clandestine contact with him. He continued publicly as a Sandinista, but began to give secret support to the Milpistas. Taking a leaf from Dimas's book, Pirata also began to recruit a new MILPAS unit of his own from among Militia companions. Like Pirata, they were highlander indio campesinos who were rapidly becoming disillusioned by the Revolution. The Sandinistas quickly became suspicious and threatened to kill him if they could confirm allegations against him.

Pirata recalled in detail the day he finally acted. On 28 January 1980, he and about twenty other indio militiamen from his comarca deserted and, taking their weapons with them, fled into the nearby mountains to join Dimas. But, after a short time with Dimas, they decided that they were not comfortable being led by an "español" former Sandinista, even one of Dimas's reputation and experience, and preferred to operate autonomously. They soon became a separate MILPAS group. By April 1980, almost one hundred men from Pirata's former militia battalion had joined him, Dimas, or one of the other MILPAS groups around Wiwilí. Fifteen stayed together to form the nucleus of what became the Grupo Pirata, which was to retain its status as an autonomous unit throughout the war. Seven of the fifteen were later killed in combat. Eight were still together when they laid down their arms in 1990.[17]

Asked why he and his group had so insistently maintained their autonomy, Pirata explained that they were indios who were deeply distrustful of all outsiders and did not like to submit to outside leadership.[18] They were unwilling to serve under former Guardia, equally resistant and suspicious of former Sandinistas, and did not even fully trust campesinos from other comarcas. Pirata ascribed these feelings to a particularly deep streak of Indian suspiciousness. Because they were excellent guerrilla fighters, their wishes were respected throughout the war. The families and friends of Pirata's group became its internal support structure, correos, clandestine comarca committee members, and popular support base.

The motives Pirata adduced to his other Militia battalion companions for rebelling were much like his own. They were unhappy at having been pressured into joining a CDS or the Militia against their will and angered by being obligated to sell their products to the state at low prices and then buy from the state at high prices. They opposed land seizures and pressuring to join new agricultural cooperatives, which they saw as threats to their land and independent survival. Coercion by security forces jeopardized their safety and limited their freedom. That the Revolution was being imposed by outsiders from the Pacific lowlands, who neither understood nor respected them, made matters infinitely worse.

THE GROUP OF FAROLÍN AND PALOMA[19]

"Segovia" remembered well his first Milpista experiences with a small MILPAS group led by "Farolín" and "Paloma."[20] Although Segovia's father was from San Juan de Limay and his mother from Condega, their children had been born and raised in the mountains near Estelí.[21] They were a rarity in one sense, a Protestant family in a very Catholic region. But like their Catholic neighbors, they made their living on a small farm, producing almost all their own food. They also grew some coffee that they sold to buy goods not made on the farm or available by barter locally.[22]

During the war against Somoza, Segovia had been a correo for Sandinista guerrilla forces operating in the region of Jalapa just south of the Honduran border in the Department of Nueva Segovia, from which he took his nom de guerre. On several occasions, he helped to evacuate wounded fighters to Honduras for medical treatment and remembered one in particular, Rufo Zeledón, who was to become a Sandinista army first sergeant after the fall of Somoza, only to change sides and become a Comando.[23] When Somoza was defeated, Segovia joined the Sandinistas' Nuevo Ejército. As a reward for his services, he was sent to study auto mechanics at a new facility in Montelimar[24] and then became a driver for Ejército Nuevo drivers. But even as he chauffeured army officers around Nicaragua, Segovia developed serious doubts about the Revolution.

On occasional trips home, Segovia found himself subjected to a steady stream of bitter complaints about how the Sandinista army was acting. People he had known all his life, including members of his own family, began to fear him. Despite Segovia's service, his father was also being harassed by the local CDS, and his mother was terrified. An uncle, Ruy Espinosa, already an early Milpista under the pseudonym Farolín, bluntly told him: "Choose. Your mother or your revolution."[25] Segovia chose.

Disillusioned with the Revolution and the Sandinistas' treatment of his family, and hurt by his family's hostility toward him, Segovia began to work as a clandestine MILPAS supporter in mid-1980 from within Sandinista army ranks. He exploited his mobility as an officer's driver to help the burgeoning insurgency by carrying supplies to the Milpistas in Sandinista vehicles, proselytizing in their favor while on official trips and then preparing with his family to launch yet another MILPAS group.

Shortly after he became a MILPAS supporter, Segovia, one of his brothers, and a first cousin went to join his uncle, Farolín, in the mountains.[26] By the end of 1980 the group had twenty-six members. Its fifteen combatants were led by Farolín and one of

Segovia's older brothers, who had taken the pseudonym Paloma. The rest were mostly family members hiding with them in the mountains to avoid Sandinista reprisals. The group was active in the hills west of Jalapa along the Honduran border. A few of its members occasionally crossed the border into Honduras to buy ammunition for their weapons and to obtain other goods. They were armed only with hunting weapons and received food and other help from nearby campesinos, including a Honduran peasant named Jorge Alvarenga, who had a farm close to Cifuentes, Honduras.[27] They had no direct contact with any of the other MILPAS until early 1981 when, for the first time, they withdrew as a group to Honduras.[28]

LAS CULEBRAS

Rubén (whose first nom de guerre was Culebra and who was cited earlier in connection with Dimas) had mixed feelings about the overthrow of Somoza since his father was a juez de mesta, or magistrate.[29] He and his family had come under pressure from the Sandinistas even before Somoza fell. In March 1979, Rubén was detained by a local Sandinista guerrilla column and sentenced to death. Friends talked the Sandinistas out of executing him, but he remarked, rather laconically, that being sentenced to death "bothered me a lot."[30] For the first several months after the Revolution, Rubén tried to avoid trouble by going about his own business quietly, but reprisals against his father and family made that impossible.

On 29 March 1980, a date engraved in Rubén's memory, a friend named Antonio Jarquín, "Chilindrín,"[31] came to the Sobalvarro's farm at Los Cedros near Kilambé. He appears to have been one of the few Guardia neither jailed or forced into exile by the Sandinistas. Jarquín had just been arrested by the Sandinistas, severely beaten, but then released. After some discussion they joined forces to organize an insurgent group. Their approach was pure Nicaraguan: they started a baseball team.[32] Jarquín and Rubén, then using the nom de guerre Culebra,[33] collected fifteen "baseball players" and, in keeping with their cover, from March through May met only on weekends at a local baseball field. Among the participants were "Ivan" (Abelardo Zelaya) and "Calambrito."[34] The group, which dubbed itself Las Culebras, began to gather hunting weapons to use in the war to come.

By the end of May, Las Culebras were ready and went in to the nearby Segovian highlands to become a MILPAS group. They soon began to capture arms and munitions from the Sandinistas' new militias. Militia members, many of them relatives or friends of the Milpistas, usually just handed over their weapons without a fight. On the few occasions when they seemed reluctant, Las Culebras would help the process along. Rubén said he did not remember this as a difficult task. It was his impression that although the militiamen were responsible for their weapons, they were not especially adverse to having the MILPAS take them as long as they could explain their loss to their Sandinista superiors. Asked why he thought the procurement of arms from the Militia went so smoothly, Rubén asked in return, "Why not? After all, they were all really on our side anyway."[35] Chilindrín was Las Culebras's first leader. They often operated as one of the MILPAS groups allied with Dimas. After Dimas was killed, Las Culebras began to cooperate with Irene Calderón. When Chilindrín was killed in combat in late 1981, Rubén, still using the nom de guerre Culebra, took his place.

Rubén believed that the campesinos' initial violent reaction to the Revolution arose from repeated Sandinista arms sweeps in May, June, July, and August 1979, which they saw as signals that the Sandinistas intended to treat them like enemies from the very beginning, especially since the sweeps began even before the fall of Somoza and well before any visible opposition to the Sandinistas among the highlanders.[36] He also elaborated at length on the early nature and conduct of the Sandinista army and State Security. He called them unprofessional forces who were being taught how to repress a general populace by Cuban and other internationalist advisors. Adding insult to injury, most of the

Sandinista officers and troops were from the Pacific coastal low-lands and displayed clear racial biases against the campesinos, whom they treated as indio inferiors. Rubén said they acted like an occupying army serving on foreign soil, behavior that generated considerable resentment among the region's peasants, already highly suspicious of outsiders, especially españoles from the Pacific.

Interestingly, Rubén also considered the Sandinista's Literacy Crusade another key cause of campesino resentments.[37] The Crusade's literacy workers, or Brigadistas, were largely urban Pacific coast student ideologues imbued with revolutionary zeal. The campesinos were eager to learn to read and write, but the political content of what the Brigadistas tried to teach along with reading and writing shocked the country folk: attacks on the traditional family and the church and effusive praise of Cuba and for Fidel Castro, often even at the expense of Sandinista heroes such as Carlos Fonseca. The Brigadistas were usually quartered on the populace, which had to feed them from its dwindling food stocks and house them in their homes, even though many Brigadistas treated them with outright contempt. Consequently, the peasants soon began to see the Brigadistas as enemies and to designate them as targets for MILPAS actions. By early 1980, MILPAS actions against Brigadistas had become so widespread that the Sandinistas had to send troops and assign special militia units to protect them,[38] and the program had become a major problem at the national level.[39]

Rubén commented with some irony that with their literacy and political consciousness-raising campaigns, the Sandinistas did, as they intended, sharply raise the political consciousness of the peasant masses. What they then failed to do was guide this new consciousness into channels that favored the Revolution.[40] The program raised political awareness among the previously apolitical peasants efficiently enough, but the peasants rejected the Sandinistas' message; instead the process backfired and served primarily to prepare the campesinos to receive the message of the Milpistas. Unlike the Sandinistas' message, that one accorded with their own interests and values systems.

HIGHLAND CLANS

In addition to the Baldivia clan of Tigrillo and Dimas Tigrillo, other prominent clans that joined the highlander Resistance movement were the Mezas, Rugamas, Sobalvarros, Herreras, and Galeanos. The Galeanos serve as an example of how important these clans were from the very beginning. The clan's homeland is near Wiwilí. Seven Galeano brothers and sisters from one nuclear family alone became Milpistas in 1979–80 and then went on to become important Comando leaders. One of the seven was killed during the war and another, Franklyn, the 1988–89 chief of staff of the FDN, died after the war in a suspicious one-car accident in 1995.[41] An assortment of uncles, aunts, and cousins of Franklyn also joined the MILPAS during the earliest years of the organization. All together, eighty-seven Galeanos were Comandos during the war, and several hundred others were correos or members of clandestine comarca committees.[42]

When the Revolution started, the Galeanos held combined properties, which were shared among some twenty nuclear families and covered about 1,250 acres, including 150 planted with coffee and about 1,100 in pasture for some 600 head of cattle. At about fifty-five acres per family, the Galeanos were classified as small or medium-sized farmers. Their farms were worked by a combination of clanspeople and sixty to seventy full-time workers, plus as many as two hundred additional hired workers to pick coffee at harvest time.[43] The Galeanos lived on their farms and were not absentee landlords. They had little formal education, and none had gone beyond primary school. Although better off than the average highlanders, they could not be classified as wealthy. All the Galeanos interviewed for this study identified themselves as peasants, indios, Liberals, and Catholics.[44] According to La Chaparra and Johnny, both Galeanos, the clan is close-knit and very resistant to outside interference.

Galeano clanspeople, with family blessings, had fought against the Somoza dictatorship as Sandinista guerrillas, including three uncles who had been with El Danto. The clan had also lent its properties to Sandinistas operating in the region and had provided food, supplies, and money to the anti-Somoza cause.[45] But despite their support for the struggle against Somoza, as landowners the Galeanos came under Sandinista pressure almost immediately after the Revolution began. The clan's patriarch and one of his older sons were arrested, and another of his sons, Pastor Galeano, disappeared. Pastor's body was recovered in 1990, when it was exhumed from a clandestine cemetery used by the Sandinistas to dispose of the bodies of campesinos killed early in the Revolution. Francisco "Foncho" Galeano, one of those who had fought on the Sandinista side, was arrested in 1983 along with his wife. La Chaparra said he was tortured at a prison known as La Perrera[46] and then castrated, after being forced to watch as his wife (her aunt) was gang-raped by their captors.[47]

The Galeanos began organizing against the Revolution as soon as they came under pressure in late July 1979. By late August they had begun preparations to fight the Sandinistas, working quietly among themselves. For the first few months, none joined the MILPAS, although whenever a nucleus of guerrillas came to their attention, such as those around Dimas, Irene Calderón, or Tigrillo, a Galeano or two would slip out to visit them. By October some Galeanos had gone to the mountains to stay. Others remained on their farms, moving quietly back and forth between them and the guerrilla camps. Although they did not create their own group, they became a prime source of combatants for several of the MILPAS groups and for the larger rebellion to follow.

Johnny recounted some of his own memories of the period.[48] Even as the Sandinistas threatened to seize Galeanos' family farms and severely mistreated members of the clan, he was being pressured by them to join their new militia and a CDS committee. When he resisted, he was publicly labeled a "Somocista" and "counterrevolutionary" and threatened with reprisals. He also remembered being concerned and frightened by the early Sandinista arms sweeps in the countryside. A neighbor, Don Alesio,[49] died of a heart attack in September 1979 when the Sandinistas took his farm. A year later Johnny joined the flood of Galeanos into the

ranks of the rebels and became the leader of a small unit in a
MILPAS group led by Tiro al Blanco.[50] As he recalled, by then
almost his entire family and most of the Galeano clan had joined
the insurgency. Tiro al Blanco's group was active in the area of
Wiwilí, Plan de Grama, El Triunfo, and Chachagüita. Only one of
its members, "Relámpago," was a former Guardia.[51] The rest were
former Milpistas or peasants ralliers. When he arrived, the group
had about thirty combatants and an extensive network of correos
and other collaborators, including many within the Sandinistas'
ranks and even some within the Sandinistas' intelligence services.
Although Johnny's group did engage in some skirmishes with
Sandinista security forces, most of its early activities were dedicated to developing its relationships with its peasant popular
support bases. He said that almost all of the Milpistas felt they had
simply exchanged a dictatorship of the right for one of the left and
harbored deep feelings of resentment for having been deceived.[52]

A number of Galeanos became key Contra commanders, including Franklyn. Johnny himself went on to command the Masaya
Task Force of the FDN's Jorge Salazar I Regional Command. Tiro
al Blanco commanded the Juan Castro Castro Regional Command.[53]
"Adolfo" led the Prudencia González Task Force, part of the Rafael
Herrera Regional Task Force.[54] La Chaparra commanded the 280
women Comandos of the Diriangen Regional Command. A younger
sister, Irma, became a head nurse at the main hospital for the
Resistance in Yamales, Honduras.

OTHER GROUPS

Other MILPAS groups were operating during 1979 and 1980 that
were less well known to those interviewed. According to La
Chaparra, two, led respectively by "Fernando"[55] and "L-20," were
operating near Matagalpa in late 1979,[56] while a third, under "El
Coyote," was active in the region of Rio Blanco, far to the south on
the border between the departments of Matagalpa and Zelaya.[57]
José Antonio Aguirre Zamora, "Chino-4,"[58] knew of a small

MILPAS group in 1979 and 1980 under one Hermia Hernández that had been active near the Jinotega hamlets of Wina, Amacona, and Waslalita. Hernández later came to be called L-20. Jimmy Leo also remembered the groups that La Chaparra mentioned, plus another under the leadership of "El Cuervo." Johnny recalled a group of twenty to twenty-five under a commander known as "Aureliano" that had been active around El Zúngano and Cerro del Cacho.[59] The Aureliano, as Johnny remembered, had fought against Somoza under El Danto.[60]

Luis Fley González, "Jhonson," who provided information on several other MILPAS groups, was an officer in the Sandinista Army from 1979 to 1981. He was later to become a Resistance comandante after he became convinced that, as he put it, "the people wanted Somoza to go . . . and things got worse."[61] But during the first phase of the highlander war, Jhonson, as a Sandinista Army officer, was kept informed by Sandinista intelligence of some eight to ten MILPAS groups operating in the highlands.[62] In addition to those of Dimas, Tigrillo, Chilindrín, Tiro al Blanco, and "El Cadejo," he remembered being told of a group near Rio Blanco (perhaps that of El Coyote) and another led by a Juan Hernández, known as "Juan:23." He recalls that Juan:23 was said to have about fifteen guerrillas, including one known as "El Sordo"[63] and another known as "Picho" Jarquín.

Jhonson is among the most quoted of the former Resistance comandantes. He served near the end of the conflict as the FDN's judge advocate general and, in that capacity, came to be known to a number of foreign journalists.[64] Born and raised in a rural comarca near El Tuma, Matagalpa, he was a correo for Omar Cabezas's forces around Kilambé during the war against Somoza. He remembered bringing food, medicine, and intelligence information.[65] He fell under suspicion and was arrested by the Somoza government. After his release, he went into the mountains to join the guerrillas and served in the Sandinistas' Bernardo Villas Ochoa Column.

Jhonson's most memorable combat experiences during the war against Somoza were attacks on Jinotega and Matagalpa. He was aware that there was a highlander MILPA unit with the Sandinistas and recalled being told that almost all its fighters were from Jinotega. As he remembered events, when the three Marxist *tendencias*, or factions, within the Sandinista Front were united by Castro in Havana,[66] the non-Marxist highlander MILPAS fell through the cracks and became a sort of fourth group.[67]

Jhonson remained in the Sandinista army for almost two years following the fall of Somoza. When he left the army in early 1981, he was rewarded by being made the manager of a government company in Managua. Soon, however, he began to have problems when he criticized policies that the Sandinistas were implementing. Labeled a reactionary by Front cadre on his staff, he was fired, and his local CDS committee began to make his life miserable. He was accused of being a counterrevolutionary and jailed. Jhonson's three brothers had stayed in the army and were able to obtain his release but warned him that the Sandinistas might kill him and recommended that he leave Managua quickly. Jhonson first returned home. But during April and May of 1981, several of his friends were killed for criticizing the Revolution. None had actively opposed the Revolution. Critical comments alone had been enough to cost them their lives. As a marked counterrevolutionary himself, he became fearful for his own safety and tried to leave the country, but was denied a passport. Finally, with six companions, he fled to the mountains and joined the MILPAS.[68]

POCOYO

One study of the period mentions a MILPAS group under a "Pocoyo" that was reportedly active near La Pita del Carmen, Yalí, and Quilalí in July 1980.[69] The group was said to have attacked a number of militia and army posts and suffered some casualties before being captured en masse on 13 September of that year.[70] It may have been led by the Pocoyo mentioned earlier, but the former Comandos who were interviewed could not remember a MILPAS group led by him.

STAY-BEHINDS AND OTHER NON-MILPAS

Not all the early armed rebel groups in 1979 were MILPAS. In addition to the highlander MILPAS that came to form the basis of the main Contra army, some small non-MILPAS armed groups of stay-behinds remained inside Nicaragua after Somoza fell. These were among a handful of other anti-Sandinistas who quickly organized themselves during this time. While relatively little information about them was uncovered, the earliest of these organizations may have been two small groups in the hills near Masaya. A former Resistance activist, Rodolfo Robles, "Raul," said that in July 1979, he and eight others organized themselves and took to the hills near Managua with the intention of engaging in guerrilla operations, but their efforts were short-lived. Sandinista security forced them to disperse within a few weeks. At the time, Raul was aware of another group of about the same number that was active nearby.[71]

One Comando remembered a group of twelve men under a leader known as "El Chino" that was active during the latter half of 1979 in eastern León; all were from the Guardia Nacional's elite EEBI (Escuela de Enseñanza Basica de Infantéria) unit.[72] The group broke up when El Chino was killed in a clash at El Roble, near El Jicaral, León, on 9 January 1980.[73] Pirata recalled another group of about fifteen others led by a "Kalimán" that had two former members of the EEBI in its ranks.[74] He had also heard of an even smaller group of five under a Frank Montenegro, "Frijol," that had been active near Masaya but was quickly pushed north into the mountains by Sandinista security patrols. He recalled that Frijol's deputy was known as "Ráfaga."[75] Jimmy Leo and La Chaparra remembered hearing of a group of about fifteen others under El Cuervo, who had been active in Matagalpa, but he did not know who they were or precisely where they had operated.[76] La Chaparra also added that she thought there had been a large group of former Guardia active near Rio Blanco led by a guerrilla who called himself El Coyote. No confirming evidence was found on any of these groups. In any case they had little lasting impact and soon disappeared.

INDEPENDENT EVIDENCE OF
MILPAS OPERATIONS:
A SANDINISTA OFFICER'S DIARY

The most convincing document used to cross-check many of the
comments by the Comandos concerning the earliest MILPAS was
the contemporary handwritten field combat diary of Lt. Fidel
Tinoco Zeledón, the commander of an elite Sandinista reconnaissance platoon. His platoon spent the better part of two years chas-
ing Milpistas in the highlands.[77] From 30 December 1980 to 29 June
1982, Tinoco led the pursuit of Milpistas as they moved in and out
of many of the mountain communities named by the Milpistas
during interviews, especially Wiwilí, Aguas Calientes, Kilambé,
Plan de Grama, and San José de Bocay. In his diary, Tinoco gives
the names of thirty-seven of the Milpistas he was pursuing, including several Sobalvarros and a number of Mezas, Herreras, and
Blandones. Irene Calderón is repeatedly mentioned, as are José
Danilo Galeano, Tiro al Blanco, and several Milpistas who were
with Tigrillo.

Tinoco's reconnaissance platoon supported the operations of
two nearby Sandinista Army units he identifies as U.M. 6027 and
B.O.N. 6009 and spent much of its time trying to obtain information from campesinos or searching for weapons.[78] It appears not to
have had much success at either mission. In one instance, Tinoco's
platoon was ordered to take up a hidden position near Aguas
Calientes to try to spot MILPAS correos and other collaborators
known to be active there. Sandinista intelligence provided them
with a clandestine peasant contact to help them. Tinoco personally
observed so many campesino-Milpista contacts that he finally
noted down in his diary, in exasperation, that it looked to him as
if all the peasants of Aguas Calientes were collaborating with the
MILPAS. After fifteen days his mission was aborted. By then he
was personally convinced that even his undercover Sandinista
contact was actually a MILPAS collaborator.[79] During his eighteen
months in the field, the only weapons Tinoco reported capturing
were four .38 caliber pistols[80] and a .22 caliber rifle, although he

did seize some ammunition and a telescopic sight for a rifle and reported seeing two M-16 rifles on 21 November 1981, in the hands of the leaders of a passing MILPAS unit.[81]

Perhaps the most striking feature of Tinoco's diary is its documentation of the rapid growth and evolution of the MILPAS rebellion. In late 1980 and early 1981, his platoon's spottings of MILPAS were usually fleeting and the number of Milpistas they saw were few. By the autumn of 1981, Tinoco was reporting larger and larger units, a group of seventeen from Aguas Calientes on 10 October, including sixteen members of the Herrera and Cornejo families, a platoon-sized unit of fifty on 21 November. By July 1982, Tinoco was reporting on company-sized units of the new FDN. One he observed even had an official name, the Grupo Lorenzo Cardenal.[82]

Tinoco's diary confirms, with individual names, places, dates, and other details, the accuracy of much of what the former Comandos said concerning the MILPAS war. All of those he mentions in the beginning were campesinos, none former Guardia; the peasantry was rebelling en masse. The diary information also confirms that the war was well under way and spreading rapidly by early 1981, and that up to the end of that year the MILPAS were the only Nicaraguans engaged in armed combat operations against the Sandinistas. Tinoco was killed in combat on 29 June 1982 during a clash with a Comando unit led by Luís Payán, "Mike Lima," who then used the diary as his own for a short period.[83] Mike Lima asked me to note that Tinoco had proven a competent foe and died courageously. (Map 5 shows the areas of operation of the MILPAS groups mentioned by Tinoco and by former Comandos.)

THE MILPAS WAR PERIOD

In addition to the above comments by early Milpistas and those found in Tinoco's diary, other independent sources confirm that there was fighting in the Segovias during this period. Many of these accounts are in press reports published by the Foreign Broadcast Information Service (FBIS).[84]

Map 5. The combined zones of operation of fifteen MILPAS groups, 1979–82. Note their spread south to Rio Blanco and east to Bocay on the Rio Coco (Coco River).

The comments of the Milpistas in particular display a high degree of internal consistency. The Milpistas who had been with the anti-Somoza MILPAS of El Danto and Dimas all said they had reached a point of disillusionment by early May 1979. Their response followed announcements, at officers' meetings in the highlands, of Sandinista plans to stage a radical revolution, not establish a Costa Rican–style democracy. Several mentioned El

Danto's open opposition to these plans, and his later death by "friendly fire," as turning points. Dimas's common-law wife, Marina, quoted Dimas himself as expressing such views at the time and dated Dimas's disillusionment and initial acts of rebellion back to May 1979. Several Milpistas, including Segovia, Dimas Tigrillo, and Tigre, traced their own active opposition to the Revolution to the same events in the same month. Others confirmed that the rebellions of Irene Calderón and Tigrillo also began during the same period. Those who had not been anti-Somoza Milpistas became disenchanted because of the same events that followed after the Sandinistas took power.

The former Milpistas were consistent in their comments on what they believed had led the peasants of the Segovian highlands to rebel. A number mentioned Sandinista arms sweeps in May, June, July, and August of 1979 as having alerted the campesinos to trouble to come. All pointed to revolutionary policies that required the campesinos to sell their crops at low prices and then buy necessities at high prices from the government, to seizures of private property "in the name of the Revolution," to coercive violence of one sort or another, and to ethnic and class tensions between the highlanders and Pacific coast revolutionary cadre. Several also mentioned land tenure problems. Unhappiness with involuntary associations, especially pressure to join new militia units and CDSs, was also cited as widespread and important. Because the Sandinistas took power on 19 July 1979, and the first Agrarian Reform Decree was issued on 22 July, the July-August period at which the Milpistas dated the beginning of the Resistance movement was historically consistent.[85]

The Milpistas also responded consistently to questions concerning their individual and family identities and their ethnic, class, and geographic origins. This was particularly suggestive. All identified themselves and their families as campesinos and small farmers. All but one, Rubén, identified themselves as indios. All said they were from particularly rural comarcas in either Nueva Segovia or Jinotega. None were former Guardia. Their information generated questions about the class, ethnic, historical, and geographic roots, not only of the Comandos, but also of the people who had given birth to the MILPAS war. It also raised another question. If the 1979–81 MILPAS war had been decidedly Segovian, peasant, indio, and non-Guardia in origin, how had these people come to be "Contras" in a so-called "Contra War"?

CHAPTER SIX

EXILE PARAMILITARY GROUPS, 1979–1982

At the same time MILPAS units were fighting inside Nicaragua, other anti-Sandinista forces were gathering outside the country. The earliest paramilitary exile groups were a small armed group in San Marcos de Colón and Choluteca, Honduras known as Los Zebras, organized in July 1979; a group of Guardia led by Major Pablo Emilio Salazar, "Comandante Bravo," that had fled to El Salvador in July and then began moving to Honduras in August; an original Southern Front that had organized in Costa Rica in August 1979 and begun some cross-border raiding into Nicaragua late that year; and the largest and best-known of these early exile paramilitary groups, the Legión 15 de Septiembre, organized in Guatemala City on 31 December 1979.

LOS ZEBRAS

The archives of the Nicaraguan Resistance contain a document dated 22 July 1979 that proved to be a personnel roster for the organization known as Los Zebras. It lists 141 members by name, noms de guerre, and function. Most of the former Comandos I interviewed were unaware of this exile group, but several, including former Guardia Col. Ricardo Lau, "Chino Lau," confirmed that Los

Zebras had, in fact, been created in July 1979, in Choluteca, Honduras, by some former Guardia and others.[1] When I showed him a copy of the roster, Chino Lau said that both the personnel named and the date of the information on it appeared correct, although the document itself seemed to be a later copy of an original list. He called Los Zebras one of the precursor groups of the Legión 15 de Septiembre, which he helped found in December 1979. Members of Los Zebras who are named on the roster later formed the nucleus for an early Legión unit known as the Base Operacional Zebra, which was established in April 1981. This was one of the first three Resistance operations bases in Honduras.[2] Of those named, fifty-seven, or 40 percent, are identified as former Guardia.[3] This percentage coincides with later data on the Base Operacional Zebra that, at 40 percent, had the highest percentage of former Guardia in any Resistance formation. Several names are also the same.[4]

Another former Comando, "Johnny II," also remembered Los Zebras and recalled that they were organized in Honduras in July 1979.[5] He remembered them as former Guardia and civilians whose intent was to organize guerrilla warfare against the Sandinistas. The group had contacts with other anti-Sandinista elements in Guatemala and Honduras.[6] Two other former Comandos, Jimmy Leo and Rubén, also remembered them,[7] although Jimmy Leo recalled little other than hearing of them during the early part of the war. Rubén was better informed and described the group as former Guardia who were active along the Honduras/Nicaragua frontier between the Gulf of Fonseca and the San Marcos de Colón/El Espino border area in 1979 and 1980. He remembered that they brought attention to themselves by stealing cattle in Nicaragua and selling them in Honduras to pay for their operations. During that period the MILPAS were also active as guerrillas but only inside Nicaragua and in regions much farther to the east in Nueva Segovia and Jinotega near the Coco River.[8] Los Zebras were probably the origin of Robert Kagan's image of the earliest Contras (see chapter 1).

On 9 April 1980, Sandinista State Security chief Lenin Cerna confirmed the presence of an active exile group in Choluteca,

complete with a board of directors, that was planning to stage guerrilla operations near Chinandega in Nicaragua's northern Pacific. Based on details given by Cerna during his public com-
• ments, the group appears to have been Los Zebras.[9] No other documents were found on the activities of Los Zebras, and none of those interviewed had been personally involved. But according to Rubén's comments and Cerna's press statements, it appears to have been this exile group that generated charges during 1979 and 1980 that former Guardia were engaged in cattle rustling raids into northern Pacific Nicaragua from Honduras. What is not clear is the real intentions of these participants.

Smuggling cattle from Nicaragua northward for sale in Honduras or El Salvador without "benefit of customs inspections" is a time-honored practice among Nicaraguan ranchers, and 1979–80 marked the beginnings of Sandinista agrarian reform efforts, with cattle growers among those most affected. By late 1979, smuggling cattle was a counterrevolutionary crime carrying harsh penalties, yet many ranchers must have felt the need to liquidate some of their assets by selling cattle, lest they be seized. Reporting them as stolen would keep them from getting into trouble with the new regime and, if done in collusion with Los Zebras or others in Honduras, both parties could profit. Thus, it is unclear whether this rustling was criminal or collusive. In either case, the region in which Los Zebras were operating is distant from the operational areas of the MILPAS. (See the upper margin of map 6.)

COMANDANTE BRAVO

The most prominent of the former Guardia to be militarily active during 1979 was Maj. Pablo Emilio Salazar, who had commanded Guardia forces opposite the Sandinistas on Nicaragua's southern front during the anti-Somoza war. Under the nom de guerre Comandante Bravo, he had been one of the few "heroes" on the Somocista side. When Somoza fled, Bravo negotiated directly by radio with the Salvadoran army to withdraw his troops by sea to

Map 6. Comparison of 1979–82 areas of operation for the Zebras, MILPAS, and First Southern Front. Note the distances between the three areas.

Puerto La Unión, El Salvador. The withdrawal took place 20–21 July, aboard a small flotilla of fishing and coastal vessels.

At first Bravo's troops, as members of Nicaragua's armed forces, assumed that once the situation inside Nicaragua settled down, they would be allowed to return home peacefully.[10] But by mid-August they realized that they would not be able to do so safely and began to think about their next move. Some joined the Salvadoran armed forces, and others sought refuge in third countries, including the United States. But most, still under the command of Bravo, began moving to Honduras.

Bravo was given some arms and ammunition from Salvadoran arsenals and encouraged by local Salvadoran army commanders to establish his force along the Honduras-Nicaragua border and to begin raiding into Nicaragua. It not clear whether this encouragement was part of an approved policy or the result of Bravo's relationships with friendly Salvadoran army officers. In any case, a logistical pipeline was established from La Unión, El Salvador, across southern Honduras to Bravo's force and was used to send his men arms, munitions, and other help as they tried to reorganize into a force that could stage cross-border guerrilla raids.[11]

Bravo's men did launch several small cross-border raids, but these apparently had little impact. Nonetheless, the Sandinistas apparently saw him as a major threat and decided to eliminate him, perhaps because, having successfully blocked their southern invasion from Costa Rica for much of the war, he was a proven combat leader and had, for some, an aura of heroism. On 10 October 1979, he was lured to a rendezvous in Tegucigalpa by a female Sandinista agent, Miriam Barbareño, and tortured to death.[12] Those who had gathered around him scattered or joined other groups.

Former top Sandinista "Pépe" Puente, cited earlier in connection with El Danto, confirmed to me during a conversation at his home in Mexico City in October 1999, that Comandante Bravo was considered by the Nine Comandantes to have the potential to be the most dangerous leader of an organized armed effort against the Revolution. He said he himself planned the operation under orders from Sandinista comandante Tomás Borge, the revolutionary government's new minister of the interior responsible for intelligence and counter-intelligence operations. At the time Puente was Borge's top intelligence aide, and his son Lenín Obidio was Borge's personal bodyguard.

THE LEGIÓN 15 DE SEPTIEMBRE

The best-known exile paramilitary organization of this early period was the Legión 15 de Septiembre, established on 31 December 1979 in Guatemala City and named for Nicaragua's Independence Day. Chino Lau was among its founders. He said that it was created by Guardia officers, some civilians then in Guatemala, and a few other Nicaraguans who flew in from Miami for the occasion.[13] They met in the home of a Guardia colonel, Juan Gomez, "Fighter," who was then working as the private pilot of Guatemalan army General Lucas.[14] Among those present were Francisco Urcuyo Maliaño, who had been president of Nicaragua for three days between the fall of Somoza and the arrival of the Sandinistas in Managua, Guardia colonels Enrique Bermúdez and Justiniano Pérez, and captains Frixione and Francisco Ribera.[15] Captain Ribera brought a small supply of propaganda leaflets from Miami. Those who met also created a parallel political organization, ADREN (Alianza Democratica Revolucionaria Nicaragüense).[16] The Legión quickly made contact with several other, smaller exile paramilitary groups that were also active in Guatemala, including the Unión Democratico Nicaragüense (UDN), the Fuerza Armada de Resistencia Nicaragüense (FARN), and the Frente Revolucionario para la Liberación de Nicaragua (FRPLN). The Legión began, too, to reach out to other groups in Costa Rica, Honduras, and the United States.

Another former Guardia who was present at the founding of the Legión 15 de Septiembre, but who did not immediately join, was Filemón Espinal Aguilera, "4-2."[17] When Somoza fled Nicaragua, 4-2 took asylum in the Guatemalan embassy in Managua.[18] Allowed to leave in late 1979, he went to Guatemala City, where he found work as a municipal garbage collector. While working for the city, he also made contact with the exiled Guardia community that was preparing to create the Legión, a number of whom were being housed and supported by Guatemalan businessmen in a safe house near Guatemala City's La Aurora International Airport. The exiles were using the house's gardens to conduct makeshift training courses while trying to keep their activities and location secret. Initially 4-2 joined the FRPLN because, although a former Guardia himself, he felt those in charge of the Legión were not the best leaders available. He held out for a few weeks but finally became a Legionnaire after he concluded that the Legión was the more viable of the two groups.[19]

"Chino 85," Later a vice minister in the 1996 Liberal government, was yet another former Guardia who went to Guatemala to join the Legión. He described the exiled group's activities during that period.[20] At first its members engaged only in limited paramilitary training on their own. But the Guatemalan army soon began to help them and Chino-85 joined a twenty-man group of Legionnaires being given basic military training at an army base known as Destacamento 110.[21] As with the Salvadoran army's support for Comandante Bravo's group, it was not entirely clear whether the Guatemalan military was acting on its own or with its government's approval.[22]

By March 1980, the Legión felt strong enough to establish a presence on the Nicaragua/Honduras border. It had continued to receive support from some Guatemalan businessmen and had also received some arms and ammunition from the Guatemalan military. Its first detachment on the Honduran border, as yet unnamed, soon began to stage small incursions into Nicaragua in the region of the Jalapa valley and managed to capture some weapons from militia units.[23] In April, the Legión increased its presence in the mountains of southern Honduras, under a plan called Proyecto Ariel, by establishing three bases of operations known as Atenas Ariel, Zebra, and Sagitario.[24]

By early 1980, the Legión was also broadcasting into Nicaragua over its own station, Radio 15 de Septiembre, a fact confirmed by regional media reports.[25] When Chino 85 later went to Honduras, he was told to report in to Legión offices at Radio 15 de Septiembre's transmitter site on top a hill known as Cerro de Hule, near Tegucigalpa. He remembers that Honduras's civilian authorities were none too happy with the radio station, but it was being protected by Honduran army officers, so there was little they could do.[26] Once the Legión's first three bases were operational, the group established three more, Pino-1, Agateite, and Arenales.[27] A seventh, Fénix, was added later in the Honduran Mosquitia and staffed by mostly former Guardia cadre to train Miskito, Sumo, and Rama Indians who were beginning to stream out of Nicaragua to join the rebellion.

THE ORIGINAL SOUTHERN FRONT

In August 1980, the Legión was asked by Argentine intelligence operatives in contact with the group through Guardia Col. Enrique Bermúdez, "Comandante 3-80,"[28] Somoza's former military attaché in Washington D.C., for a favor in return for more support. (Argentina's 1979–84 role in the Contra War is discussed in chapter 7.) In this instance, in Guatemala City, the Argentine military said it was interested in helping the Legión, but first wanted the members to demonstrate their ability to stage a paramilitary operation. If the Argentines were satisfied, they would take three groups of twenty-two Comandos each to Argentina for courses in intelligence, counter-intelligence, and special warfare. The Argentines specified that for the Legión to demonstrate its seriousness it needed to stage a commando raid in Costa Rica. At the time, leftist Argentine Montonero guerrillas opposed to the Argentine government were operating a powerful short-wave radio transmitter at Punta Piedras near Grecia, Costa Rica, known as Radio Noticias del Continente, broadcasting southward into Argentina, and Argentine intelligence wanted it silenced. Johnny II remembered that the Nicaraguans fully understood that the Argentines had made its destruction the price of their support.[29]

The Legión, with no presence of its own in Costa Rica, turned to the original Southern Front, a small non-Guardia exile group that had been active there since 1979 but was not part of the Legión. (The better-known second Southern Front led by Edén Pastora, "Comandante Zero," did not appear until later.)[30] The group's raids had already caused the Sandinistas, on several occasions, to send troops to Nicaragua's southern border in reaction to its attacks.[31] By mid-1980 the original Southern Front had some 174 combatants. Most were peasants from Nicaragua's Pacific lowlands. About 10 percent were former Pacific lowland businessmen. Several dozen were former Sandinistas, and seven were former Guardia.[32] The group agreed to stage the raid on behalf of the Legión and, shortly thereafter, attacked the Radio Noticias transmitter site, knocking it off the air for a short time.

A former business manager who was to go on to command an FDN Special Forces unit had been a member of the original Southern Front. A third-generation native of Managua, his parents were both "muy indios y muy Liberales" (both very Indian and very Liberal).[33] To protect him from possible reprisals, his name is withheld. His father was a sugar cane specialist who helped manage several Somoza farms; the Sandinistas consequently labeled the family as Somocista. When the Salvadoran company he worked for closed its offices in Managua, it transferred him to Costa Rica. He did not become involved in exile activities until late 1980, when he joined the original Southern Front. From then until late May 1982 he was actively involved in supporting cross-border raids into Nicaragua from Costa Rica.

This Comando and another Comando, Johnny II, who was interviewed separately, both remembered several raids the group had staged during 1980–81 from Costa Rica against Sandinista targets at Los Chiles, Peñas Blancas, Naranjo-Conventillos, and Cárdenas. A June 1981 attack on a military basic training camp at a place called La Cruz that was under the direction of three Cubans was the most successful. The Comando claimed that they inflicted twenty-seven casualties, including wounding all three Cubans. Only one of the raiders, a Costa Rican known as "El Tico," was wounded.[34] Both he and Johnny II recalled that although they were not officially welcome in Costa Rica, they received considerable informal help from Costa Rican Guardia Civil officers and other officials, including protection, arms, munitions, and other equipment. He remembered three or four Guardia with the group. Johnny II placed the number at four.

This Comando also recalled that on one occasion in early 1981 the original Southern Front was contacted by another group that had been hiding for over a month in the hills inside Nicaragua near San Carlos on Lake Nicaragua just north of Los Chiles, Costa Rica. Of the twenty-six members, eighteen were former Sandinistas, but they had no weapons. Costa Rican officials gave the first Southern Front some rifles and three LAW rockets from leftover Sandinista arms caches.[35] They thought it ironic that the weapons were from stocks the Sandinistas had left behind in Costa Rica. It turned out that none of the new group's members knew how to use any of them, so the Comando's group also had to give them a crash weapons course.[36] He finally left Costa Rica for Honduras when pressure was applied on the Costa Rican government by the second Southern Front of Edén Pastora, after it began to organize in 1982. By then the Argentines had made good on their promises. According to a handwritten personnel report dated 20 December 1981 (see appendix A), sixty-two had been trained in Argentina and sixteen in Guatemala. By then the Legión also had fifteen *oficiales* in the United States, ten in Miami, and five in "projects."[37] The implications of this are discussed in the forthcoming chapter.

CHAPTER SEVEN

FOREIGN ENTANGLEMENTS

Cuba, Costa Rica, and the CIA

SUPPORT FOR THE SANDINISTAS AGAINST SOMOZA

Alone among the major antagonists in Nicaragua's recent wars, the MILPAS of 1979–82 had no foreign military support. All the others did, including those who made earlier attempts to overthrow the Somozas, the Sandinistas both during their struggle against the Somozas and later when in power, the FDN alliance, even Augusto César Sandino in his time.

The Somoza dynasty, which was widely described by its critics as a "client" of the United States, probably could not have retained power for so long without American political support.[1] Although some scholars have expressed doubts that this was so categorically true, little question exists that part of this support—the provision of arms—was of major value to the Somozas.[2] But the Somozas were not the only players with foreign government support in Nicaragua's wars.

Attempt after attempt to overthrow the Somozas by force were also supported by other countries. Foreign governments had armed and sustained several guerrilla incursions against Somoza—for example, the repeated efforts by former Sandino Gen. Ramon Raudáles,[3] the Olama y Mojellones incursion of Pedro Joaquín

Chamorro, and other efforts to topple the dynasty.[4] Costa Rica,
Venezuela, Mexico, and Guatemala were especially involved.[5] But
a former senior Sandinista, who participated for over eighteen
years, labeled all such foreign-trained, armed, and supported efforts
to eject the Somozas "injertos rechazados," attempts to graft outsider guerrilla groups onto an unreceptive host that were rejected.[6]

The final and successful push to oust the last Somoza came only
after 1977. At that time, Nicaragua's traditional oligarchy, which
until then had largely sat out the process, finally made common
cause with the country's radical revolutionaries. This occurred for
a number of reasons, not least because the third Somoza, unlike his
father and older brother who had been presidents before him, had
become excessively forceful not just as a competitor for political
power but also as a rival for economic dominance. The Carter
administration of the United States also turned its back on the third
Somoza, and Fidel Castro flooded the Sandinistas with arms and
other war materiel from Cuba. In order to mask their actual origin
in Cuba, a widely reported cover story was put out that the arms
that flowed to the Sandinista Front in 1978–79 were from Panama
and Colombia, but this was never true. According to Costa Rican
congressional investigative archives, confirmed by the minister
who had been personally charged by the Costa Rican president
with facilitating movement of the arms, by a senior Sandinista field
commander who had been directly involved, and by numerous
others who had seen or monitored various shipments from early
1978 through July 1979, Cuba shipped at least two thousand tons
of arms and munitions to the Sandinista Front in Costa Rica alone
and did so with the active cooperation and support of the Costa
Rican government. The materiel arrived via more than four hundred cargo flights directly from Cuba.[7] Other shipments arrived by
way of Honduras or directly by air drop. Former Costa Rican president José "Pepe" Figúeres said flatly of the final 1978–79 push
against the Somozas that had it not been for arms from Cuba and
Costa Rican government support for Sandinista operations, the
"war [against Somoza] could not have been fought. It would not
have been possible."[8]

When the Sandinistas took power, they brought most of this Cuban-supplied arsenal with them from Costa Rica. At the same time, they also began to benefit from a second flood of foreign aid, advisors, and arms.[9] During their first three years in power, the Sandinistas received an estimated $310 million in military assistance.[10] According to Sandinista military inventories classified Muy Secreto, or Top Secret, that were brought out by a defector, by October 1987 the Sandinista Army had 420,000 small arms and 567 million rounds of ammunition in its official arsenals and was asking for 149,056 more small arms, mostly automatic rifles, and 230 million more rounds of ammunition.[11] These inventories, several pages of which are reproduced in appendix E, did not include about 180,000 small arms left over from the estimated 267,000 Cuba had supplied to overthrow Somoza.[12] By comparison, during their first years, the MILPAS inside received no foreign help and the exiled paramilitary elsewhere got a mere trickle.

THE CIA'S FIRST INVOLVEMENT, 1979–80

The first serious offers of covert American paramilitary help made to those who were to become Nicaragua's Contras were reportedly presented to the Legión 15 de Septiembre in Guatemala at the very end of 1979 and early 1980. They involved both Americans and Argentines, with the Argentines acting as the CIA's cover. The evidence became convincing because so many separate sources that were unacquainted with one another described initial contacts during that period with American and Argentine intelligence agents.

According to eyewitnesses, also in December 1979, two American CIA agents visited the Nicaraguan exile's safe house near Guatemala City's La Aurora airport. The senior of the two told them he was the agency's chief of station in Tegucigalpa and that the United States was ready to give them covert paramilitary help if they could show that they were serious.[13] He suggested that they demonstrate their resolve by generating some funds independently.

Desperate for the legitimacy that would come with American involvement in their struggle, as well as for the help itself, they staged a series of kidnappings and bank robberies in Guatemala. The senior CIA officer rushed back, appalled by what they had done, but convinced they meant what they said. He told them that kidnapping and robbing were unacceptable but that he was satisfied they meant business. Shortly thereafter, the Argentines made their first contact, the exiles organized themselves as the Legión 15 de Septiembre, and the Legión began to receive funds and paramilitary support from Argentine operatives.[14]

Apparently these contacts led to late-1980 efforts to enroll a non-Guardia commander for the enterprise. After several approaches, CIA operatives and Argentine military intelligence officers tried to recruit a very experienced guerrilla combat leader who was well known both for his earlier fierce opposition to the Somoza dictatorship and his equally fierce opposition to the new Sandinista revolutionary government. Alejandro Martínez Saenz, an anti-Somoza guerilla since 1948 and an original member of the Fuerza Revolucionaria Sandino (FRS) that predated the FSLN by more than ten years, was approached in December 1980 in San José, Costa Rica. A Conservative and son of a Conservative national deputy who had been forced into exile in Costa Rica by Somoza, Martínez had fought as a Sandinista commander from 1972 through August 1979. But, as with El Danto, when in May 1979 he became convinced that his Sandinista comrades intended to stage a socialist revolution, he openly rebelled. His erstwhile comrades-in-arms made attempts to kill him. In August 1979 a bullet was fired from within his unit's own ranks that took off part of his left ear, and he decided to retire from the battlefield. A subsequent attempt in Costa Rica to assassinate him was also unsuccessful. Presumably the CIA and Argentines looked at him as a potential leader of the paramilitary forces they were building. Martínez went to Washington, D.C., in early January 1981 to discuss the project in detail but decided not to cooperate when he was told he would have to accept a general staff of former Guardia.[15]

ARGENTINA AND THE CIA

The widely believed story that Argentine military intelligence had become independently involved in the nascent Central American Contra guerrilla enterprise seems on the surface hard to understand. Central America is, after all, of far greater interest to the United States than to distant Argentina. That they would have done so against the wishes of the United States seems even bizarre, and the idea that they could possibly have mounted such a major operation in cooperation with the Honduran government without American knowledge and acquiescence seems, simply put, not credible. It was only after I heard witness after witness insist that the Argentines had been enthusiastic cut-outs for the CIA that Argentina's reasons for becoming involved made sense. After all, Argentina's then-military government was unhappy with the Sandinistas well before they took power, and many Argentine Montonero guerrillas had served in the Sandinistas' ranks during the war to overthrow Somoza.[16]

Covert Argentine interest in anti-Sandinista guerrillas appears to have begun in late 1979, but the Argentines' real passion for the project was greatly increased at the first anniversary celebration of the Sandinista Revolution when the Sandinistas deliberately and publicly insulted the Argentine ambassador before numerous international delegations, including some heads of state. When the Argentine ambassador arrived to take his place of honor on the reviewing stand at the celebration's parade, the official Argentine box was already occupied, at the invitation of the Sandinista Foreign Ministry, by Montonero guerrillas who were under sentence of death in Argentina for terrorist acts. The ambassador and his government were incensed.[17] Later, the former Costa Rican minister of public security, "Johnny" Echeverría Brealy, who had been responsible for ensuring that the Sandinistas received their arms shipments from Cuba during the war against Somoza, suggested that this was the event that triggered Argentine involvement.[18] But, in fact, the Argentines had already been involved for many months.

In any case, according to other witnesses, the next month two American and two Argentine agents also visited a small group of Milpistas at the farm of Jorge Alvarenga, near the town of Cifuentes in southern Honduras.[19] They were accompanied by two Legión 15 de Septiembre leaders, one of whom was Col. Enrique Bermúdez, plus some Honduran military personnel.[20] By then the Legión had already been working for some four months with Honduran military protection and help to establish its first bases near the Honduras-Nicaragua border. The presence of American and Argentine agents with the Hondurans strongly suggests that by then the three countries were working together.[21]

If true, this meant that American involvement with Nicaragua's Contras began with President Carter, not President Reagan, a finding that came as a surprise to me, since I had previously accepted as true the conventional wisdom that Reagan had been first. Because of the implications, I explored the question of the earliest date of U.S. involvement during numerous additonal interviews. Among those I reinterviewed were several former senior Costa Rican officials, three Costa Rican security operatives, seven intelligence professionals from three other countries who had detailed information on events of the times, and a number of Nicaraguan Resistance personnel. All of those contacted were surprised that I was surprised. Three responded with the same Spanish phrase. "Por supuesto. No lo sabías?" (Of course. Didn't you know?)

Adolfo Calero, one of the most prominent longtime activists in the Resistance, said categorically and repeatedly during a reinterview in Managua that he and all of the movements leaders had understood from the very beginning that the Argentines were never more than a front for the CIA. He commented that it should have been obvious. The Argentines lacked the money, supplies, and expertise and, even if they had these, would never have engaged in an extensive clandestine paramilitary operation in Central America without American involvement. Such CIA involvement in a covert operation would, of course, have required a formal Presidential Finding and notification to the Senate Select

Committee on Intelligence (SSCI). Carter reportedly made two Nicaragua-related findings in 1979–80, but these have not been made fully public. Regardless, Calero insisted that he had been told by Americans with whom he later had contact that covert paramilitary support to the Legión 15 de Septiembre was started during the Carter administration using the Argentines as a front to cover the CIA's involvement.[22]

Another longtime Resistance activist, a medical doctor known as "Doctor Javier," who joined the FDN in 1981, confirmed Calero's claim, saying that he too had been made fully aware from the beginning that the Argentines were acting as front men for the CIA. Several of the Argentine operatives with whom he worked daily told him privately, during drinking bouts, that they were being paid by the CIA and were sometimes made to feel very uncomfortable by the cavalier fashion in which their American case officers treated them in private. As an officer of the FDN's headquarters staff in 1984, Doctor Javier also recalled being present at a small change-of-command ceremony at a Honduran base at which direct control of clandestine paramilitary support operations for the FDN was passed from Argentine military intelligence to American CIA hands. The Argentines were being roughly and abruptly ejected by their American counterparts, and he recalls that the way the Americans went about dismissing them made the Argentines feel more than a little insulted and abused. Nonetheless, the Argentines tried to keep their dignity as best they could. He still remembers verbatim what the senior Argentine colonel said as he passed control over to the Americans:

Hace cuatro años ustedes nos encomendaron una misión. Hoy podemos decir, con orgullo y dignidad: Misión cumplida!

(Four years ago you [the Americans] entrusted us with a mission. Today, with pride and dignity we can honestly say: Mission accomplished!)[23]

"Four years ago" was 1979.

CHAPTER EIGHT

BIRTH OF THE FDN

A Guardia/MILPAS Alliance

After the original Southern Front attacked the Montonero's Radio Noticias in Costa Rica at the behest of the Legión, arms, money, and training support began to reach the Legión through the Argentines. Several months later, in April 1981, the Legión took the lead in the creation of a new umbrella organization, the Fuerza Democratica Nicaragüense (FDN) which became the principal conduit for help from Argentina, the United States, and other foreign sponsors. It was to the FDN that the CIA director, William Casey, referred in November 1981 and that Clarridge called "five hundred rag-tag troopers."[1]

Although precise details cannot at this time be uncovered, available evidence strongly suggests what happened next. The FDN was not large enough to accomplish much more than the limited missions that Casey had envisioned when he formally told the Senate Select Committee on Intelligence (SSCI) in December 1981 of CIA plans to mount the covert operation that came to be known as the Contra project. The Sandinistas later claimed, even in Top Secret documents circulated to their own senior staff, that the FDN had ten thousand former Guardia in Honduras on whom it could draw.[2] In reality, the presence of so many Guardia in Honduras was a mathematical impossibility, since the Guardia's peak combat strength in July 1979 had been at most six thousand,[3] and of them, more than three thousand were in Sandinista prisons and several thousand more in the United States or other countries. According to internal FDN documents, the former Guardia in the FDN peaked in strength at 437 in August 1982, well within the CIA's estimate as reported by Casey to Congress but clearly not enough to wage a serious war.

What did exist, however, were the MILPAS, an already mobilized and operational army of highland peasants who had been fighting for well over two years in Nicaragua's central mountains. By the end of 1981, the MILPAS had from 2,000 to 3,000 armed combatants, plus several times that number of already mobilized auxiliary combatants ready to join as soon as weapons became available. The MILPAS also could draw on a large manpower pool of highland peasants:[4] a ready-made guerrilla army. Even more important than the numbers, however, was that these potential fighters were members of the very large, homogeneous, and geographically distinctive populace of actual or potential campesino supporters from which the MILPAS had emerged. The FDN had only to tap into this pool.

Nevertheless, serious obstacles remained. Almost all the Milpistas and their commanders, and much of the peasantry, had been anti-Somocista, and the FDN was led by former Guardia. Furthermore, Pacific coast urban ethnocentrism was a principal generator of highland anger against the Sandinistas, and most of the Guardia were from Pacific coastal towns or cities. But the major incentive that overrode the obstacles were the arms and other resources that the Americans promised to deliver through the Argentines. The Sandinistas were rapidly growing in strength and, especially after Dimas's attack on Quilalí, were using helicopters, artillery, and other systems from which the MILPAS could no longer defend themselves independently. The rebellion was also rapidly outstripping locally available arms and other resources.

Again, it is not exactly clear who then decided to do what when, but circumstances and available information suggest that the Argentines and Americans were acquainted with the FDN in exile in Honduras but apparently knew little if anything about those fighting inside Nicaragua. So when the Argentines and the CIA settled on the new FDN as their instrument for harassing the Sandinistas, they inadvertently decided the issue. In their decision to choose a Guardia-led organization as their preferred conduit for paramilitary covert aid, they transmuted what had been a sponta- neous highland peasant MILPAS rebellion into an alliance with the Guardia.

The FDN's Guardia leaders moved quickly to take advantage of the opportunity. In June 1981, they started a careful campaign to attract the Milpistas under their umbrella, using their monopoly over foreign resources as the main inducement. A special recruit- ing unit was set up, of which 4-2 was a member. The unit devel- oped a list of prospects and began a carefully planned campaign, offering resources to selected MILPAS groups and to individual Milpistas if they joined the FDN.[5] Among its earliest recruits were Tigrillo; Tiro al Blanco; several Galeanos, including Franklyn and La Chaparra;[6] Irene Calderon; and according to one source, Dimas himself.[7]

As the Milpistas rallied to the new alliance, they were sent to a camp known as La Lodosa, (The Mud Patch), for basic training. Some remembered being less than impressed. La Lodosa's train- ing program was run by former Guardia advised by Argentines. Although neither the Guardia nor the Argentines had any experi- ence as rural insurgents, they treated the Milpistas like raw recruits. The Milpistas themselves, as seasoned mountain guerrilla fight- ers, often with many years combat experience, should have been teaching the Guardia and the Argentines, not the other way around.[8] But in the characteristic peasant way, they smiled and buried their feelings in exchange for the resources and support the Guardia promised them.

The process of amalgamating the Guardia and Milpistas went slowly at first, since the Milpistas were skeptical about whether the Guardia would really deliver on their promises. But once Ameri- can support began to arrive in quantity in early 1982, and to reach MILPAS hands, the alliance grew quickly. By August 1982, the FDN was telling the Argentines that they had about 3,700 combatants under arms. Internally, however, the FDN estimated its actual combatant strength at 11,270. Almost all, an estimated 96 percent, were Milpistas. The number of Milpistas officially enrolled in the FDN's ranks was only 1,571, but an additional 2,200 armed combatants were not formally on its rosters. There were also 6,100 auxiliaries (see table 2). The number 3,700 appears to have stood only for those Comandos formally engaged in the new Argentine-American covert project, and the 6,100 others were a sort of army-in-waiting of organized but not yet armed peasants. This in turn suggests the project had a limited budget that did not provide sufficient support to all the organized peasants of the highlander Resistance movement, a challenge that became evident at the end of the Contra War when first the U.S. Agency for International Development and then CIAV/OAS found that the actual number of rebels greatly outstripped their expectations.

The army produced by the FDN/Milpista alliance process was a curious hybrid. Colonel Céspedes, "Cyro," who directed FDN air logistical operations throughout the war, described it as two armies in one. The face was Guardia, but the body was Milpista.[9] The two armies were fundamentally different in several ways. Many of the Guardia were of urban Pacific coast origins, and literate, with at least several years of formal education. The Milpistas were, with few exceptions, illiterate highlander owners of small farms with an average of fewer than two years of formal schooling. But there were also similarities. Perhaps the most striking was that most of the Guardia, and virtually all of the Milpistas, identified themselves as indios, considered themselves members of the masses, not the oligarchy, and were Liberals. At least some of the key Guardia were also highlanders, especially combat leaders. Of fifteen mid-level Guardia Contra Comandantes, nine, including the most prominent commander in Chontales and Boaco, Juan Ramón Rivas "Quiché," were from the mountains.[10] A third stream of Comandos later also became important Sandinista ralliers. This mixture gave the postalliance FDN three institutional origins, which sometimes caused tensions, but these were normally sub-ordinated to the larger interest. On occasion, the tensions caused

TABLE 2
Guardia vs. Non-Guardia, 12 August 1982

	GUARDIA	MILPAS/OTHER	TOTAL
FDN BASE CAMP			
Sagitario	58	83	141
Ariel	7	113	120
Pino-1	20	151	171
Zebra	57	80	137
Nicarao	41	76	117
Agateyte	64	58	120
SUBTOTAL	247 (31%)	571 (69%)	808
MILPISTAS (IN FDN)			
Kilambé Tigrillo	–	300	300
Pino-II	–	100	100
Flecha	–	300	300
Aguila	–	100	100
Matagalpa y Boaco	–	200	200
SUBTOTAL	–	1,000 (86%)	1,000
NOT YET ENROLLED			
Base Operativo	–	2,200	2,200
Base Clandestino	–	1,800	1,800
Reservas	–	4,300	4,300
SUBTOTAL	–	8,300	8,300
GRAND TOTAL	247	9,871	10,118
Percentage	**3%**	**97%**	

SOURCE: "Estado de Fuerza local y general, porcentaje ex-G.N. en las bases, e informe de bajas a la fecha," Cuartel General General Fuerza Democratica Nicaraguense, 12 Agosto 1982. ACRN archives.

problems, but by and large the groups worked effectively together throughout most of the war. (See table 2 for data on the relative importance of the MILPAS and former Guardia in 1982.)

It seems clear that the main 1982–88 "Contra" FDN army was primarily a Milpista/peasant force. The Guardia brought military professionalism and were the conduit for covert aid. But the MILPAS comarca campesino base was the element in which they all had to operate. Without the MILPAS and their campesino supporters, the Guardia could not have survived as guerrillas among the highlanders.

CHAPTER NINE

Structure and Organization of the Highlander Resistance Movement

Beyond serving as the source of its Comandos, the highlander Resistance movement provided the entire FDN/MILPAS alliance with its popular support base, without which it simply could not have functioned successfully. At first the internal dynamics of the highlander Resistance movement may seem baffling to the Western observer. The confusion occurs when one applies a Western cultural model to this decidedly non-Western organization. Within this movement, power and authority flowed upward from the peasantry, not downward from a government, military headquarters, or ideological elite. Unlike any other insurgency, it had no intellectual author or articulated unifying ideology, nor was it the product of an external conflict. The Resistance movement was a spontaneous grassroots rebellion and drew its strength and raison d'etre from the individual comarca communities that produced it.

The Resistance, thus, can best be visualized not as a unified hierarchical organization similar to a Western army or ideological movement, but as a series of small pyramids, each planted in a comarca community, with Comando combat formations at their tops. Rather like locally raised British regiments in the days of the British Empire, most units came from and relied on a particular local populace. When tactically feasible, a unit was most active militarily in or near the communities from which its Comandos came. Just below the Comandos in each comarca pyramid was a thin layer of correos. Directly below them lay a larger strata of clandestine comarca committees. And beneath these committees lay yet another, and even larger, layer of supporting activists, a popular support base. At the foundation of each pyramid was a final layer of peasant sympathizers, without whom the entire edifice would have collapsed. The FDN as a whole relied on hundreds of such pyramids.

SUPPORT STRUCTURES

The vast majority of the activist participants in the highland rebellion remained hidden from public view throughout the war. Even the closest of outside observers were not aware of them. For security reasons, each comarca's system of correos, clandestine committees, and popular support bases were free-standing and compartmentalized, existing only in relation to the local community. FDN's Strategic Headquarters knew of and promoted their existence, but they were not centrally organized at that level and had no headquarters. In all but rare instances, the identities, numbers, and activities of correos, clandestine comarca committee members, and popular base supporters were kept secret by the units that they served and almost never reported to higher headquarters.

The general staff knew how the system worked, but security at the local level was exceedingly tight. Compartmentalization assured that no one had more than a tiny fraction of data concerning individual identities, precise numbers, or specific missions, so very little was recorded in central FDN files. Even after the war ended, the Comandos kept the identities of almost all their correos and clandestine committee members secret, and neither group participated in the demobilization process. Postwar events, especially the Re-Contra war of 1990–96 and the 1996 ad hoc electoral registration process (see chapters 15 and 16), indicate that these networks remained intact, strongly suggesting that they had and still have an existence and strength independent of the rebellion itself.

The support structure of the Resistance movement provided most of what was needed to sustain Comando units in the field. Clandestine committees organized the movement of goods and services supplied by the popular support base and provided them to the Comandos via the correos. The system also provided them with food, shelter, political support, local security, and intelligence information while they were in their operational zones. Unlike the Comandos, who occasionally moved in and out of Nicaragua, correos, committee members, and popular base supporters stayed permanently in their comarcas.

CORREOS

The correos were the eyes, ears, and brains of the Resistance. Without them it could not have succeeded.

—EMILIANO[1]

Angel Sosa, "Emiliano," one of the FDN's most successful field commanders, considered the correos the most important part of the insurgency and believed that they were vital to the operations of every major Comando unit. A former anti-Somoza Milpista, and then for a short while a Sandinista People's Army soldier, Emiliano joined the Resistance in its earliest days. He helped organize the correo networks that later supported the five Jorge Salazar Regional Commands. For him an effective system of correos was vital.

Because correos had to move around to perform their missions, they lived and worked covertly within communities. Normally they were neither uniformed nor armed; they were therefore especially vulnerable to discovery and reprisals. Many former Comandos considered the mission of the correos the most dangerous of all those performed by Resistance activists. Because they were more familiar than anyone with the current tactical situation and the terrain in a comarca, the correos were the key cadre on the ground. Their primary missions were to act as links between clandestine comarca committees and the local combat unit and to help Comandos and supporters from other comarcas move across their zone of operations from one area of conflict to another. When they did have weapons, correos sometimes also served as clandestine auxiliary forces.[2] Because they were so exposed to danger or compromise and were trusted and experienced, correos who feared exposure, or simply wanted to become combatants, were a prime source of new Comandos. Within the highlander Resistance army, it was normal for a person to progress from correo to combatant.

Because their activities placed them in constant peril of discovery, many hundreds if not thousands of correos were arrested or killed. Partial data presented below suggest just how dangerous their work was and why security surrounding correo networks was so exceedingly tight. Even in the year 2000, prudence continues to dictate that their identities be protected. Consequently, not only is this discussion based on limited documentary evidence, many of the details that are available to me have been deliberately omitted or masked. Even so, enough usable information is available and can be disclosed here to give a partial picture of the situation.

The few available reports on correo strengths found in the FDN archives reveal an average ratio of one active correo to every 2.5 Comandos. This suggests, albeit with limited statistical confidence, that, assuming an average troop strength of 17,000, the correo networks consisted of 6,000–7,000 members during much of the war. A few other documents support this estimate. A handwritten report of 12 August 1982, on one of several FDN operational zones of varying sizes indicates that 735 Comandos and 143 *agregados*, or correos, were operating inside Nicaragua in Zona V.[3] A typed memorandum of 20 October 1983 gives similar numbers for Zonas I–IV.[4] A May 1987 report by the Jorge Salazar Regional Command notes that this command had 299 active correos in 6 comarcas near Quilalí.[5] No data were found on correos in the Zones VI and VII. The Jorge Salazars had about 1,300 Comandos in Zone V at that time. Partial data on correos found in several 1988 Status of Forces reports have been combined in table 3 below.[6]

TABLE 3
Correos by Regional Command (10 of 23 units)
(partial data)

REGIONAL COMMAND	TROOP STRENGTH	CORREOS
Jorge Salazar ('82)	735	143
Nicarao ('83)	1,241	300
Segovia ('83)	515	50
San Jacinto ('83)	1,080	627
Diriangen ('83)	1,507	600
Jorge Salazar ('83)	1,809	800
Jorge Estrada ('83)	361	100
Jorge Salazar I ('87)	1,300	299
Jorge Salazar IV ('88)	668	150
Santiago Meza ('88)	861	130
TOTALS	10,077	3,299

The number of mentions that correos received in combat communications generated by both the Resistance and several Sandinista military headquarters confirms their importance to military operations.[7] FDN message traffic for September 1984 includes eleven mentions of correos. For example, on 11 September, FDN Comandante Chicle reported that 29 new correos in the comarca of Runflín were asking for weapons to establish a self-defense unit. On 17 September, he reported having given them several Mauser rifles and some ammunition.[8] On 15 September, he noted the presence of 272 correos and clandestine comarca committee members in 7 comarcas and mentioned 11 other correos from two comarcas two days later.[9] In an intercepted radio message dated 26 September, a Sandinista army regional headquarters reported on correo and clandestine committee activities in support of the Comandos. Other messages contain similar information (see table 3).

Data from 1986 documents allow for some individualized breakdown of correos by dates of entry into service. Of 124 identifiable by year of entry, 15 had joined in 1980, 43 in 1981, 23 in 1982, and 20 in 1983. Some 101, or 80 percent, had been active by 1983. The remainder joined during the following three years. Assuming this pattern was typical, it seems evident that correos on average entered the Resistance movement much earlier and stayed much longer than did Comandos. This finding is consistent with comments by Comandos who were interviewed.

CLANDESTINE COMARCA COMMITTEES

Scant as documentary information is on the correos, it is abundant compared to what can be presented on the clandestine comarca committees. At the same time, the Comandos consistently described the clandestine comarca committees as by far the largest group of Resistance activists. The committees, made up of civilian supporters, collected food, provided shelter, and gathered intelligence information for the Comandos. They were organized according to function, with several committees in each comarca, each with a specific mission. In some comarcas they were further compartmentalized along societal lines that took in to account such factors as religion (Catholic or Protestant), local hierarchies, and the like. Different committees performed distinct functions, the most important being intelligence, logistics, and recruitment. Insofar as was possible, each committee had independent communications both upward toward the Comandos via correos and downward into the Resistance movement's popular support base. Committees tried to avoid engaging in activities that were the responsibilities of other committees. Logistics committees did not recruit, recruitment committees did not engage in intelligence activities, and so forth.

If, as Mao Tse Tung said, a guerrilla movement survives by swimming among the masses, then, in the highlander Resistance movement, the clandestine comarca committees did most of the swimming. Multiplying the approximate number of campesino comarcas in the highlands by the average number of committees per comarca and the estimated number of members per committee yields a rough figure of around ninety thousand active clandestine committee members in the highlands.

One document found in the ACRN's archives describes the system in several comarcas in some detail, listing nine principal missions they performed.[10] It is the only documentary description available of clandestine comarca committee operations.[11] This particular report was generated by a special operations group of the Base Operacional Nicarao, working from the comarca of San Fernando. It identifies the committees in each of eight comarcas, Mosonte, Achuapa, Salamají, Ciudad Antigua, Arrayán, San Fernando, and San Nicolás.[12] Each comarca had six committees: one for political matters, one for military matters, one for propaganda, one for logistics, one for finances, and one for central coordination.

The team from Base Nicarao established in each comarca *buzones,* or supply and weapons caches, that were under the responsibility of a member of a clandestine comarca committee. Two of the buzones were under comarca coordinators, two under members of finance committees, one under a member of a political committee, and two under other collaborators. The team also described the missions of the committees:

> *Mission 1:* To coordinate both overt and covert operations in their comarcas. [As Emiliano and other Comandos described this, once a unit entered the area of activities of a comarca Resistance network, its operations were normally subject to that network's control. Even when a mission had been assigned by a higher military command, the decision on whether or not it would be carried out was subject to comarca-level approval.]
>
> *Mission 2:* To manage local contributions in kind or in currency. [In practice, this rarely involved cash, as the campesinos were almost always cash poor.]
>
> *Mission 3:* To direct pro-Resistance political activities in their comarca. [Committee members proselytized one-on-one and also organized meetings and rallies by the Comandos.]

Mission 4: To collect and disseminate military and political intelligence on Sandinista activities in and near the comarca. [In this role, the committees, through the correos, became the eyes and ears of the Comandos.]

Mission 5: To establish and maintain safe houses and weapons caches. [Small Comando detachments and even individuals on special missions often moved in and out of the comarcas. Larger units infiltrating in or out of the zones of conflict often left weapons and supplies behind for their own use or the use of others. The widespread system of buzones reduced problems of resupply.]

Mission 6: To establish and operate escape and evasion networks. [These served many customers, from Comandos who had been separated from their units, through Sandinista deserters or escaping civilian supporters, to ralliers exfiltrating to sanctuary.]

Mission 7: To collect and provide logistical support to the combat units. [Usually this support included food, medicines, and incidental materials such as shelter and rain boots. The Comandos had only three other alternative sources of supplies—rare air-drops, shank's mare,[13] and supplies captured from the Sandinistas. Capture could provide weapons and military supplies[14] but not daily rations.]

Mission 8: To organize, equip, and train a warning network that could give the alarm in case of Sandinista army or other suspicious movements near Comando units.

Mission 9: To recruit new Comandos. [The number of Comandos interviewed who had once been correos demonstrated that in practice the correos were often the main pool on which the committees drew.]

POPULAR BASE SUPPORT

A number of Resistance comandantes who were interviewed confirmed that the committee structure described above was the usual pattern, although they explained that it was often flexible and subject to variation. But they were also quick to point out that the committees were only the coordinators of popular base support. Emiliano, Rubén, Chino-4, and others said that throughout the rebellion, it was the mass of campesinos, not just the committees or correos, who actively helped the Comandos. Their help took the form of direct assistance with food, clothing, shelter, transportation, raw intelligence, rudimentary medical assistance, and myriad other needs. In areas where preinsurgency populations remained, almost all the campesinos were sympathizers-in-place, and many had friends or family members among the Comandos. This was the rebellion's first and largest source of supporters. In October 1982, a Resistance report on Nueva Segovia estimated its popular support in one operating area at 98 percent.

A second type of popular-base support involved peasants living in areas beyond the effective control of Sandinista troops or administrators. These were usually internal refugees who had fled the region's more populated areas for many of the same reasons the Comandos had joined the insurgency. Their only other alternatives were to be forced into state farms or resettlement camps, or to leave Nicaragua for refugee camps in Honduras or Costa Rica. These peasants chose instead to withdraw into even more remote areas and survive by returning to their traditional practice of slash-and-burn agriculture, used by their indio ancestors. Among these internal refugees, all the inhabitants of a given zone were sympathizers, and they shared whatever they could with Comandos moving through their areas. These supporters were especially valuable to Comando units infiltrating or exfiltrating the zones of conflict by way of Nicaragua's more remote wilderness areas. The Comandantes described the campesinos living in such regions as among the poorest of the poor but usually able to provide water, shelter, information, guide services, and some food.

A third important set of popular base supporters lived in the region's rural market centers or small towns where they had access to supplies, transport, or other goods or services not available in the countryside. Although less numerous and more susceptible to

Sandinista detection, these supporters were especially helpful to units that remained in nearby operational areas for extended periods of time.

THE WEBS THE CORREOS WOVE

One unexpected finding of this study was the convincing evidence that the Resistance movement had successfully woven a web of correos across the entire highlands. Initially, this seemed to contradict what had been learned about the carefully compartmentalized comarca-level nature of the movement and its networks. That description fit nicely into a schema of geographically isolated corps of correos each in comarca serving only nearby units. A successful comarca-to-comarca network of correos seemed anomolous because it placed the safety of correos from one comarca in the hands of people from the next mountain valley, requiring confidence between comarcas beyond the local level. The existence of a highlands-wide network of correos seemed at first to contradict the nature of the movement.

Because of the implications of this finding, I felt it important to substantiate it with extensive interviews. Those consulted included Rubén, La Chaparra, and numerous other Comandos, as well as knowledgeable religious leaders, merchants who worked in the mountains, Nicaraguan government officials who worked in the highlands, and informed international observers with years of experience in the region. Because the Comandos and the highland peasants were still very protective of the system even in 1996 and 1997, many asked not to be identified.

Their unexpected answer was that in the highlands there is, and apparently always has been, a previously unrecognized but dense web of highlands-wide loyalties and relationships of mutual trust. These are based on intracampesino comarca-to-comarca social and economic relationships that completely bypass Nicaragua's urban-centered economic and social systems. The campesinos live, in effect, in a second Nicaragua. Nicaragua's first world is on the peasants' periphery at Nicaragua's center: an urban-based set of economic, political, and social networks that reach out from the Pacific coastal lowland cities. With these the highland campesinos have only episodic contact. At the center of their universe lies a second campesino world where they live most of their lives.[15]

The great majority of the highland campesinos make their living by working relatively independent small farmsteads, mostly producing food crops for their own consumption. Any surplus products are sold to buy items not available locally, such as salt, spices, cloth, thread, needles, kerosene for lamps, batteries for radios, and the like. Until the Revolution, the process of exchanging surplus products for such goods relied on merchants in the region's market centers. For a traditional peasant, a trip to a market center was and is a major undertaking. Not only must he or she leave a familiar environment for one that is socially threatening, but the journey itself often requires several days' travel and involves risks and relationships that can generate considerable unease.[16] Some campesinos develop sufficient social skills to be comfortable with the process, but for most it is an excursion into an alien and disconcerting world. Marketing visits are therefore often limited to only one or two trips a year, with many family members never going at all.

But this social unease relates only to the web that links the campesinos to Nicaragua's formal market economy, not their daily lives. Within their own world the campesinos enjoy a great deal of social interaction at the local level. They may live in scattered farmsteads or clusters of houses too small even to be called hamlets, but they are not isolated from their fellow campesinos. To the contrary, while contact with outsiders is rare, interaction with neighbors is constant and a favorite form of both recreation and social intercourse. With no electricity, television, newspapers, or town centers, and few radios, personal interaction is the main entertainment.

Family relationships, both nuclear and extended, lie at the heart of this social interaction among campesinos. *Extended* in this context is very extended indeed and embraces a large number of connections at three levels—relatives by blood (siblings, uncles and aunts, cousins to several removes), by marriage (in-laws become like blood relatives), and by choice (compadres, or godparents).[17] These extended families and clans often live not in one, but in several neighboring comarcas. Furthermore, despite many exceptions, by and large the highlanders honor a system of what might best be described as extended incest taboos. In addition to condemning parent-child, sibling, and first/second cousin unions, unions are also discouraged between other residents of the same comarca.

These patterns result in highly developed networks of comarca-to-comarca relationships. Visiting and social exchange between comarcas occur daily. These may be visits to relatives, friends or compadres (literally coparents), courting excursions by the young (and sometimes the not-so-young), economic barter exchange trips (your beans for my corn, your *guaro*[18] for my chicken, and so forth), attendance at religious services or such social events as birthdays, weddings, marriages, wakes, "Quince Añera" (fifteenth birthday) coming-out parties, or visits to folk-medicine practitioners. The dense, constant and long-standing networks of family and peer relationships among nearby comarcas generated by these daily activities, family ties, relationships by marriages, friendships, code-pendencies for barter exchange, multicomarca systems of inter-relationships and trust are ubiquitous throughout the highlands.

As their autonomous small guerrilla groups began to coalesce, the Comandos understood that they would need a regionwide network of contacts. They also understood that creating one would require only linking these comarca-to-comarca relationships into a sort of regional daisy-chain. By linking each comarca to its neigh-bors via correos who had long-established ties to the correos of the next comarca, they could cast a web across the entire highlands region from Nueva Segovia and Jinotega to southern Chontales almost to Costa Rica. This web would be all but impenetrable to Sandinista intelligence infiltration.

To the Comandos' surprise, when they started trying to weave a regional web, they found the campesinos who had remained in the comercas were well ahead of them; they had already begun to weave one in anticipation of the emergence of a region-wide Resistance movement. Using this precreated network, La Chaparra traveled in mid-1981 alone, on foot, and in absolute security, passing from comarca correo to comarca correo all the way from Honduras to Chontales, even though the southern comarcas she traversed in Boaco and Chontales did not even have guerrilla units. The MILPAS had not reached south of Matagalpa, but the campesinos had already rebelled, and correo webs had been woven by them that completely bypassed Nicaragua's formal farm-to-market and government networks.

The existence of such networks seems reasonable. Nicaragua's formal networks extend outward from the core Pacific coast lowland cities into the peripheral countryside using Pacific-centered roads and communications systems that can be drawn on maps. They are densest in the Pacific coast lowlands but in general do not penetrate deeply into the peripheral highlands where the campesinos live. In the highlands, comarca-to-comarca relationships among campesinos are more important.

These two Nicaraguan worlds, the one of its formal core, the other of its highland peasantry, often touch one another but each leads a largely independent existence. The first Nicaragua is relatively modern, the second more traditional. When the Sandinistas triumphed, they took control only of the first Nicaragua's networks, and it was these that they used to try to revolutionize the country. But the highlanders controlled the second Nicaragua, and they used its networks to defend themselves. The Sandinistas were to find the comarca campesino networks virtually impenetrable.

RESISTANCE NUMBERS

Most correos and clandestine committee members remained in place and were continuously active in support of the insurgency during the entire period of the conflict. A number of the Comandantes interviewed insisted that, on average, 25 to 30 percent of the inhabitants of the comarcas with which they were personally familiar were active supporters, while the remainder were almost universally sympathizers. It was not possible to establish a statistical base against which to measure these claims, but historical evidence confirms that the Comandos operated throughout the region with a great deal of security of movement.

Based on fragmentary evidence in published sources,[19] the few available documents, interviews, and Comando estimates, it seems reasonable to believe that almost all the peasants in most rural highland comarcas were either Comandos, correos, committee members, popular-base activists, or sympathizers. The weakest support for the Resistance in the highlands was apparently in the region's market centers and scattered areas of plantation agriculture. But even there the movement's leaders appear usually to have been able to count on extensive assistance when needed. In the countryside, even many members of Sandinista organizations, such as the militias and CDS, sympathized with the rebels. According to those interviewed, corroborated by archival evidence, this sympathy extended even into the ranks of the Sandinista army and security services.

An account by a Sandinista supports this finding. In 1986, Maj. Roger Miranda, in his capacity as personal aide to Sandinista People's Army Commanding General Humberto Ortega, made an inspection tour of much of the highlands. Miranda commented that when visiting remote villages he found he was "looked on with suspicion, fear and hatred." Surprised, he asked a local brigade commander, Major Lorente, about this hostility. Lorente's response, which Miranda remembered verbatim, was both categorical and significant: "Look chief, all these peasants you have seen, all these little villages we have passed through, all these sons-of-bitches are Contras. All of them."[20]

In 1987, in connection with an FDN offensive known as Operation Olivaro, a major attack on the three northern Zelaya mining towns of Siuna, Bonanza, and La Rosita, more than half the Comandos inside Nicaragua, about six thousand combatants, withdrew from their normal positions and marched for more than six weeks through inhabited rural areas from as far away as southern Chontales and the Rama road to reach the attack zone more than halfway across Nicaragua. The attack came as a complete surprise to the Sandinistas. Executing such a sophisticated and extensive maneuver through inhabited territory without being detected by Sandinista intelligence required near-perfect operational security that, in turn, would have required virtually universal popular cooperation in the areas traversed. Because the peasants were fully aware that failure to report Comando movements to the Sandinistas was a major counterrevolutionary crime and would be severely punished, their silence implied active complicity, not merely passive sympathy. Considering the several groups that combined to form the Resistance—Comandos, correos, comarca committees, and activists—it would seem that, conservatively, at least half the peasants of the Segovian highlands were involved in the effort, or between 500,000 and 600,000 people.

FORMAL MILITARY STRUCTURE

In 1982 the structure of the armed forces of the highland Resistance movement changed, although its support system remained the same. From 1979 through 1981, only individual MILPAS groups operated without a central structure in the field. But when the Milpistas allied themselves with the FDN in early 1982, they found themselves part of a formally organized force. Although this force was later reorganized several times, during most of the war it was divided into regional commands, each with several subordinate task forces that, in turn, had several subordinate groups. By the end of the war twenty-four regional commands were in place, well over a hundred task forces, and several hundred groups. Completing the structure were three independent task forces, an artillery unit, a naval (riverine) force, a Special Forces command with two Special Forces groups, a Center for Military Instruction (CIM), and the Grupo Pirata (discussed in chapter 5).[21] The alliance had a central administrative structure, and the FDN's Strategic Headquarters had a formal staff similar to a classic military headquarters, including G1 (personnel), G2 (intelligence), G3 (operations), and G4 (logistics).

It is essential to note, however, that FDN Strategic Headquarters did not exercise the sort of command authority it would have in a traditional army. The general staff managed logistics, central communications, medical services, base operations, intelligence and police functions, air operations, training and transport, and coordinated overall military operational planning. But the actual flow of authority was the reverse of that of a classical army because Strategic Headquarters derived its authority from both the commanders of the individual regional commands and from a council of commanders. Combat unit commanders were not generally appointed from above by headquarters but rather elected from below. With some exceptions, a group's members selected their group leader. The group leaders then selected the commander of their task force, and task force commanders, in turn, selected the commander of their regional command.[22] The latter became members of a committee of commanders that evolved into a formal Consejo de Comandantes (council of commanders) with decision-making authority. The minutes of numerous Consejo meetings were found in the archives of the Resistance.

Toward the end of the war, the Consejo de Comandantes exercised its rarely used authority to appoint or remove the FDN's overall Jefe de Estado Mayor (chief of the general staff), the army's titular top commander, and its senior general staff members. In one sense this made all the more remarkable the stability displayed by strategic headquarters, which was led from the beginning almost to the end by Enrique Bermúdez, Comandante 3-80. To keep that position and maintain such stability, he had both to satisfy the FDN's American suppliers and maintain the confidence of the combat commanders below him.

When a regional commander was inside Nicaragua, as most usually were, he kept a representative at headquarters to act on his behalf. Field commanders and various subcommands normally had the authority to initiate local operations and to approve or disapprove those that Strategic Headquarters suggested.[23] Occasionally, the chain of command functioned as though the FDN were a conventional army, but normally it was more like a confederation.

This was because the movement itself had been created from below by the comarca peasantry, and its ultimate authority rested with them, not with Strategic Headquarters, and authority flowed from the bottom up, not from the top down. Task forces and regional commands were thus representative of the populace from which they were drawn. The movement was neither a creation of outsiders nor a centrally coordinated insurrection but essentially a confederation of local rebellions. In 1981–82, when the alliance first took shape, the highland rebels viewed the FDN, but not the MILPAS, as the outside group. At the same time, to succeed, the alliance depended absolutely on an extensive, organized, and secure support structure, and that structure, belonged lock, stock, and barrel to the campesinos of the comarcas and the MILPAS.

The structure, nature, and extent of the highlander Resistance movement, hidden throughout the war, was partially revealed in 1990, when the Comandos laid down their arms, and the geographic, historic, and social origins of the rebellion became visible. The following chapters attempt to provide an overview of what was revealed. One of the more noteworthy and surprising revelations was the important role played by women in the rebellion.

CHAPTER TEN

WOMEN COMANDOS

Heroes, Combatants, and Comarca Leaders

Women played a crucial role in the rebellion. "Legionnaire L-332," Juan José Martínez Tercero, was killed in combat in November 1983, two years after he entered the Resistance in 1981. His mother, Dominga, could not mourn his death. She had died in battle earlier in 1983 during Operation Marathon.[1] On 5 September 1984, in the middle of an extended combat patrol inside Nicaragua, FDN Comandante "Dimas Negro" received a message from fellow Comandante "Toro" that forced him to perform one of a commanding officer's saddest tasks. He had to tell a Comando serving under him, "Pablo," that his wife had been killed that day in combat while serving as a frontline Comando with another unit, that of Toro.[2]

"Angelica María" was a Comando in the Jorge Salazar Regional Command for more than six years, remaining inside Nicaragua almost the entire time although wounded more than once.[3] A campesina, she was offered a "battlefield commission" as a group leader[4] after she took command of her unit during a firefight in which all its officers had been killed. She is still widely recognized by her peers for her heroism. Another female Comando became recognized as one of the FDN's most heroic fighters. Maritza Zeledón, "Daysi," joined the Resistance in January 1983 as a combatant of the Salvador Pérez Regional Command. Although trained as a paramedic, whenever her task force went into battle, Daysi would lay aside her medical kit and join the fray as an infantry combatant, AK-47 in hand, returning to her kit to treat the wounded when necessary. On 6 April 1985, Daysi was fatally wounded by an incoming round of 105 mm artillery during a firefight at Cerro El Guapinol in Jinotega. To honor her service and heroism, her comrades in arms renamed their unit the Maritza Zeledón Task Force.[5]

Although recognized for their bravery, female Comandos faced a glass ceiling. No woman ever became an official member of the Council of Regional Commanders or commanded a task force. Although they did not advance in rank or power to the very top, women Resistance fighters played key roles during the insurgency. They served by the hundreds as frontline Comandos with FDN combat units. Others were radio operators, nurses, or trained cadre. They were fully integrated into infantry task forces, carried the same backpacks, ate the same food, slept under the same conditions, wore the same kinds of uniforms, and carried the same weapons as the male Comandos. They also engaged in the same skirmishes and fire-fights, and paid the same price in lost health and injury. Like the men, many gave their lives. Some adjustments had to be made of course. They did need smaller uniforms and combat boots, different underwear, and items to use during their menstrual cycles and to serve a few other feminine needs.[6] Because the Resistance was often a family or comarca affair, many women Comandos served alongside brothers, other relatives, or life-long friends. In other instances, they were as much on their own as their male combat companions.

Most of the male and female comandantes and Comandos interviewed estimated that about 10 percent of the combatants were women. This was a slight exaggeration, as according to documents in the FDN's archives the actual number was closer to 7 percent. But the 10 percent estimate demonstrated that the Comandos clearly viewed women as a major element within the military formations of the Resistance. That their numbers were overestimated said much for how their peers perceived them. The Comandos' estimates were cross-checked against the ACRN's archives, which contained several documents that permitted estimates of the number of female

Comandos. An April 1989 memorandum listed 272 women Comandos whose names were to be added to the rosters of combat units.[7] Two other documents give data for women Comandos in sanctuary (Honduran rear areas) as of September 1988. According to these sources, they totaled 885 of the 12,615 Comandos reported and included women in noncombat units such as medical personnel, rear-echelon staff workers, and the like.[8] If a similar percentage of the 4,572 Comandos then inside Nicaragua were also women, that would add 275, for a total at that time of more than 1,160, or almost 7 percent.

Once a woman joined a frontline unit and developed some experience in military matters, she was marginally more likely to be assigned certain tasks. Within a combat task force, a woman Comando was somewhat more likely to rise to a technical position, such as radio operator or paramedic. And because most Comandos, both male and female, were young and healthy, and women were mixed into mostly male units, many women Comandos married their male comrades and even more established stable liaisons outside of marriage. About half of all women Comandos had at least one child while with the Resistance. Once a woman Comando's pregnancy was advanced, and especially after her child was born, units normally retained her as a task force member but tried to assign her to rear echelon duties.[9]

According to a September 1988 Status of Forces report, 456 of the women in rear echelon positions had a total of 867 children at that time. In some instances a Comando mother might ask for reassignment to other duties and leave her unit to work in a rear-echelon hospital, a headquarters operation, a training center, in a communications and intelligence office, with a military police detachment, or the like. She might then formally become a member of a rear echelon organization although, as was also the case with male combatants assuming similar duty changes, her primary identification usually remained with her home regional task force. This did not necessarily excuse her from combat duties. A set of poignant photographs taken during the last battle of Bocay in 1988 shows woman Comandos with babies in their arms, AK-47s on their shoulders, and combat packs on their backs moving forward toward the front lines.[10]

The casualty lists found in the Resistance archives disclose the names of 504 Comandos killed in action during 1982–84 and 1988. I reviewed the lists to determine what percentage of those killed were women, even though they do not separate names according to sex. Because Latin American men sometimes have apparently feminine first names—for example, Dolores, María, or Irene (as in Calderón)—I excluded such names from the count. I identified with certainty twenty-nine women Comandos by name, and the conservative methodology I used probably makes this an undercount. Even so, in this limited sampling, it appears that 5.7 percent of the Comandos killed were women. Extrapolation from the estimated 8,500–10,500 total of FDN Comandos killed in action suggests that from 456 to 570 women Comandos died in combat.

Frontline Comando was not, however, the most dangerous role a woman could play during the rebellion. Serving as a correo or member of a clandestine comarca committee was even more hazardous, and women played a crucial role at this level. Correo lists found in the archives suggest that close to 20 percent of jefes de correos, or chiefs of correo networks, were female, almost triple the percentage of female Comandos in the combat units. This figure probably greatly understates the percentage of women in the networks themselves. According to two female jefes de correos, Marina and La Chaparra, women were often preferred as correos over men because they tended to attract less attention, could move about more freely, and were not subject to conscription. In their own two networks, more than 50 percent of those serving were women. Of the few names I found of clandestine committee heads, 15 percent were female. Given the relative absence of young men in the comarcas during the war, and with women relatively less suspect than men, a reasonable assumption is that half or more of the movement's clandestine committee members were women.

Most of the comandantes interviewed considered the missions of correo or clandestine committee member the most dangerous in the Resistance. The Comandos also insisted that the correos and committees were key to the movement's success because the combat units depended heavily on them. If, then, as this review indicates, about half the correos and committee members were women, the importance of women in the highland Resistance movement was extraordinary, and the casualties they suffered while serving with these two corps would have been correspondingly high. It proved impossible to develop from available data a dependable estimate of the number of women correos or clandestine comarca committee members killed. But because these corps were both more numerous and more exposed to reprisals than were the Comandos, their casualties must have pushed the number of female deaths during the Resistance to well over one thousand.

In sum, while the Resistance made no special effort to enlist female combatants and activists, they were welcomed as participants at all levels below that of comandante. The price they paid is visible in the casualty reports. But it was as correos and clandestine committee members that they played their most decisive role. It seems no exaggeration to suggest that without the active involvement of women, the highlands war would have gone very differently.

CHAPTER ELEVEN

GEOGRAPHY OF THE REBELLION

In 1990, eleven years after the first Nicaraguan highlands comarcas rose up in rebellion, the FDN and the two smaller Resistance armies, YATAMA and the second Southern Front, had more than twenty-four thousand Comandos formally enrolled in their ranks. Following the defeat of the Sandinistas at the polls in 1990, newly elected Nicaraguan President Violeta Chamorro[1] asked the Comandos, as part of the peace process, to lay down their arms and return to their homes. The new president enlisted the United Nations and the Organization of American States (OAS) to comanage the process. The Comandos reluctantly agreed.[2] By far the largest army of Comandos to demobilize was the FDN.

As we have already seen, the nature and identity of those who disarmed bore little or no resemblance to their demonized wartime image defining them as Somoza Guardia with no geographic or popular base. Even more unexpected was the size and nature of the movement on which their army had rested. Those FDN Comandos who returned from outside Nicaragua, about half the FDN's Comandos, were accompanied by more than eighty thousand civilian supporters and were welcomed home by hundreds of thousands of others. Given the wartime image of the Resistance, this was totally unexpected both by the UN and OAS, and even by the best-informed Americans.

By June 1991, some 22,340 former Comandos of all fronts[3] had presented their weapons to a new UN peacekeeping organization, Observadores de Naciones Unidas en Centramerica (ONUCA), a multinational military force.[4] About 80 percent were FDN. By November 1992, the Centro Nacional de Planificación y Apoyo a Polos de Desarrollo (CENPAP), a postwar Resistance-oriented nongovernmental organization (NGO), was reporting that 27,450 former Comandos had demobilized, a number confirmed separately by CIAV/OAS. Most, but not all, had been active Comandos at war's end. Since mid-1991, more than five thousand additional combatants had deposited their arms. In terms of the total number of Comandos who had served during the war, this was many more than had been expected by the UN, OAS, or even the Americans closest to the project, to comply. An estimated 2,500–3,000 Comandos did not participate in the process.[5]

Over the course of the conflict the Comandos' ranks had been subject to constant change as new Comandos enrolled and others left or were killed in combat. At the rank-and-file level they were an unpaid volunteer force.[6] The repeated charges during the war of forced recruitment by the Contras had led to the contracting by the U.S. government of a professional sociologist, Robert Gersony, to study the problem. Gersony spent several months living in FDN and YATAMA camps interviewing hundreds of Comandos. He found "no/no evidence of forced recruitment." The Comandos told him that they were volunteers but that their parents either had to lie and say they had been forcibly recruited or risk losing their land and being jailed for having children who participated in the Resistance. Captured Comandos routinely made the same claim to protect themselves and their families.

Although a surprisingly high percentage of the Comandos who volunteered early on stayed the course, they were not forced to do so, and thousands departed voluntarily. Also, some 8,500 to 10,500 FDN Comandos were killed in action.[7] All together, perhaps 45,000 to 50,000 Nicaraguans served at one time or another as FDN combatants.[8] According to CIAV/OAS estimates, of those who laid down their arms in 1990–91, not only were 97 percent campesinos, 64 percent had no formal schooling, only 1 percent had gone beyond the fifth grade of primary school, and 70 percent were under the age of twenty-four.[9] Fewer than 1 percent had been Guardia.[10]

More than 100,000 other persons[11] accompanied the Comandos back to their communities, where they were received by an additional 400,000 to 500,000 other Resistance activists. Beyond the numbers, their return demonstrated the impressive homogeneity of the geographic and social origins of the rebels, especially in the case of the FDN. The great majority of FDN Comandos and supporters returned to communities along the Rio Coco and Bocay River valley corridors in the heart of Nicaragua's northern highlands, or those of the Tuma/Rio Grande de Matagalpa to the south.[12] As was discussed earlier, almost 9,000 Comandos and a proportional number of their supporters went back to only seventeen rural locales.[13] (Table 1 shows these places of return.) The much-feared and widely demonized "Contras" turned out to be only poor dirt farmers from Nicaragua's equivalent of Appalachia, historically marginalized but insistently independent mountain "hillbillies."

In addition to what was reported at an earlier time, the demography and geography of the FDN Comandos and the regional nature of the war were documented from a number of later sources as well. Table 4 is constructed from the data in more than twenty thousand FDN personnel dossiers, some compiled by the Legión 15 de Septiembre.[14] Among other information, each gives the Comandos' place of birth and year of entry into the Resistance.[15] This archive may well constitute a unique window into a guerrilla movement. Table 5 is developed from separate postwar data provided by CIAV/OAS that identify the department of origin of Comandos who came under its aegis after they were demobilized. The regional nature of the war is also demonstrated by table 6, which is constructed from postwar Nicaraguan government data on war claims, and by table 7, which is developed from data in the ACRN's postwar files on the process of integrating the Comandos into society.

TABLE 4

Earliest Comandos by Department of Birth and Year of Entry

	1979–80	1981	1982–3
HIGHLANDS/OTHER			
Jinotega	24	37	42
Nueva Segovia	19	36	32
Madríz	12	22	6
Estelí	9	15	18
Chinandega	8	25	1
Matagalpa	4	21	0
Zelaya	6	3	2
Boaco	1	0	0
Chontales	0	1	5
Rio San Juan	0	0	0
Honduras	1	4	3
SUBTOTAL	84	159	110
% OF TOTAL	(86%)	(93%)	(89%)
PACIFIC LOWLANDS			
León	7	6	6
Managua	3	4	5
Carazo	1	2	0
Masaya	1	1	1
Rivas	1	1	0
Granada	0	0	1
SUBTOTAL	13	14	13
% OF TOTAL	(13%)	(8%)	(11%)
TOTAL	97	173	123

NOTE: The highlanders were mostly Milpistas. During 1979, 1980, and 1981 most of the lowlanders were with exile paramilitary groups, not the MILPAS.

SOURCE: FDN records.

TABLE 5
Demobilized Comandos by Department of Origin, 1991

	COMANDOS	(1991 POP.)	PER 1,000
HIGHLANDS			
Matagalpa	3,808	322,333	11.81
Nueva Segovia	2,692	122,101	22.04
Jinotega	4,117	175,633	23.40
Chontales	2,653	129,632	20.50
Boaco	557	117,924	4.70
Estelí	602	169,125	3.60
Madríz	27	88,682	0.30
Unspecified, est.	1,547	—	—
TOTAL	16,003[a]	1,125,630	14.21
PACIFIC			
Managua	304	1,026,119	0.30
León	198	344,451	0.60
Chinandega	137	330,498	0.40
Masaya	36	230,834	0.20
Rivas	21	149,783	0.10
Granada	15	162,563	0.10
Carazo	7	149,996	0.05
Unspecified, est.	77	—	—
SUBTOTAL	719	2,394,385	0.30
ATLANTIC (EST.)	5,585	298,944	18.68
TOTAL	22,597	3,748,959	

SOURCE: CIAV/OAS data. This table does not account for 5,000 who disarmed later or an estimated 2,500 to 3,000 who did not disarm at all.

TABLE 6
Resistance Victims by Region

	PACIFIC	HIGHLANDS	RATIO
Sandinista	9,587	14,637	1:1.5
Resistance	470	7,058	1:15
Ratio	20:1	2:1	

SOURCE: *Nicaragua: Boletín Estadístico Sobre la Población Afectada por la Guerra por Departamento y Region* (Managua: INR, October 1992) and monthly reports of the Instituto Nicaragüense de Repatriación, January–November 1991, to Minister Jaime Incer, Managua.

A high percentage of Sandinista casualties were reservists or militia. Even Salman Rushdie in his book on revolution-era Nicaragua, *The Jaguar Smiles*, despite his sympathy for the Revolution, expressed shock that so many militia and so few soldiers of the regular army were among the Sandinista wounded he saw.[16] Sandinista casualties were more often suffered in firefights, whereas many FDN casualties were caused by land mines, artillery, or air bombardments.

An examination of the geographic and social origins of the FDN provides answers to important questions. A preliminary review of available texts clearly reveals a number of correlations between the historically dominant ethnic group in the highlands, the birthplaces of the earliest FDN Comandos, and key historical events. Maps 1 and 7–9 demonstrate correlations between the homeland of South American Chibchan Indian groups in pre-Columbian Nicaragua as of 1523 and the birthplaces of 274 Comandos identified as having entered the Resistance in 1979, 1980, or 1981.[17] As is discussed in the next chapter, the great majority of Comando birthplaces fell within the 1523 Chibchan region or straddled a colonial-era divide known as the Spanish Line, or "La Linea de la Frontera Espanola," that divided Chibchan from Spanish Nicaragua for

TABLE 7
Resistance War Claims by Department

	% RURAL (1970)	CLAIMS PER 1,000 INHABITANTS (1991)
HIGHLANDS		
Jinotega	86.2%	61.1
Nueva Segovia	80.8%	43.6
Zelaya Sur/Norte	67.2%	33.0
Rio San Juan	79.4%	27.6
Chontales	78.1%	15.2
Estelí	68.2%	9.9
Matagalpa	80.1%	9.1
Madríz	80.2%	7.8
Boaco	83.2%	2.7
PACIFIC COAST		
Managua	23.7%	1.3
Chinandega	52.1%	0.5
León	51.2%	0.1
Masaya	46.4%	0.0
Carazo	49.9%	0.0
Rivas	66.2%	0.0
Granada	35.4%	0.0

NOTE: Claims by widows, orphans, and the disabled serve as surro-
gates for casualties. All Fronts are included, not only the FDN.
Claims in Zelaya were mostly YATAMA.
SOURCE: Resistance postwar data.

over three centuries.[18] Most of the Comandos whose places of
origin fell outside the Chibchan region were former Guardia.

These correlations strongly suggest that the highlander Resistance movement was actually part of a centuries-old historic pattern,
not simply an isolated late twentieth-century aberration. Additional review of the literature on Nicaraguan history allows identification of places where Indian-Spanish clashes have taken place

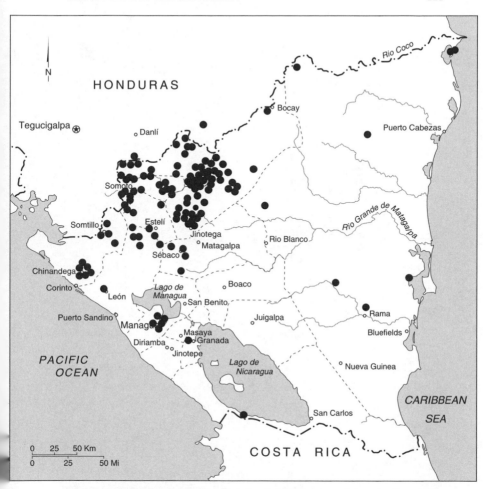

Map 7. Birthplaces of Comandos (both Milpistas and former Guardia) known to have enrolled in the Resistance in 1979 and 1980. Given the map scale, a great many of the birthplaces overlap as many Comandos were from the same family or comarca. Note the close correlation with pre-Columbian Chibchan Nicaragua (see map 1). Source: Legion 15 de Septiembre and FDN personnel files.

since the Conquest. The CIAV/OAS list of communities to which FDN Comandos returned can be compared to these historical data.[19] Of the top seventeen communities on the CIAV/OAS list, fifteen are places where Indian-Spanish clashes recurred over four

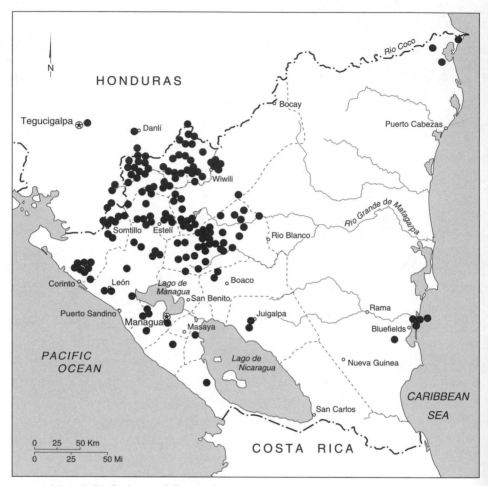

Map 8. Birthplaces of Comandos known to have enrolled in the Resistance in 1981. Milpistas, former Guardia, and others are not differentiated. The many overlaps are due to the identical family and/or comarca origins of most of the Comandos. Source: FDN personnel files.

centuries, between 1526 and 1923. To emphasize this point, these data were presented in map 1. The other two are settlements on Nicaragua's twentieth-century southern agricultural frontier. Both lists also correlate closely with the birthplaces of the FDN Comandos. These correlations suggest that the highlander rebellion had ethnic roots that had gone unnoticed.

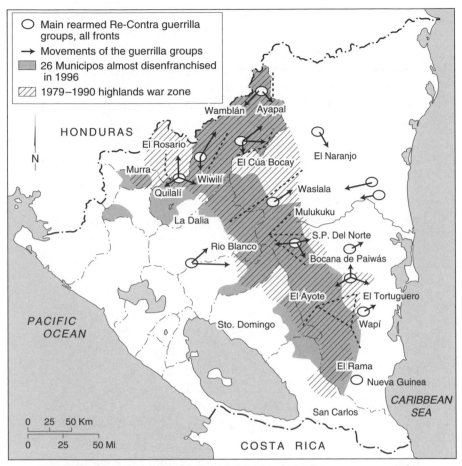

Map 9. Comparison of the 1979–1990 highlands Resistance war zone, the 1990–96 Re-Contra silent war zone, and the 26 municipios nearly disenfranchised in 1996. Note the correlations with map 1 to the pre-Columbian Chichba/Nahua division, the 1523–1920s Indian wars, and the 17 municipios to which almost 9,000 Comandos returned most frequently in 1990–91.

Beyond the geography of the rebellion, this concept can also be cross-checked by comparing pre-Columbian Chibchan sociological markers to modern patterns in the highlands described by former Comandos. Closely correlated markers that possibly link today's highlands to a Chibchan social ancestry include settlement patterns, kinship structures, agricultural practices, house construction methods, forms of sorcery and witchcraft, and attitudes toward authority. Some 97 percent of the Comandos lived on dispersed homesteads, a Chibchan pattern; the Nahua lived in cluster or line communities. About 70 percent of the highlander Comandos were linked by blood or marriage as members of some thirty extended family/comarca clans, and most lived in traditional huts of highland architecture, not Spanish or lowland houses. Popular forms of sorcery and witchcraft followed Chibchan, not Nahua models.[20] The Comandos were decidedly libertarian in their attitudes and lack of local authority structures; the Nahua had been hierarchical. Most of the Comandos, including all those interviewed who were highlanders, identified themselves as ethnic indios, a practice rare among Pacific coast mestizos, most of whom consider that label pejorative.[21]

A significant finding is that colonial-era commentaries on the Chibchans parallel FDN accounts of organizational structure and authority patterns, which reflect Chibchan-like rejection of centralized authority and an insistence on near-absolute individual and family autonomy. These were certainly unusual, if not unique, for an army, and decidedly non-Western. They were also distinctly different from the pre-colonial authority patterns of Pacific coast lowland Nicaragua. In judging the Contras, outside observers erroneously projected conventional Western command models onto them and their army. But its structure and authority patterns were far less conventional and far more Chibchan than these models suggested (see maps 7–9).

Dimas (Pedro Joaquín González), *left*, the father of the "real" Contras, in 1977 while still a top anti-Somoza Sandinista MILPA guerrilla commander. Beside him are Sandinista guerrillas Marianela, González, and Pinell. Author's collection, courtesy of Marina (Andrea Pinell).

Dimas (Pedro Joaquín González), *center*, with four unidentified Sandinista activists, 1977. Author's collection, courtesy of Marina (Andrea Pinell).

A press briefing in the White House in 1989. Vice President Dan Quayle is flanked on his right by Comandante Franklyn (Israel Galeano Cornejo), then chief of staff of the FDN/ERN army (and later killed in a suspicious one-car accident in 1994), and Rubén/Culebra (Oscar Sobalvarro) on his left, later to fill the same position. Both were founding members of the 1979–82 MILPAS movement. The woman beside Franklyn is a State Department interpreter. Author's collection, courtesy of Comandante Franklyn.

Chino Lau (Ricardo Lau), *second from right*, with three Argentine intelligence operatives in 1982 at the Honduran army's Quinta Escuela near Tegucigalpa. Author's collection.

Resistance unit led by Suicida, inside Nicaragua, May 1983. Author's collection.

Comandante 3-80 (Enrique Bermúdez), in his headquarters in Yamales, Honduras, in 1987. Under CIA pressure, the FDN had officially been renamed the ERN by this time. But most Comandos did not agree, and 3-80's FDN patch is still on his left arm. Author's collection.

Mike Lima (Luis Moreno Payán), in Yamales circa 1986. His right arm was blown off by an 82mm mortar round. Author's collection, courtesy of Mike Lima.

A Comando unit planning an ambush inside Nicaragua, circa 1985. Author's collection.

Villagers feeding a Resistance force. The Comandos depended on the peasantry for food. Author's collection.

A YATAMA Indian Task Force crosses open terrain in the Nicaraguan Mosquitia in 1986, well spread out to minimize casualties in case of attack. Author's collection, courtesy of Comandante Blass (Salomón Osorno Coleman).

A Comando gunner sighting a Red-Eye surface-to-air missile. Although not as lethal as the Stinger supplied to Afghanistan's Mujahadin, the Red-Eye still sharply limited the effectiveness of the Sandinistas' helicopter transports and gun-ships. Author's collection.

Sandinista AK-47s, SAMs (surface-to-air missiles), and munitions captured by Comando fighters. The Resistance filled at least half its military through such captures. Author's collection.

Comandos in training in the use of command-detonated Claymore mines, a deadly antipersonnel weapon. The United States did not normally supply pressure mines to the Resistance, although it did capture many from the Sandinistas. Author's collection.

A Comando on combat patrol inside Nicaragua. His expression tells its own story. Author's collection.

A Comando wounded in a skirmish on a hill in La Salvadora near El Cuartelon, Jinotega, in May 1987. Shrapnel from an 82mm mortar had ripped a large piece out of his left shoulder. Author's collection.

FDN headquarters cook Ciriaco, in front of his kitchen in Yamales, circa 1986. Wounded in combat and unable to return to the front lines, Ciriaco found another way to be useful. Author's collection.

YATAMA Comando Fernando Chow in front of his Mosquitia home, circa 1986. His daughter Alvia is playing with his grenade launcher. Chow is half-Chinese, half-Miskito Indian. Author's collection, courtesy of Comandante Blass (Salomón Osorno Coleman).

A sniper from Regional Command San Jacinto, upon completion of May 1987 training by a U.S. CIA team on Swan Island in the Caribbean. The rifle is a Czech version of a Soviet 7.62mm Dragunov (SVD) with a 4x scope. Author's collection.

An air drop under way inside Nicaragua in Jinotega in 1987. Air drops were conducted whenever possible and provided much-needed supplies otherwise unavailable, but they were expensive, risky, and too often unreliable. Author's collection.

A cache of munitions captured from retreating Sandinistas in May 1988 during the battle of Bocay: 82mm mortar rounds, plastic antipersonnel pressure mines, an AK-47, and munitions. These mines, undetectable by sweepers, are especially dangerous. Of perhaps 150,000 planted by the Sandinistas in Nicaragua and Honduras, about 90,000 remained in the ground in the year 2000. Author's collection.

HISTORY OF THE HIGHLANDERS

THE NAHUA CONQUEST

Beginning in the ninth century, Nahua groups started arriving in what was later to become Nicaragua, as part of a centuries-long march southward from central Mexico.[1] Skirting the Maya highlands, they moved slowly down the Pacific coastal plains of the narrowing Central American land bridge. As they advanced, they either conquered or displaced earlier inhabitants.[2] In the region that would become Nicaragua, they encountered Chibchan hunter-gatherers with rudimentary farming skills, who themselves had been drifting northward from South America for about four thousand years.[3] By the time Columbus first visited the New World in 1492, the Nahua had seized and settled Soconusco,[4] the Pacific lowlands of Guatemala, all of El Salvador, much of Honduras, and Pacific lowland Nicaragua and Costa Rica as far south as the Gulf of Nicoya. In Nicaragua they had established a number of proto city-states, the most recent dating from less than a century before the Spanish Conquest.

When the conquistador Gil González reached Nicaragua in 1523, its Pacific lowlands were one of the most heavily populated regions of the Americas. Although the precise number is still subject to debate, two of the best-informed modern students of fifteenth- and sixteenth-century Nicaragua, Linda Newson and William Denevan, after reviewing many archives, have estimated its population in the 1520s at around 1.4 million. Over one million were Nahua living in the Pacific lowlands. The remainder were almost all Chibcha in the central highlands.[5]

Pre-Spanish Nahua Nicaragua was surprisingly urbanized. Managua alone reportedly had a population of some 40,000 and was as large as any city of Spain in the same period.[6] Other large settlements were Imabíte, with 15,000, Jalteba with 8,000,[7] and Denochari, the latter a collection of six villages with a total of 2,000 inhabitants.[8]

Although the Nahua had a writing system, no Nicaraguan Nahua written records survive. Nevertheless, surviving commentaries by Spanish colonial chroniclers reveal glimpses of their society and culture.[9] Modern historians caution readers that the chroniclers were often prone to hyperbole and excessive zeal.[10] To this should be added another caveat. They were all also outsiders and, although occasionally critical of Spanish behavior, were themselves participants and beneficiaries of the Conquest. Some objected to tactics, but none opposed the Conquest itself.

According to the early Spanish colonial chroniclers, the Nahua city-states of Pacific lowlands Nicaragua were centralized autocratic chiefdoms with top-down power structures.[11] With population densities of about thirty people per square kilometer, and many large settlements, their social, political, and economic systems were densely organized. They had highly developed pyramidal class systems. For example one of the most prominent city-states, Nicarao, had as its ruler a hereditary chief, also named Nicarao, after whom Nicaragua is named. He ruled with the support of a small upper class of nobles, priests, warriors, and managers. They, in turn, were lords over a middle class of artisans and a lower class of laborers. At the bottom were numerous slaves, either captured in battle, purchased at market, or enslaved as a form of punishment for transgressions.[12]

Economic activity was centrally organized. Plantation agriculture was a major source of income, and cacao plantations were especially prominent. As cacao served as both a medium of exchange (money) and a sumptuary good for the privileged elite of the entire Nahua region from Nicoya to Mexico, it was especially valuable.[13] Cacao was exported to Nahua centers to the north on the backs of *tamemes,* human porters,[14] or in coastal vessels, to be paid as tribute or in exchange for import luxury goods for the elite.

The invaders had displaced Chibchan groups of South American origin that had drifted into Nicaragua several millennia prior to the Nahuas' arrival.[15] They had conquered the Pacific lowlands, which the Chibcha had previously occupied, but Chibcha continued to dominate the central highlands.[16] The Nahua and Chibcha were continuously at war with one another.[17] Unlike the hierarchically organized and class-riven Nahua city-states, the sixteenth-century Chibchan groups were "smaller societies which were essentially egalitarian and did not possess idols, temples, or an instituted priesthood."[18] They had no large urbanized settlements but rather lived in scattered individual farmsteads in the mountains. The Chibcha shared amongst themselves a common linguistic heritage and culture. One of their most important characteristics was that they were not, and apparently did not want to be, centrally organized. Because their population was close to the maximum carrying capacity of the mountains in which they lived, they were apparently well adjusted to their environment. Socially they preferred individual family group independence and freedom from external interference. Most of the few settled locales in the highlands were small outposts of Pacific Nahua known as *pocheca* that mostly lay along a trade route reaching through the mountains to other Nahua groups in present-day Honduras.[19] Although fewer in number than the Nahua, the Chibchan population of the mountains was not small. Newson estimates that at the time of the Conquest, they numbered about 358,000, an estimate that Denevan accepts.[20]

According to Nicaraguan historian Jaime Incer, "When the Conquistadores first arrived the Nahua and Chibchans were at war. In the mountains to the north of the lakes and volcanoes. . . . lived the much-feared Chontales, whom the Chorotegas and

Nicaraos[21] considered crude and ill-spoken, and with whom they engaged in constant warfare."[22] Thus, even centuries after the Nahua invasion had begun, the Chibcha continued successfully to offer resistance. In addition to warding off continuing Nahua efforts at domination, the Chibcha were reacting to sporadic armed "entradas," many of which were slaving raids.[23] They appear to have limited their responses to defensive actions. Reports of large standing armies among the Nahua may attest more to the extent of these hostilities than to clashes between Nahua city-states.

Nicaraguan historians such as Incer, as well as Jaime Wheelock, the husband-and-wife team of Julian Guerrero and Lola Soriano, Germán Romero, and Cecilia Guillén de Herrera, consider this Chibcha-Nahua division critical to understanding modern Nicaragua.[24] As Incer comments:

> To the west, on the dry plains [of the Pacific] lived indigenous groups whose historic roots and culture were tied to the notable civilizations of Mexico; to the east [the highlands], among rain drenched mountains and torrential rivers wandered tribes of clearly circumcaribbean origins and customs. As a consequence of these differences of geography and of origins, Nicaragua is really made up of two nations living in one country, sharing an isthmian bridge where the natural and the cultural have come together from the most remote of times to allow the passage of both biological and ethnic migrations from North to South America, and vice versa.[25]

Pablo Antonio Cuadra, one of modern Nicaragua's grand men of letters, goes so far as to call this ethnic division the founding duality of modern Nicaraguan character.[26]

THE SPANISH CONQUEST

Spain's conquistadores arrived in Nicaragua in the early 1520s from both Panama and Mexico, entering Nicaragua via its Pacific coast lowland Nahua region. Those from recently conquered Mexico were accompanied by Nahua-speaking guides and, on occasion, Nahua auxiliary troops. The conquistadores found Nicaragua extraordinarily attractive. One of the earliest conquistadores, Lopez de Gomara, described it as "healthy, fertile and full of gardens and orchards." Bishop Bartolomé de las Casas called the province "a delightful and happy find for the human race . . . which fills me with more wonder than any other place I know, so fertile, so abundant, so fresh and agreeable, so healthy, so filled with fruitfulness, as orderly as the orchards and villages of Castilla, and completely provisioned to comfortably house, entertain and provide gracefully for man."[27]

Another conquistador, Jeronimo Benzóni, reported that the Spanish "for the abundance of all they found there, called [Nicaragua] the Paradise of Mohammed."[28] In his monumental *Conquest of Peru*, Prescott remarked that conquistadores who had been in Nicaragua before joining Pizarro, when faced by the dreary Peruvian landscape, longingly remembered "their pleasant quarters in their luxurious land, [and] sighed only to return to their Mahometan paradise."[29]

Perhaps the conquistadores who had departed for Peru sighed for Nicaragua, but those who stayed quickly converted it into a purgatory for the Nahua. The Spanish came armed with modern steeds and the steel of Castile, a hunger for fortune and power, and the missionary zealotry of true believers in the era of the Spanish Inquisition. To advance all these interests simultaneously, the Spanish employed a procedure known as a *requerimiento*. This involved reading to each native group as it was encountered (no doubt to the complete bewilderment of its members) declarations that henceforth they would be required, *requerido*, to convert to a new ideology, Spanish Catholicism, and to submit to a new master, the king of Spain. Submission to the king was to be demonstrated by acts of fealty and payments of tribute. Acceptance of Catholic Christianity was to be demonstrated by baptism followed by participation in activities and organizations led by the priests. Those who refused to do either voluntarily would be forced to comply. The requierimiento is perhaps understandable in the context of the times. The Spanish state and Catholic Church were inextricably intertwined. From the perspective of the state, absolute submission and loyalty to the king was (at least in theory) mandatory for all subjects of the realm, no matter how recently enrolled or how bewildered. From the perspective of the church, a person who had never been exposed to Christianity might die in limbo and would not go to hell, but once offered an opportunity to convert, refusal was a mortal sin. The demands of this duality made concurrent political and ideological conquest both mandatory and inevitable.

In their very first meeting in 1522, Spanish conquistador Gil González offered Nahua-Chorotega Chief Nicarao[30] the stark choices of a requierimiento: accept Catholic Christianity and baptism and become a vassal of the king of Spain or meet the Spanish on the field of battle. In either case, bring gold. Nicarao chose to submit, bringing with him as tribute gold worth 18,500 Castillian pesos. He accepted baptism and became a vassal of the king. Gil González reciprocated by giving him a linen shirt and a red cap.[31]

The second important Nicaraguan Nahua chief to meet with Gil González, also in 1522, was Diriangen,[32] accompanied by over five hundred retainers. He brought an even larger tribute of gold, worth over nineteen thousand Castillian pesos. But unlike Nicarao, Diriangen was not submissive. Asked why he had come, Diriangen replied that he wanted to meet the Spaniards, to touch them, and to see if they really did have beards and travel astride beasts of prey. But he did not promptly submit to baptism nor did he agree to become a vassal of the Spanish king. Instead, he left, promising to return in three days. Return he did, but at the head of a Nahua army of some three thousand warriors. The battle that followed appears to have been noisy and, for the Nahua, bloody. But the Spanish emerged triumphant, reportedly without the loss of a single soldier. Other battles followed the González-Diriangen confrontation. The city-state of Managua alone reportedly fielded ten thousand archers during one battle against the conquistadores.[33] But, on balance, the conquest of the Nicaraguan Nahua took place swiftly and with minimal Spanish casualties, leading Newson to say that the Spanish "conquest of Pacific Nicaragua was relatively easy."[34]

DECIMATION OF THE NAHUA

For the Nahua, the price of defeat was appalling. In one genera-tion, the Spanish annihilated almost the entire population of Pacific lowland Nicaragua. In 1544 Spanish *oidor*, or crown inspector, Diego de Herrera, reported that the population in the Nahua region had been reduced to only thirty thousand.[35] By 1548 Managua had only 265 tributary Indians while Jalteba had been reduced to 195 tributary Indians.[36] The principal cause of this decline was trading Indians as slaves.[37]

The supply of existing gold and other precious goods available in Nicaragua was exhausted almost immediately by early Spanish exactions of tribute. With the exception of a small mining district in the highlands at Nueva Segovia, Nicaragua had no other substantial sources of gold or silver.[38] Farming was the most impor-tant remaining generator of riches Nicaragua offered, but that was hardly an attractive option to the early conquistadores. They were extractors of existing wealth, not long-term foreign investors. With the native populations of the Antilles disappearing rapidly and every Spaniard demanding personal servants and concubines as his price for continued service in the New World, Indian slaves quickly became colonial Nicaragua's second-most valuable export commodity.[39] Pedro de Alvarado brought commercial Indian slaving to Nicaragua by way of Soconusco, Guatemala, and El Salvador.[40] MacLeod, in his study *Spanish Central America*, calls the amassing of existing stock of gold and silver and the trade in Indian slaves the two "golden keys to wealth" for the conquista-dores.[41] For the slave trade, "Central America was the most con-venient center of large Indian populations, and within Central America lacustrine Nicaragua was the closest nucleus. Thus it became the main center of the slave trade in Indians."[42]

The Spanish also quickly replaced the Nahua oligarchy as Pacific coast Nicaragua's rulers and installed themselves and their descendants as its new hereditary elite,[43] employing both the ideology of the Catholic Church and the power of the Spanish state to establish and retain control. Because relatively few Spaniards were present, even after the destruction of most of the Nahua masses, they resorted to a series of institutions and instruments to dominate the Pacific lowland's remaining Indians and a slowly growing number of mestizos. At first, when a Nahua chief or leader submitted to a requerimiento, the Spanish exerted control through the Indians' own pre-Conquest hierarchy. But such indirect methods quickly gave way to other approaches, especially direct military coercion combined with religious persuasion, each reinforcing the other.

The most important early institution of domination was the *encomienda*, a state grant to a Spaniard of a tract of land and of authority over the Indians living on it. In return the grantee, or *encomendero*, was supposed to provide "his" Indians with "protection and instruction in the Catholic faith."[44] Its principal real effect was to remove land from Indian control and put both it and an Indian labor force under the control of the new Spanish elite. But by and large, because the Spanish were interested in living like Europeans, not Indians, they were more concerned with generating income than with protecting Indians. Many maximized their immediate incomes by stripping their properties of workers; encomienda Indians quickly became a prime source of slaves for export. Because the Pacific coast was the only region under effective Spanish control, the highlands were largely spared.[45] Soon slaving, excessive labor demands, and disease took a major toll and caused what one writer laconically called "a drop in labor supplies."[46]

Faced by a severe labor shortage of their own making, the Spanish created another new institution, the *repartimiento*, or forced assignment of Indians to the control of selected Spaniards, a system designed to mobilize remaining manpower to the benefit of the now labor-short new regime.[47] The repartimiento process swiftly became a key instrument for generating free forced Indian labor for the dominant Spanish elite.[48] Within a decade, stripping the countryside to profit urban Pacific coast Spanish communities had become a Spanish-Nicaraguan habit.

Survival of the Chibcha

In the highlands, "resistance to Spanish colonization was vastly different and, in fact, persisted throughout the colonial period."[49] The first two Spanish soldiers killed in combat against Nicaraguan Indians were to die in the mountains at the hands of Chibchan Chontals, not Nahuas.[50] This resistance to the Conquest by the highland Chibcha resulted in their survival as a group, a result not unrelated to the fierce resistance they put up against Spanish domination, and standing in sharp contrast to the relatively quick submission and subsequent near-annihilation of the Pacific coast lowland Nahua.

The differing responses of the two groups had multiple origins. The Chibcha had little that the Spanish could exploit for profit. They had no gold or silver and did not offer the Spanish, as did the Pacific Nahua, an already organized system of agricultural plantations complete with proletarian labor forces of docile workers accustomed to taking orders. But, also unlike the Nahua, the Chibcha put up a fierce, constant, and violent resistance.

By the mid-1500s, the few remaining Nahua were launched into a process of deracination from the Indian and acculturation to the Spanish. Although some cultural and social markers survive, and certain communities such as Subtiava and Monimbo still retain a strong sense of indio identity,[51] by the early eighteenth century the Pacific coast region was essentially hispanicized.[52] By way of contrast, the use of Indian languages as mother tongues in the highlands continued into the twentieth century, and important vestiges of Indian religions and folk customs, as well as pre-Columbian cultural patterns, are still found.[53] In a 1994 study, Costa Rican ethnosociologist Eugenia Ibarra found that in the highlands of Nicaragua, descendants of the Chontals and Mata-galpans retained cultural traits identifiable as Chibchan.[54]

The case, however, should not be overstated. Over the ensuing centuries, Spanish did gradually became the highlanders' mother tongue and Catholicism their predominant religion.[55] Mestizaje and ladinoization made considerable inroads. Migration into the highland small towns and agricultural frontier increased the percentage of mestizos, especially in the towns, and some mestizo peasants established themselves in the agricultural hinterlands, as did small enclaves of Europeans. But the most indio of the campe-sinos continue to this day to retreat further and further into the region's agricultural frontier, and many settled areas and comarcas remain heavily, if not entirely, indio. Pre-Columbian practices such as the extensive use of sorcery, witchcraft, and native medicine continue. I even heard tantalizing hints that a few native speakers of Chibchan languages continue to live in isolation, carefully hidden from outside eyes, although I was not able to find any.[56]

COLONIAL-ERA HIGHLANDER RESISTANCE

The Spanish, then, did not subjugate the highlands. They did stage entradas, or incursions, and Catholic priests tried periodically to establish *reducciones*, or frontier missions. But these rarely pros-pered for long. In only one place, Nueva Segovia's gold fields, were the Spanish prepared to pay the price the Chibchan *indios bravos*[57] of the highlands extracted for maintaining a long-term full-time presence. The result was the Spanish Line that since the earli-est years of the Conquest divided the territory in two.[58] West of the Line Spain's fiat was supreme, but to the east it was not. Several historians trace the Line as running through the middle of the high-lands through Nueva Segovia into Honduras, but this appears actually to trace a Spanish salient that roughly followed the line of pre-Columbian Nahua pocheca, outposts northward toward Hon-duras from their Pacific city-states, since the highlands to the west of that salient also appear to have remained Chibchan.

Resistance in the highlands continued throughout the three centuries of the Spanish colonial era.[59] Some of the most violent early Spanish-Indian battles in the highlands (see map 1 for specific locations) took place near Nueva Segovia.[60] Founded in 1527 to exploit nearby gold deposits, Nueva Segovia was attacked and destroyed repeatedly throughout the sixteenth and seventeenth centuries by Chibchan warriors from the surrounding mountains. The town had to be moved several times before it finally came to rest in its present location where, in 1611, it became Ciudad Antigua.[61] The Chibcha also attacked a second small mining region on the Rio Segovia north of Ciudad Nueva. Guillén de Herrera notes that "aggressions of the natives, especially those then called Jicaques, who came from the mountains continued for . . . centuries.[62] She also states "Lencas who killed with witchcraft and hordes of Jicaques poured forth from the Rio Pantasma region[63] to attack and pillage Christian settlements."[64]

Several histories of the sixteenth, seventeenth, and eighteenth centuries give the place-names of locales where particularly notable battles took place between the Spanish and Indians.[65] Prominent among them were Kilambé, El Cuá Bocay, Pantasma, Wamblán, Bocay, Peñas Blancas, Matagalpa, Wiwilí, Quilalí, Somoto, and Jalapa, several of which are the locales to which large numbers of FDN Comandos returned in 1990–91 (see table 1).[66] Many of the early clashes were described as Indian reactions to efforts by zealous Catholic priests, supported by Spanish army units, to collect the Chibcha into mission reducciones to convert and indoctrinate them, combined exercises in ideological proselytizing and military coercion. Later conflicts tended to revolve around land tenure and coercive attempts by the central government to conscript peasants to work on the farms of the ruling class.

During much of the colonial period, the Spanish also suffered repeated incursions by pirates, Zambo-Miskitos,[67] and Sumu Indians, many of these joint incursions led by the British. Essentially raids on colonial outposts or cities, these were often brutal and highly destructive. Incer is among those who describe several of these raids in detail.[68] The mountain indios had mixed reactions to

Zambo-Miskito and other raiding parties from the Atlantic Mosquito Coast that passed through the highlands. Because the raiders sometimes also took slaves, the Chibcha feared them. But on occasion they joined forces to attack the Spanish. On balance, the main difference between the Zambo-Miskito raiders and the highlanders' resistance appears to have been one of objectives. The pirate and Zambo-Miskito raids were offensive operations targeting Nicaragua's cities, especially those in the Pacific coast region, in search of fortune. The Chibcha rarely raided far from home and appear to have mostly acted in self-defense.

INDEPENDENCE-ERA HIGHLANDER RESISTANCE

Nicaragua's independence from Spain, a process that began in 1821, did not end ongoing attempts by the heirs of the Spanish to dominate the highlands. To the contrary, it exacerbated the highlanders' problem. From their perspective, the principal change was that the independence-era dominant elite was no longer fettered by the concerns of Spanish bureaucrats or by the moral queasiness of a distant crown. E. Bradford Burns, writing about the postcolonial Nicaragua of the eighteenth and nineteenth centuries, finds that it was sharply divided between a Spanish patriarchy and mestizo and Indian folk masses. The dominant patriarchs were the espanoles; the subordinate folk were the indios. The patriarchs were extremely quarrelsome amongst themselves, but as a group they consistently used their collective control of the country's power structures to seek economic, social, and political advantage for themselves at the expense of the folk. As Burns puts it, "The Indians shared none of the elite's vision of a nation-state, or even the city-state, and of expanded commerce. They preferred to adhere to their own cultural traditions, and to grow their subsistence with just enough surplus for the local market."[69]

Tensions and outright violence often resulted when the patriarchy pushed its advantages too far too fast. This most often occurred in the agricultural sector when the elite decided it needed more land on which to produce a new export crop to generate hard currency, such as sugar, cotton, indigo, coffee, or cattle, or when it felt the pinch of labor shortages that necessitated the recruitment of cheap rural labor, willing or not. Burns comments that as a consequence, "the extremes of European and Indian institutions defined and perpetuated two different social patterns."[70]

The fundamental problem continued to be what it had been in the colonial period, that Nicaragua produced like the rest of Central America but the patriarchs, as had their Spanish colonial forefathers, insisted on living like Europeans. To pay for their preferred lifestyle, the patriarchs had to generate hard currencies with which to buy the foreign "necessities" and luxuries that they demanded but Nicaragua could not produce. This, in turn, required them to produce export crops at minimal costs to generate sufficient surplus cash to import their "needs." That process required cheap land and even cheaper labor. Because of these efforts to support European lifestyles for the few, extracted from the land and labor of the many, the elite made repeated forays against the indios and their land in search of cheap land and all but free labor. Because the patriarchy dominated the government, the elite routinely enrolled its power to advance its interests. But because these forays also threatened the indio lifestyle, the masses often resisted violently.[71]

Occasionally the folk, the indios, would find a champion. Among the more fascinating incidents were attacks in 1845, 1847, and 1849 on Pacific coastal cities, led by a charismatic leader, General Bernabé Somoza, an ancestor of Anastacio "Tacho" Somoza Garcia, founder of the twentieth-century Somoza dynasty. Bernabé Somoza was a Liberal, and the conflict he headed had political roots. But he was also a populist and a natural leader. In addition to occupying Chinandega, Managua, and Rivas at various times, Somoza twice sacked the city of León, against which he had a strong personal grudge. Burns finds that the patriarchs reacted to Bernabé Somoza with exceptional virulence. What they seemed to fear most was that "Somoza would win the confidence of the Indians and unite

them . . . [so the elite's press] . . . fired a ceaseless barrage of pejo-
ratives 'barbarian,' 'cannibal,' 'savage,' 'bandit,' 'madman,' and
'brigand' [and] accused him of burning haciendas and killing at
least one patriarch."[72]

Burns's own conclusion is less apocalyptical than that of the
patriarchs: Bernabé Somoza's sackings of León were not especially
different from other incidents of the period, but "what doubtless
intensified the heat of rhetoric in this case was the popular dimensions of this war, its potential threat to all patriarchs. . . . If the popular and dashing figure of Bernabé Somoza succeeded in coalescing
discontent, the elites would confront a formidable foe. They feared
a unified and popular agrarian movement [and] persuaded themselves that nothing less than Western civilization was at stake."[73] In
short, the elite's fear of the indio masses that had followed Somoza
had bordered on hysteria.[74] It was one of those rare occasions when
the patriarchs put aside their internal political competition for
advantage long enough to unite against the masses.

In 1881, almost two generations after Bernabé Somoza's rebellion, another major Indian rebellion occurred in Matagalpa, triggered by a combination of patriarchal grabs for remaining Indian
lands, government attempts to establish involuntary military
service, and efforts to forcibly recruit Indian campesino labor in
the nearby highlands to work on the patriarchy's estates for marginal wages. As Europeanate Nicaraguan historians Guerrero and
Soriano de Guerrero later put it, the Indians "prepared their rebellion in secret and with the 'traditional slyness and malice' which
has always characterized our aborigines."[75] The first attack took
place on March 30. "A large party of armed Indians attacked the
city for over three hours. The city's residents, remembering depre-
dations during similar attacks in 1824, 1827, and 1844, reacted in
panic. Twenty-five Indians and three city residents were killed."[76]
The people of Matagalpa petitioned the government to save them
"lest they be exterminated."[77]

Jeffrey Gould, a leading scholar of the period, suggests that the
1881 Matagalpan rebellion is best understood "in the context of five
years of violent changes in the Indians' lives; losses of thousands

of acres of communal land, forced labor, internal economic and political divisions, and a conflict with the church over ownership of their *cofradías,* lay brotherhoods,[78] and possession of images that included representations of the 'apostles.' The movement responded to and fomented ethnic strife."[79]

Gould concludes that the Matagalpan Indian rebellion of 1881 compelled the state to devise methods to contain the Indian military potential once and for all.[80] After the rebellion had been squashed, the government and patriarchy launched a combined and apparently orchestrated assault on Indian society and identity that included further expropriations of land and coercion of Indian labor, attacks on remaining Indian social markers such as religious symbols, and assaults on their communities' ethnic cohesion.[81] Concurrently, Nicaragua's intellectual elite set out to define away the Indian-ness of the highland campesinos by establishing a new hegemonic discourse. This discourse promoted a "myth of mestizaje" that redefined Nicaragua as a homogeneous society of mixed-blood mestizos within which, save for the Mosquitia, Indians no longer existed.[82]

Gould believes that the Nicaraguan patriarchy, as it combined the process of creating a new hegemonic discourse with direct assaults on Indian cultures and ways of life, set an example that was emulated elsewhere in Central America. Consequently, in El Salvador, Honduras, as well as in Nicaragua,

> between 1880 and 1950, the Indians suffered dramatic losses of land, language, and identity. Those losses were codified in census returns that reported the virtual disappearance of the Indians into the ladino population. So powerful was the dominant discourse that hundreds of thousands of Central American Indians . . . became "ashamed" of their ethnic markers as the word *Indian* became a synonym for "ignorant" or "savage."[83]

But in the case of Nicaragua, Gould also has found that the onslaught elicited Indian resistance that "thwarted eight governmental attempts to abolish [indigenous] comunidades between 1877 and 1923."[84] Nonetheless, the Nicaraguan elite did create a "myth of mestizaje" that tried to suppress the real ethnic dimensions of contemporary Nicaragua. In so doing, it constructed an important hegemonic form, a mirror of Nicaraguan society that reflected only the faces of mestizos and Spaniards.[85] Gould argues that this mirror reflected a deliberately falsified image. He demonstrates this by listing subsequent Matagalpan Indian uprisings in 1898, 1904, 1909, 1915, 1919, and the 1920s. Gould's list brings the history of violent Chibchan Indian resistance during the period of "patriarchal independence" up to the era of the Marine-Sandino war. But he may have ended his catalog of violent Indian resistance at too early a point. Other scholars find that patriarchal use of a discourse of hysteria directed against the Indians did not end in 1920. Michael Schroeder, in a study of the Sandino affair, explains that

> Bourgeois [patriarchal] representations of the [Augusto César Sandino] Rebellion emerged from the wider semantic field of "civilization versus barbarism" [and] were deeply inscribed with imageries of *lower class savagery, disorder, and violence, of the racial inferiority of the Indians and primitivism of the countryside* . . . [Sandino's] Rebellion came to represent something truly frightening: the specter of the rural lower orders committing organized and directed violence against the ideals [the patriarchy] held most dear.[86]

Schroeder quotes an editor for Managua's *La Prensa*, who wrote on 2 April 1932 that "the hordes of Sandino are made up of mercenaries and men without scruples. . . . I find only in these dry and cold-blooded names, thieves, assassins, and incendiaries."[87]

In the 1980s, the 1881 Matagalpan Chibchan rebellion was to serve historian Jaime Wheelock, who is both an aristocrat[88] and Sandinista, as the watermark event from which to date the end of Nicaraguan Indian resistance to Spanish control.[89] But, again, a declaration of an end to the highlander resistance proved premature.

THE 1990s

Costa Rican ethnohistorian Eugenia Ibarra brings the survival of highland Chibchan Indian identities into the 1990s. A student of Matagalpan ethnohistorical markers, Ibarra has concluded that a separate Chibchan Indian sense of identity based on shared cultural characteristics continues to exist in Nicaragua today.[90] The highlanders I interviewed agreed. The pride that the former FDN Comandos expressed in their indio roots in the mid-1990s demonstrated the failure of all these efforts to define Nicaragua's highland Indians out of existence. Highlander self-identification as indio has survived.

This historical review appears strongly to reinforce the suggestion that the highland rebellion had deep ethnohistoric roots. The distinctiveness of the Chibchan identity in the region may have blurred over the centuries, but deep regional differences remain.

CHAPTER THIRTEEN

THE HIGHLANDERS' SOCIAL PLACE

As the previous chapter has shown, the highlanders of Nicaragua have for several centuries, and perhaps for more than a millennium, resisted attempts by the Pacific lowlanders to control the region. The highlanders first resisted the Nahua, then the Spanish, then the patriarchy. If the Nahua-Chibcha conflict was intertribal, if the conflict with the Spanish was colonial, and if the Spanish patriarchy versus Indian folk was economic, then the question arises of how to classify the highlanders' resistance to the Sandinista Revolution. A number of options are possible: core vs. periphery, modern vs. traditional, urban vs. rural. Each has validity. But for me the most fruitful means of understanding the Resistance movement is to look at it as an ethno-class conflict related to the highlanders' place in modern Nicaraguan society.

Richard N. Adams, in a seminal cultural survey, describes Nicaraguan social divisions of the 1950s in considerable detail. The picture he paints is of an unamalgamated composite of social subgroups with deep fault lines dividing classes, ethnicities and regions. He identifies the largely Pacific coast urban upper class as *la sociedad, la aristocracia,* or simply *los ricos,* the rich, with the term *aristocracia* reserved for "members of the old families of León, Granada, Managua, and some of the older towns, such as Ocotal, Masaya, etc."[1] He calls the heavily rural lower classes *campesinos proletariado,* or simply *los pobres,* the poor. These terms reflect race and ethnicity as much as wealth, although the two usually go hand in hand. The upper class is widely perceived as whiter, more Spanish, or more European. The lower classes are *mas indígena,* more Indian.[2] In 1976, based both on extensive interviewing and on experience in-country, Harry Strachan divided the upper class into business groups. The three most important were the Pellas, the Montealegres, and the Somozas. The six second-tier families, included, as the most prominent, the Lacayos, Chamorros, and Cuadras. But one of his sources argued strongly that in Nicaragua "the real group is the family group; business groups are simply a manifestation in the economic sphere of these family groups."[3] Samuel Stone brings the class question into the period of recent conflicts and labels the war between the Sandinistas and the Somozas as no more than "a violent eruption of economic and political differentiation within Nicaragua's ruling class."[4]

But the highlander–Sandinista conflict was different. The Milpistas were a phenomenon of the Indian highland peasantry, of Burns's "Folk," not his "Patriarchy." More precisely, based on the geography of their rebellion and the history of the highlands, the highlander Resistance movement and the Milpistas were a phenomenon of only part of Burns's "Folk," those who were also independent microbourgeois campesinos of the mountains. Even after 1981, with the exception of a handful of Comandos, neither Pacific coast lowland peasants nor urban workers formed part of the FDN.

All of the highland Comandos the FDN interviewed for this study belonged to this peasant group. They or their families controlled small-to-medium farming plots sufficient to sustain themselves and their families, placing them squarely within the group of Nicaraguan Indians who, in Burns's words, "preferred to adhere to their own cultural traditions, and to grow their subsistence with just enough surplus for the local market."[5] Strong indio self-identification of all but one of the Comandos interviewed reinforced this conclusion. Thus, in addition to their geographic and historical distinctiveness, the Comandos' social place was squarely within the lower classes. Comparing their class origins to those of the Sandinistas produces an interesting contrast.

NICARAGUA'S ELITE

As Burns, Stone, and Adams describe it, the Nicaraguan upper class is composed of a hereditary patriarchy, with the more well-to-do professionals and smaller businesspeople ranged beneath them. The handful of "Spanish" families that have traditionally ruled Nicaragua comprises perhaps 1 percent of the country's population. Entrance into this aristocracy is normally by birth, sometimes by marriage, but rarely by merit. From the perspective of family and social class origins, the pre- and post-Somoza Nicaraguan patriarchal class is a continuum, with the upper echelon of the Sandinista movement a part of the elite. Their intimate blood and business relationships with the traditional aristocracy demonstrate that key members of the Sandinista vanguard are part of the elite.[6]

Radell describes the patriarchal families as divided by rivalries between Granada and León that are themselves the products of different social origins, ethnicity, and class:

> Granada was settled by aristocratic officers . . . León was settled by humble foot soldiers. . . . [Managua is the capital, but its] most influential residents do not consider Managua their real home. Their economic influence is exerted from the capital, not in the name of that city but in the name of either Granada or León, or more recently, Chinandega.[7]

Strachan, discussing elite divisions in terms of major family groups,[8] notes that the richest and most powerful of these in 1976 was the Grupo Banco de America (Bank of America) of the Pellas family group[9] that had "its roots . . . in Granada, an ancient city of Nicaragua . . . generally identified with the Conservative party in politics."[10] The second most important family group was the Montealegres, built around the Banco de Nicaragua (BANIC-Wells

Fargo), that had "its roots in León, another ancient city of Nicaragua, and is identified with the Liberal Party." The third most
important family group was the Somozas, which, led by social
upstarts, was climbing quickly up the social ladder.[11] The inter-
vening Sandinista Revolution notwithstanding, in 1997 the aristocracy remained essentially intact and dominant. The Pellas and
Montealegre family groups remained largely intact, although the
Somoza group had disappeared and had been replaced by the
Sandinista leadership group. This was clearly demonstrated by
the make-up of Nicaragua's 1990–96 post-Revolution government
of Violeta Chamorro.[12]

In contrast with the closed system of the aristocracy, entry into
the upper classes beneath the patriarchal families can be earned.
This group is made up largely of businessmen, export agricultur-
alists, leading professionals, senior bureaucrats, and their families.
This second layer of the elite contains about 4 to 5 percent of the
population. Together, the aristocracy and bourgeois contain perhaps 6 percent of the population.

THE DIVIDED FOLK

About 85 to 86 percent of Nicaragua's population is either Pacific
mestizo or highland indio, with the Comandos and their families
within the latter subgroup. When conducting his survey, Adams
found deep differences between these two groups. He heard
"comments which suggested that the campesinos of the more
densely populated Pacific Coast plains and valleys tended to
regard themselves as more 'civilized' than those who occupy the
rougher country, the 'montaña.'"[13]

The difference between Pacific mestizos and highland indios is
historically and socially significant. Besides the historical divisions
described above, the modern Pacific coast is 60 percent urban and
40 percent rural and highly mestizoized. Pacific urban mestizos are
mostly wage laborers, while its rural population is mostly made
up of proletarian agricultural workers. The mestizos may have

small farming plots, but these are usually too small to sustain a family. In contrast, most highlanders are small farmers who control sufficient land to feed their families, making them rural micro-bourgeois.

MARGINAL MINORITIES

Several minority groups that live on the Atlantic littoral make up the remaining 8 to 9 percent of Nicaragua's population. Nicaragua's tribal Miskito, Sumu, and Rama Indians are well-defined ethnic minorities that constitute about 4 percent of the country's population. Several excellent studies of these Indian groups are those of Ephraim Squier, Eduardo Conzemius, and Bernard Nietzchmann.[14] Lazlo Pataky also describes the region's distinctive ways of life in fascinating detail.[15] Black Creoles are Nicaragua's second-largest marginal Atlantic coast minority. They possess many of the characteristics of a protonation, and recently a few have begun to demand outright independence.[16] They are of Afro-Caribbean origin, speak English, and are mostly Protestants. Sources on the Creoles are limited but do include a study of the region during the Revolution by Costa Rican scholars[17] and a report prepared by the Creoles themselves.[18] There is also a small Garífuna community. Including "españoles" who live in the region, as of 1989, the peoples of the Atlantic Coast numbered almost 400,000.[19]

SANDINISTA/COMANDO
CLASS DIFFERENCES

In addition to the interviews, I also reviewed more than 350 biographies of Sandinistas and Resistance activists. I determined that 299 of them could be classified with some confidence by social class.[20] Table 8 shows the findings. The results may be considered conservative because all former officers of either the Guardia or the Sandinista army, regardless of rank, have been tallied as elite.

TABLE 8
Social Origins

		ELITE	LOWER CLASS
SANDINISTA			
Heroes		6	13
Leaders		18	4
Cadre		56	4
	TOTAL	89	21
RESISTANCE			
Heroes		6	15
Leaders			
	Political	11	7
	Military	31	108
	TOTAL	48	132

SANDINISTA VS. RESISTANCE SOCIAL CLASS RATIO

SANDINISTAS	RESISTANCE
4:1 Elite	3:1 Peasant/proletarian

Nonetheless, it is clear that majorities of both the Sandinista vanguard and the leadership of the Nicaraguan civilian Resistance were of elite origins.[21] The social place of the Comandos was just as clearly lower class. These class differences not only had a major impact on the war, they also had an impact on how the war ended and on its aftermath.

CHAPTER FOURTEEN

THE FDN RETURNS TO ITS MILPAS ROOTS, 1988–1990

The last major battle of the Contra War was fought just sixty miles from where the MILPAS war had begun, in a remote region known as the Bocay. Following peace negotiations between Central American presidents in late 1987, the Honduran government had forced the FDN to abandon its main sanctuary at Yamales and move to the Bocay, a remote region of triple canopy rain forest. The U.S. Congress then permanently ended American lethal aid to the Contras on 3 February 1988. On March 10, shortly after this congressional action, the Sandinistas launched a major attack on the Resistance's Bocay sanctuary, using eight elite counterinsurgency and irregular warfare battalions, known as BLIs and BLCs. Assistant Secretary of State Elliott Abrams warned Secretary of State George Schultz that the Sandinista army was trying to land a killing blow.[1] With Enrique Bermúdez, Comandante 3-80, in personal command on the battlefield,[2] the heavily outnumbered FDN defenders held, and the attack failed to reach any of its primary objectives.[3] It was later falsely alleged by would-be detractors, who were not present at the scene, that the FDN's commander fled from the battlefield as soon as the shooting started. This was not true. He directed the FDN's side of the battle from his jungle headquarters at Bocay from beginning to end.

Following the battle, the FDN settled into both a new relationship with the United States and a new phase of the war with the Sandinistas. A tentative cease-fire was negotiated. Sporadic clashes continued, but both sides spent as much time maneuvering for advantage as fighting. An AID Task Force for Humanitarian Assistance (TFHA) took over support for the FDN from the CIA, with the mission of providing it with "humanitarian" assistance. This took the form of goods and services to the FDN forces while they were in sanctuary in Honduras and of cash in the form of Nicaraguan Cordobas for them to take to Comando forces inside Nicaragua to buy what AID was not allowed to deliver to them. Despite the loss of lethal aid, the armed Resistance inside Nicaragua remained organized and effective and was able to keep more Comandos inside Nicaragua than out.

In May 1988, a team from the U.S. Embassy in Managua visited the highlands to assess the situation of the armed Resistance in the region. A Liberal Independent Party leader in Ocotal, Luís Moreno Ponce, told them that "while few rural residents will openly admit that they support the armed opposition Contras, in reality, they constitute the 'social base' of the Resistance." Carlos Olivas, the chief of the Popular Social Christian Party in Nueva Segovia, said "the peasants are supplying the Resistance with food." A businessman in Quilalí said that the "armed opposition was obtaining food from the local populace and seemed to have no problems with uniforms or arms." A small farmer near San Rafael del Norte said that the Comandos "were asking the peasants for food, and the rural populace was responding to such requests." The Sandinistas had launched an intensive psychological warfare campaign to try to convince the Comandos to lay down their arms and accept amnesty. The Embassy Managua team reported that, on one occasion, a Sandinista army sub-lieutenant, Harold Moreno, "attempted to disarm a Resistance band near Quilalí. The Resistance . . . responded by disarming the Sub-Lieutenant instead." In another instance the Sandinistas enlisted the help of a local priest for a meeting at El Naranjo near San Rafael. But "although the priest had celebrated a mass, the Resistance had kept its weapons throughout the meeting. No Resistance member had surrendered his arms." On "May 4 at Sabana Grande the EPS had asked the Resistance force to lay down its arms and return to civilian life." Not only did no Comando do so, "some youths fleeing Sandinista military recruiters had reportedly gone over to the armed opposition during the meeting." Officials of the Sandinista government's Institute for Agrarian Reform told an Embassy Managua officer privately that "popular resentment against the regime remains high."[4]

The Embassy team concluded that "Resistance forces appear to enjoy significant support from the peasantry throughout the area visit by EmbOffs [Embassy officers]." The team actually saw only part of what was happening. Not only were the peasants helping the Comandos with food, they were trying to join the FDN's ranks in unprecedented numbers.[5] As had happened repeatedly, in the absence of American lethal aid, the rebellion had simply turned to its peasant roots for support.

The sheer numbers of peasants trying to join the FDN forced AID to set a maximum manpower quota on the number of Comandos it would assist. By doing so, it unwittingly returned to a policy that the CIA had been required to adopt earlier for the same reason. During periods when the CIA was providing the bulk of lethal assistance to the Resistance, the FDN's requests for support had regularly exceeded available funds. Many of the Americans involved suspected at the time that the Resistance was inflating its numbers to maximize its income, suspicions probably reinforced by Sandinista allegations, even to their allies, that the Resistance armies were far smaller than they claimed. But postwar data in the Resistance archives, the postwar experiences of both the UN and OAS, as well as all other indicators, support a contrary conclusion. Not only did the Resistance have even more Comandos under arms during the war than it was reporting, but had it had sufficient logistical and financial help, it could have enlisted thousands more. Enrique Bermúdez's briefcase was jammed during 1989–90 with requests from hundreds, perhaps even thousands, of highland campesinos who wanted to be Comandos. He had to refuse all of them.[6] Shortly after Congress cut off lethal funding, Comandante 3-80 commented that "the NR [Nicaraguan Resistance] [which] had gotten spoiled with the success of the air supply program and ignored the ground option was going back to the old way of doing business."[7]

In 1989, a large number of Comandos were directed by their headquarters to withdraw from the combat zones of Nicaragua to sanctuary in Yamales. Some FDN commanders were surprised by this. Lethal aid or no, they were having no real problems sustaining themselves inside. Typical were comments by Comandante "Nelson," the S-3 of the Jorge Salazar II Regional Command who, under orders, withdrew with 330 men all the way from Nueva Guinea. In my role as chief of the Special Liaison Office (SLO) of the U.S. Embassy in Tegucigalpa, I reported to the Department of State:

> [Comandante] Nelson said that Jorge Salazar II had been able to sustain itself without aerial resupply. Food was obtained from supporters in the civilian population, and munitions from enemy forces. . . . His unit was frequently able to take weapons and ammunition from civilians who had been the object of hasty Sandinista "Militias formation" efforts. These people often had no loyalty to the Sandinistas and no wish to fight the Resistance . . . they frequently surrendered their weapons and ammunition without opposition.[8]

A handful of the FDN Comandos who withdrew to their camps in sanctuary in Honduras were in poor physical condition or short of supplies, but the great majority were not. About a third of the Comandos, all the movement's correos, clandestine committees, and popular support bases remained inside Nicaragua. The withdrawals were apparently intended to protect the force while it awaited new lethal aid, which never materialized. Nonetheless, sporadic combat continued inside Nicaragua. Between April 1988 and September 1989, the FDN sustained 392 casualties, including 236 killed.[9]

In the end, the "killing blow" against which Abrams had warned Secretary of State Schultz was delivered to the FDN by its erstwhile American allies, not by the Sandinista army. When George Bush was elected president of the United States, American government attitudes toward the Resistance changed dramatically. In early 1989, Bush's new secretary of state, James Baker, refused to meet with representatives of the Resistance. His press advisor, Margaret Tutwiler, privately let the comandantes know that they should go back to Central America where "we know how to find you if we want to." To others, she called the armed Resistance a "lose-lose proposition." The new secretary of state was heard to label them as "Reagan's project, not ours,"[10] and cautioned Reagan holdovers not to think that the transition from Reagan to Bush was a "friendly takeover." Certainly for the Comandos, change came quickly. Bush's assistant secretary for Latin America, Bernie Aronson, later said that "the peace of Managua was signed in Moscow."[11] After several meetings between Aronson and his Soviet counterpart early in the Bush administration, Soviet aid levels to Nicaragua began to drop, and Bush did not push for more lethal aid for the Resistance.

In the Yamales salient in Honduras, to which the FDN's headquarters, hospitals, and logistical operations had returned after the May 1988 battle at Bocay, things also changed. By the spring of 1989, Bush-era American maneuvering had successfully removed Comandante 3-80 as chief of the general staff, although he stayed on as commanding general, headquartered in Tegucigalpa. He was first replaced by a highland campesino from Boaco who was also a former guardia sergeant, Juan Ramon Rivas, Quiché, an outstanding combat leader who had been crucial to the organization of the five Jorge Salazar Regional Commands.[12] But he too was quickly forced out. Such maneuvering, pressure to minimize combat operations, redoubled attacks from both inside and outside the movement over real and alleged human rights violations, and garrison duty, exacerbated MILPAS/Guardia/Sandinista tensions at FDN headquarters in Yamales, which, on occasion, turned nasty. Many former Guardia saw the end approach and began drifting away in search of postwar futures.[13]

With many of the former Guardia gone, military leadership reverted to Milpistas who had been with the movement from the beginning. The first original Milpista to become chief of staff was Franklyn, a Galeano clansman and Milpista. In August 1989, after the Central American presidents signed a second agreement known as the Tela Accord, the FDN realized that it had been waiting in vain for renewal of lethal aid, and Franklyn started a major program of re-infiltration. The announced purpose was "to limit ERN losses in case of a future demobilization."[14] Comandos remaining in Honduran sanctuary were deployed closer to the border. Low-level combat operations by the FDN inside Nicaragua were to continue into 1990. Toward the end, yet another original MILPAS leader, Rubén (discussed extensively at the beginning of this book), became chief of staff. It fell to Rubén to lead the FDN during its final days before demobilization and to become the president of its post-war ACRN, a position he continued to hold in the year 2000.

CHAPTER FIFTEEN

THE SILENT WAR AGAINST THE HIGHLANDERS CONTINUES, 1990–1996

In 1990, the Revolution ended when the Sandinistas lost a national election, the "peace process" advanced, the Comandos began to lay down their arms, and officers of the American Embassy in Managua traveled once again into "Contra country." One officer who penetrated deep into the highlands in August reported on what they found in a cable entitled "Quilali, Yali, and Parts Beyond."

> The narrow roads leading from San Sebastian de Yali to the remote hamlets of interior Jinotega are littered with the rusting carcasses of Soviet-made armored personnel carriers and IFA trucks, the victims of Contra ambushes throughout the years of the war. They remain a witness to the failure of the Sandinistas to win the hearts and minds of the highlands peasants.[1]

The region they visited was in 1979 the birthplace of the highland Resistance movement, and a faithful area of support during the war. It should have been the safest of havens for the returning Comando. But it was not.

A Monteforte Missionary Father told the visiting diplomat that in February a Sandinista army patrol had come "to a recently amnestied Resistance member's home in Villa Sandino, Chontales, shot him, and then chopped his head off and ripped his face from his skull."[2] Both the brutality and the pre-Columbian Indian methodology were reminiscent of how the war had started in the first place. The killing was merely a taste of what was to come. For the highland campesinos and the Comandos the war did not end in 1990.

When the Comandos laid down their arms, they expected to be treated as respected combatants of a war that had led to the defeat of the Sandinista Revolution. In return for their disarming, both their American allies and the new Nicaraguan government of Violeta Chamorro had promised them protection, assistance, and land on which to resettle and restart their lives.

The Comandos kept their promises but both the Americans and the Chamorro government broke theirs. As Catholic Cardinal Miguel Obando y Bravo said three years later, "All the promises made to [the Comandos] were broken. As a result, frustration and fear among the campesinos in the countryside is greater than ever, and growing."[3] Newly elected President Chamorro, herself a director of the Sandinista Front in 1979 and with both children and many close relatives among the Sandinistas, chose against all expectations to govern not in alliance with those who elected her but rather in conjunction with the Sandinistas. As part of an *acuerdo*, or agreement, she made with them, she let the Sandinistas continue to command the army without civilian supervision and let their intelligence apparatus keep its autonomy, authority, and power.[4] The army slowly down-sized from its 1990 high of 90,000 troops to 14,500 in 1996, still 3,500 more than Somoza's Guardia Nacional at its wartime peak in 1979.[5] Although there was some quiet grumbling from the American Embassy in Managua, the U.S. government made no serious visible effort to address the problems that this created for its erstwhile "allies," although American and other foreign economic assistance did pour in to Nicaragua, reaching a combined total of over $4.5 billion by 1997.[6] Most of this money was American and appears either to have gone into the coffers of the wealthy or powerful or to have been wasted. Six years later, Nicaragua still had unemployment rates above 50 percent.[7]

Less than a penny of each dollar trickled down to Reagan's former "Freedom Fighters."[8] Privately, AID officials in Managua complained that they had received clear guidance from AID in Washington to favor the Sandinistas while ignoring the former Contras, and they could do nothing to redress the imbalance.

Largely as a consequence of the Chamorro-Sandinista pact, not only did prosperity not arrive in the highlands, but armed violence continued. By December 1996, CIAV/OAS had documented 1,932 violent attacks against former Comandos or their families, including 708 homicides. A few of these had been committed by re-armed Contras. But according to these international observers, the vast majority of the perpetrators of these acts were Sandinista army, police, or party activists.[9] Those who compiled the data told me they had often deliberately erred on the side of caution and included only clearly political crimes that they had thoroughly investigated and extensively documented. Less "conservative" observers said that the real number of homicides against former Comandos or their families was closer to three thousand, and the number of violent incidents against them closer to five thousand.[10] Independent Nicaraguan human rights organizations agreed, especially the Asociación Nicaragüense Pro-Derechos Humanos.[11]

The former Comandos and the highland peasants could do little more than try to weather the storm. But they were embittered and angry with Chamorro, the Sandinistas, and their own former civilian Resistance political leadership, which they felt had simply used and then abandoned them. Some Comandos, however, had never trusted the process and had not laid down their arms, while others had retained arms in secret caches, just in case, as had the Sandinistas. When it became clear to them that the government did not intend to honor its commitments, several hundred dug up their guns and returned to the mountains, becoming what was known as Re-Contras. Their move was quickly countered by the Sandinistas, who put some EPS soldiers in civilian disguises and sent them into the field to fight the Re-Contras. These thinly disguised Sandinista army soldiers became known as Re-Compas.[12] In a few cases, Re-Contras and previously pro-Sandinista campesinos joined together to create bands known as Revueltos.[13] To add to the confusion further, a few criminals who had been neither Resistance Contras nor Sandinistas took advantage of the melee to engage in banditry. The result was an ongoing war. (See map 9.)

A 1995 study by the OAS describes the continuing highland conflict that ensued in vivid terms.

> During the last five years [1990–95] there have been more than 1,500 armed confrontations, seventeen towns and hundreds of farms have been besieged, producing a great number of victims, considerable economic damage and enormous losses in terms of "opportunity costs."[14] For an important segment of the populace on the agricultural frontier, [official] impunity, defenselessness and criminality engulfed entire communities, leaving three in every ten Nicaraguans to live in zones of conflict, the vast majority also in conditions of extreme poverty.[15]. . . [In 1995] basic human rights were being violated systematically. Some 79 percent of complaints received by CIAV/OAS were produced in the Departments of Matagalpa, Jinotega, Estelí, Nueva Segovia and Boaco; 77% of the murders reported took place in the Departments of Jinotega, Matagalpa and Chontales.[16]

As late as March 1997, well over five hundred Re-Contras divided into forty-seven small groups were still active in the highlands. The number of Re-Compas was unknown. When the OAS produced the map on which map 9 is based, which showed the area at war in 1990–95, the striking geographic correlations were apparent between the ancient Nahua/Chibcha divisions, the 1979–90 Contra War rebellion, and this post-Contra violence.[17]

In June 1996, dozens of international observers from organizations as diverse as the OAS, the Carter Center, the Center for Democracy, and the International Republican Institute (IRI) descended on Nicaragua in response to electoral problems in the highlands. Ranging from a former president of Ecuador to conservative college student activists, they were responding to allegations that Nicaragua's government had failed to enfranchise the rural highlanders to vote in forthcoming October 1996 national elections. Almost all the disenfranchised were campesino indios of the twenty-six municipios that comprised the heart of Contra country.

In response to international pressures, the government had agreed to reopen voter registration stations in these municipios,[18] and the observers had come to watch the process. I went to Managua to observe the observers. What they saw showed that these concerns were valid.[19] In just two weekends, some 325,135 previously disenfranchised highlanders registered to vote.[20] Almost all were campesinos from a population that had not been counted during Nicaragua's 1995 census. Almost all were also from the same comarcas that had rebelled in 1979.

The observer groups made carefully measured public statements. But in private several of them described to me how the process had really gone.[21] Observer after observer told me off the record that they had been taken by Nicaraguan government escorts to highland voter registration centers at which no one appeared to be registering. Their escorts then launched into speeches asserting that the lack of registrants was clear evidence that allegations of massive disenfranchisement were false. Their speeches ended abruptly when groups of campesinos began to appear out of nearby woodlands or mountainsides to register. The explanation was that in anticipation of the event, although they had received neither official notification of the process nor official forms on which to register, when they learned the ad hoc registration process was to take place, they organized themselves by preparing their own registration documents, awaiting the arrival of the observers and then presenting themselves to the government's registrars only after the international observers appeared. This spontaneous, regionwide, and obviously well-organized peasant action was called by a former Democratic governor of Nevada, a widely experienced Carter Center observer, "the most heartening example of grassroots democracy in action" he had ever seen.[22] Apart from what the peasants' actions suggested in terms of their distrust of the government and its intentions, from the perspective of this book, it also was strong evidence that the highlands-wide comarca-to-comarca network of the second Nicaragua which had produced the Resistance movement's systems of correos, clandestine comarca committees, and the Comando army itself, was still functioning efficiently in mid-1996.

The attempted disenfranchisement of the highland peasantry was almost certainly not accidental. During the interviews I conducted, I asked all participants to define their political party preference. What emerged was a universal correlation between Comando and Liberal. Not one single FDN Comando identified himself or herself as a Conservative. Even with a small and not entirely random sampling, a correlation of +1.0 can be considered significant, and the highlanders' Liberal political preferences were no secret. The leading early contenders for Nicaragua's presidency at the time these events took place were Violeta Chamorro's son-in-law and de facto prime minister Antonio Lacayo, a Conservative, and Daniel Ortega, the former Sandinista president. Both knew that neither could win if the highlander peasants voted. The disenfranchisement attempt probably began in 1995, when a national census by Chamorro's government reported that only 36 percent of Nicaragua's population lived in the country's nine highland provinces.[23] Subsequent government voter registration programs were then based on this number, and even they were indefinitely "delayed" in the twenty-six municipios discussed above, known Liberal strongholds.

But 1995 was not 1881, when the patriarchy had successfully manipulated census data as part of its attempts to define the Indian population of the highlands out of existence. In 1995, education, health, and social welfare programs were beginning to reach the highlanders, and Nicaragua's Ministries of Education, Health, and Social Action apparently knew full well that the official census had sharply undercounted the highland population. To administer their programs efficiently, these ministries had to know how many highlanders there actually were. Further, the official census did not meet their programming needs, as it had missed 40 percent of this region's population. So they came together and performed a second, secret "administrative" census of their own, which was completed in early 1996. Taken on a house-by-house basis, it showed that in 1995 the highland population had been undercounted by at least 600,000,[24] that 52 percent, not 36 percent, of all Nicaraguans live in the region, and that over 70 percent of the highlanders, or more than one in three of all Nicaraguans, were rural campesinos.[25]

In March 1997, this second census was still being kept secret from other government agencies that could make good use of it.[26] But major sections, especially those directly related to the twenty-six municipios, came into my hands just before the ad hoc registration process took place, and I made them available to some of the observers, the American Embassy in Managua, the OAS, and others as a benchmark against which the success of the ad hoc registration process could be measured. When the ad hoc highland voter registration of June 1997 added 352,135 new voters to the roles, the size of Nicaragua's registered electorate increased by almost 15 percent.[27] Because the voting age in Nicaragua is fifteen years of age, given the demographics of the country, the number of new voters almost precisely equals the number that would be found in a population of 600,000, which is the exact difference between the 1995 official and 1996 secret censuses.

The ad hoc registration process did not entirely end attempts to keep the highland campesinos from voting in 1996. Confidential sources privately warned me and others that in case the attempt to disenfranchise the campesinos failed, a contingency plan had been prepared to provoke Re-Contra/Re-Compa violence just before the actual elections and then to have Nicaraguan security forces seal off major areas of the highlands. The violence could then be used as an excuse for excluding the highlanders from the October election even though they had been registered in June.[28] A column I wrote in the 11 October 1996 Wall Street Journal called international attention to this plan and, I am privately told, helped forestall its implementation.[29] The newly enfranchised campesino vote, 15 percent of the national total, proved decisive to the 1996 election of Liberal Arnoldo Aleman to the presidency. Although several highland departments and market towns split their votes, in the most rural Resistance comarca precincts the Liberal vote exceeded 90 percent.[30] Including the highlanders in the process changed the outcome.

CHAPTER SIXTEEN

FROM POOR PEASANTS
TO POWER BLOC

The Difference Democracy Can Make

Nicaragua's 1996 election was unlike any other in its history. For one thing, it was the country's first ever truly open election, free of excessive pressures from a powerful central government, whether Somocista prior to the 1980s or Sandinista as in 1990.[1] It also marked a fundamental change from exclusionary backroom politics dominated by the elite to relatively inclusionary politics involving active and meaningful public participation. It was widely remarked that for the first time in Nicaraguan history the election was also followed by a peaceful transfer of power from one democratically elected president to another. Even more remarkably, if less remarked, it also involved the transfer of public power from the hands of a traditional Conservative aristocrat into those of an elected populist Liberal.

And yet from the perspectives both of this book and of the future of Nicaragua, the most remarkable change of all may have been the legitimation of the Contras—the Comandos—the Resistance supporters, and Nicaragua's highland peasants who emerged as a potent presence on the national political scene. With no known exceptions, those who accompanied newly elected Liberal President Arnoldo Alemán into power were either Resistance sympathizers, activists, or former Comandos.

Legitimation was bestowed on the Contras not only by the Liberals but also, amazingly, by the Sandinistas. The process began during the 1996 presidential campaign. When it became evident in spite of earlier efforts to disenfranchise them and plans to keep them from reaching the polls, that the highland peasants would vote en masse, Sandinista presidential candidate Daniel Ortega tried to woo the highlanders by recruiting the FDN's former chief of intelligence, José Benito Bravo Centeno, "Mack," to campaign at his side. Ortega appeared repeatedly at public rallies with former Contra comandante Mack at his side and promised that, if elected, he would make Mack his minister of government.[2] Because Mack was not only a former sergeant in Somoza's Guardia Nacional but also was separated from the FDN for alleged human rights violations,[3] the image of a former Sandinista president trying to win election to the presidency by recruiting him as his new minister of government seemed decidedly ironic. But ironic or not, it demonstrated how far the Resistance and the former Comandos had traveled politically since 1990. Ortega's argument that a former Comando would make a good minister sent a crystal-clear signal that, even to the Sandinistas, the Contras had in fact, never been the unmitigated pariahs that the wartime rhetoric had said they were.

Not to be outdone, Liberal presidential candidate Arnoldo Alemán, the former mayor of Managua, during a visit to Miami, asked Elsa Ilitali vda de Bermúdez, the widow of FDN Commander Enrique Bermúdez, Comandante 3-80, to endorse him publicly and to go to Nicaragua to campaign for him, especially in the highlands and among the poor. After much soul-searching, she did so, and appeared at his side at several rallies dressed in the combat fatigues of a Contra comandante. Given the popularity of the Resistance and of Bermúdez in the highlands, her appearances had far more impact than those of Mack, who was actually out of favor with his former comrades. Several observers went so far as to say that it was Elsa Bermúdez's endorsement in the name of the FDN's former commander that assured Alemán's substantial margins of victory in the Resistance comarcas.[4] By enlisting her help, Alemán also greatly enhanced the legitimacy of the former Comandos and of the Resistance.

Other developments advanced the legitimation of the Comandos and the Resistance as well. A small political party known as the Partido de la Resistencia participated in the 1996 elections. It represented only a faction of the former Comandos and their supporters, but its presence as a registered political party sent a message. Alemán won the presidency by less than a 1 percent majority, with almost half his votes, more than 400,000, coming from the nine highland provinces or equally rebellious regions of the Atlantic coast. Of these 400,000 votes, 232,000, much greater than his margin over Ortega, were cast in municipios, or counties, that were home to the comarcas that had been among the first to rebel in 1979–80. In municipio after municipio, the campesinos voted by margins of 4, 5, or even 8 to 1 for Alemán over Ortega. The campesinos emerged as a major presence in Nicaraguan politics.

The transformation of the Resistance and the Comandos from maligned pariahs into major and legitimate political actors on the national scene became most evident when Alemán began to put his administration in place. Civilian Resistance wartime supporters, activists, or former Comandos were appointed to dozens of senior positions. Alemán's two closest personal collaborators were Jaime Morales Carazo and René Herrera Zúñiga. Morales, Alemán's baptismal godfather and best friend, was one of only two civilian Resistance activists ever to have actually gone into combat, however briefly, with a Comando unit. Alemán made Morales his *asesor personal,* or personal advisor, with cabinet rank, a position close to that of prime minister. A wealthy financier, Morales had been an anti-Somoza activist and had provided the Sandinista front with money to help it overthrow the dynasty. His reward was to have Daniel Ortega seize his Managua home. Ortega was still living in it in 1997.[5] Herrera, a university professor and intellectual who had also been a Resistance activist, became the president's confidential secretary. Another supporter of the Resistance, Jaime Cuadra, became minister of defense. During the war, one of Cuadra's rural haciendas, El Gorrión in Matagalpa, had been a

Comando safe haven. The new minister of tourism, Pedro Joaquín Chamorro Barrios, son of the martyred editor of Managua's major newspaper, *La Prensa,* and of the previous president Violeta Chamorro, had been a civilian Resistance director.[6] The minister of education was Humberto Belli, another pro-Resistance political leader and the author of several works critical of the Sandinista Revolution.

While it did not entirely disappear, violence in the countryside against former Resistance campesinos dropped sharply. With the Contras legitimized by a national election, a sympathizer as president, and former Comandos in key government positions, the security forces and army could no longer count on the "official impunity" they had enjoyed during the Chamorro administration, and the violence of the 1990–96 Re-Contra, Re-Compa, Revueltos silent war slowly came to an end. During my 1997 and 1998 visits to the highlands, from Estelí to Matagalpa, I found the changes the 1996 election had wrought remarkable. Roadblocks had disappeared, construction crews were upgrading the region's main roads, schools and public health facilities were being improved, and former Contras and Re-Contras were in key positions throughout the region. While problems and tensions remained, the reversal of the fortunes of the highlanders of the Resistance was nothing short of extraordinary. Judging by the impact a single fair election had on the region, I could only conclude that, entirely contrary to the Black Legend, the Contras had indeed been the legitimate representatives of an important societal group: the highlanders. And even more. In addition to representing the highlanders, they had also represented a major, if not dominant, constituency from within one of Nicaragua's two major traditional political parties, the Liberals, who had been almost entirely absent from both the Sandinista revolutionary and Chamorro administrations.

Equally striking was the transformation of former FDN Comandantes from outcasts to legitimate political leaders at the national level. In 1994, when I conducted initial interviews in preparation for this study, many had to be done in secret because the Comandos lived in fear for their lives. In March 1997, when I conducted follow-up interviews, several Comandos held high-level government positions, and the interviews took place in their offices. Two FDN Comandantes whom I randomly selected as oral history subjects in 1994 and whom I cited extensively earlier in this study, Carlos Garcia, Chino-85, and José Filadelfia Rivas, "José," were vice ministers. Chino-85 had gone from being a feared former enemy of the state to being Vice Minister Carlos Garcia of the Ministry of Natural Resources and the Environment, with extensive professional responsibilities in the highlands and on the Atlantic littoral. After having been an outcast working quietly in a municipal garage, José found himself in an even more sensitive position than was Chino-85, becoming Vice Minister José Rivas of the Ministry of Government, with special responsibilities for the highlands and former Resistance areas. A third former Comandante was vice minister of the Institute for Agrarian Reform (INRA),[7] and a fourth was director general of the Ministry of Social Welfare.[8] Another, Maximinimo Rodríguez, "Wilmer," had been elected to the National Assembly,[9] and another was a member of the Central American Parliament. Literally hundreds of former Comandos or Resistance leaders or members of their families were in other elected or appointed positions, from deputy director of customs to positions in dozens of smaller agencies at the national, departmental, and local levels. Others were elected council members in almost half of Nicaragua's municipios, including those in which their constituencies had been temporarily disenfranchised. Others ran unsuccessfully for high office. Three former Comandantes or civilian Resistance directors had been small-party candidates either for president or vice president.

Even non-Liberal political leaders, if they had been active Resistance participants, benefitted from the association. Adolfo Calero, a former civilian Resistance director, was one of very few Conservatives elected to the National Assembly. He was also the only other Resistance civilian leader besides Jaime Morales to have gone into combat, however briefly, with a Comando unit. Asked why the Conservative Party had all but disappeared, Calero commented that former President Chamorro's 1990 deal with the

Sandinista Front was so unpopular that it had made it impossible for the Conservatives, until then Nicaragua's second major political party, even to field a viable presidential candidate. He ascribed his own ability to survive in large part to having allied himself early on with the armed Resistance movement.[10]

Colonel Bermúdez's widow, Elsa, his family, and those closest to him were not forgotten. The ink had hardly dried on the country's ballots when Alemán personally telephoned to offer diplomatic appointments. Elsa Bermúdez had just become a naturalized citizen of the United States, and the State Department would not accredit her as consul general in Miami, one of Nicaragua's key diplomatic posts, so as an alternative Alemán appointed her ambassador to the Dominican Republic. She was also under consideration for appointment as official ombudsman for the former Comandos. Bermúdez's son Enrique, Jr., who had not become an American citizen, was made a consul in Miami. Harry Bodan, Bermúdez's personal lawyer and a former deputy foreign minister, became ambassador to Japan. Two other key Resistance activists, Bosco Matamoros and Domingo Salinas, became ambassadors to The Netherlands and Colombia, respectively.

In addition to offering political and diplomatic appointments, the Alemán government initiated plans that would reward the highlanders for their electoral support. These included extending public services much more vigorously into the highland comarcas, especially education, health, social services, and agricultural extension programs. Discussion was also under way about how to reverse Nicaragua's tradition of top-down development efforts in favor of peasant-based micro-enterprise programs intended to help small farmers at the grass roots. This approach would especially benefit the highland campesinos, who had the most to gain from agricultural minifinancing programs and local level agricultural extension technology transfers. In addition, the Ministry of Agriculture was working to reestablish the marketing links between peasant producers and the national market. The destruction of these links had been a major objective of Sandinista revolutionary efforts to "descampesinizar" and then "proletarianizar" the highlands. Former Comandos and others with close contacts with the peasant community were recruited to serve as the government's liaisons to its newly discovered major peasant constituency. One possible channel to be favored was the Asociación Cívica Resistencia Nicaragüense (ACRN), the only existing efficient link to the highlands peasantry that had not been politicized during the 1996 elections.

President Alemán himself was clear in his recognition of the peasantry as a major part of his Liberal constituency. During my interview with him in March 1997, he made it plain that while the highland rebels had not been a formal part of his campaign entourage, without them and their sympathizers his candidacy would probably not have prospered.[11] Particularly concerned with Nicaragua's exceedingly high unemployment rates and unfavorable balance of payments, he also recognized the peasants as potential producers who, if given a sense of security and minimal assistance, could feed Nicaragua and produce a major quantity of agricultural exports while simultaneously employing tens if not hundreds of thousands of people. In short, the highland campesinos of the Resistance were not only crucial to Alemán's 1996 electoral victory. They had emerged from their faceless past to become major players on the Nicaraguan political scene and potential determiners of its future.

CHAPTER SEVENTEEN

RESISTANCE AND SURVIVAL

Genio y cultura hasta la sepultura
(Personality and identity, from the womb to the tomb)
—PEASANT PROVERB

As we have seen, examination of the historical, geographic, and social context within which the highlander Resistance war was fought provides ample perspective on the divisions that led to the conflict. But even divisions as deep as these do not inevitably lead to war. This leads to the intriguing question of whether the highlander Resistance movement was unique or if there were other comparable cases of peasant-Marxist conflicts. And what internal processes triggered the highland war? Political psychology offers the best set of tools for understanding how a Marxist revolution can trigger an extremely violent peasant reaction, and two historical examples seem especially useful as comparative cases: the Marxist-kulak peasant clash that led to efforts to "de-kulakize" (in Spanish, *descampesinizar*) the Soviet Union and the 1959–65 Escambray peasant rebellion against the Cuban Revolution. Because it has been studied intensively, the Russian case, discussed later in this chapter, produces the more fruitful theoretical insights. The Escambray case is more productive in terms of pertinent parallels.

When they are compared, it seems the Escambray rebellion, which took place in the Sierra Escambray mountains of western Cuba, was a rehearsal for Nicaragua's highlander peasant rebellion. It has been described in some detail by a participant, Dariel Alarcón, "Benigno," who first secretly followed its development for Cuban Intelligence and then infiltrated its top ranks on Castro's behalf to become in 1964 the movement's chief of logistics. Benigno was a peasant guerrilla of Castro's Sierra Maestra campaign, was later with Ché Guevara in Africa, and is one of only a handful of survivors of Guevara's ill-fated Bolivia campaign. Guevara mentions him more than forty times in his personal diary on his Bolivia campaign.[1] Benigno recounts the story of the Escambray rebellion in a recent book edited and translated by Elizabeth Burgos, the wife of French revolutionary Regis Debray, whose involvement gives it a seal of special authenticity.[2] He describes the Escambray rebellion as beginning in 1959, immediately after Castro took power, and as being led by former anti-Batista peasant guerrillas of Castro's rebel army who were deeply disillusioned when Castro suddenly veered sharply to the left once he took power. The army was made up of independent mountain peasants angered by efforts to collectivize their farms, new state control over the sales and purchases of previously free-flowing goods, demands they join new "popular" mass organizations, attacks on the Catholic Church, and the arrival in their midst of urban literacy brigadistas demanding they learn Marxism. Each of these complaints was made almost verbatim twenty years later by Nicaragua's highlander peasants against the Sandinistas. By 1962, three years after the Escambray rebellion had started, several thousand peasants under arms had joined the movement, and the rebels were receiving arms and materials from the United States. These developments also parallel Nicaraguan experience.

Declassified U.S. government documents confirm Benigno's story. By 1960–61 "a limited air capability for resupply and for infiltration and exfiltration [from the Escambray] already exist[ed] under CIA control."[3] Other declassified documents confirm that the CIA considered "the Sierra Escambray and Sierra Maestra the only areas of Cuba with terrain of sufficient extent and ruggedness for guerrilla operations" and that originally the Bay of Pigs force was intended to land near the Escambray rebels and link up with them.[4] After walking much of the terrain during 1999 visits both to the Bay of Pigs [Playa Jirón] and the Sierra Escambray, I am convinced that the Bay of Pigs is a terrible site for an amphibious landing and that moving the landing there from its originally planned site near the Escambray is what sealed the fate of the Escambray rebellion, even though it took Cuba until 1965 to stamp it out completely. By 1999 all that remained of the Escambray rebellion was *pueblos cautivos*, captive towns, inhabited by peasant former supporters of the Escambray rebellion who had been forcibly removed from their farms to urban centers and whose movements even thirty-four years later were still tightly controlled by the Cuban government.

It is impossible to know whether the Cuban Revolution would have gone the way of the Sandinista Revolution had the U.S.-backed invasion succeeded, largely because the two rebellions are not exact parallels. The Cold War was at its height in 1963; by 1979 it was winding down. Cuba is an island; Nicaragua has extensive land frontiers with worried neighbors possessing their own armies. The Escambray peasantry is small; the highlanders are half of Nicaragua's population. There is no millennia-old ethnic conflict in the Escambray. But one similarity between the two—Castro's Escambray rebellion and Nicaragua's highlander Resistance movement—stands out above all the others. Each was the consequence of irreconcilable differences between independent peasants who own the means of production and dispose of its surplus, making them by Marxist definition bourgeois enemies of any Marxist revolution and of revolutionaries bent on creating an all-proletarian society. (Russia's kulak program also falls into this category.)

There is also another important difference between the Escambray and Nicaraguan highlander rebellions. In both Cuba and Nicaragua the revolutionaries expected counterrevolutions. But in Nicaragua the central mountain peasants were doubly dangerous because they were not just micro-bourgeoisie class enemies of revolution, they were also ethnically distinctive. As their pre-victory 1979 arms sweeps in the highlands but not elsewhere demonstrate, the Sandinistas had expected the highlander peasants to try to rebel and had planned for this eventuality. What they had not planned for was a war fought by an entire people who were historically primed to resist domination by any Pacific lowlanders, whether colonial, patriarchal, or Marxist. It was the ethno-historical dimension of the highlanders' rebellion that made its virulence far deeper than the Sandinistas ever expected and that led to the failure of their Revolution.

An examination of the process that led to the highlander rebellion yields particularly useful insights into how peasants such as the highland Indians react to the challenges of a revolution. As we have seen, the highlanders have certain defining characteristics. Ethnically, although they have no recognized tribal identity, they nonetheless identify themselves as indio and explicitly differentiate themselves from Nicaragua's dominant "españoles." They are inward-looking, have a centuries-old history of organizing to resist outsiders, and are geographically enclosed against outsiders, especially from Nicaragua's Pacific coast lowlands. They have strong family structures that extend from nuclear family parent-sibling cores to distant cousins of the same clan, reinforced by overlapping networks of godparenting and comarca neighbor/peer relationships. Webs of loyalties based on mutual interests and interdependencies exist within this structure: distrust radiates outward from it.

The highlanders are microbourgeoisie, but they are at the bottom of Nicaragua's pecking order. In economic terms they live marginal lives largely outside the country's money economy. Land is the key to their survival and independence. They place a high value on personal freedom. Religion is an important social cement. Politically they are supporters of the traditional Liberal Party but libertarian in ideology. They distrust government, although they are prepared to selectively accept its services. Largely preliterate, their world views come less from schools, books, radios, or television than from peers, priests, elders, and personal experiences. These characteristics suggest how they might respond to such challenges as those generated by the Sandinista's revolutionary policies.

My content analysis of the oral histories of former Comandos found 261 specific mentions of reasons why the campesinos rebelled. I divided these into three categories: political, physical, and economic.

Political

One hundred fourteen (44 percent) of the 261 mentions were political. Most often cited was a feeling of having been deliberately deceived by the Sandinistas as to their true political intentions, both during and immediately after the anti-Somoza war. This feeling of deception, along with coercive pressure to join new Sandinista organizations, generated a great deal of anger among the campesinos. The other causes that they mentioned repeatedly were the loss of personal freedoms, especially freedom of speech, and the Revolution's assault on the family and the church.

Physical

Physical abuse by Sandinista authorities, even in the earliest days of the Revolution, was the second-most frequently cited category of motives for joining the rebellion (eighty-seven mentions, or 33 percent). Assaults, beatings and torture, killings, and arrests and detentions without due process were most often mentioned, in that order.

Economic

Economic causes came third (sixty-one mentions, or 23%). Most often given as reasons were forcible seizures or the outright theft of crops and food supplies, farm animals, personal items, or individual property by Sandinista military or State Security personnel. Another factor of almost equal importance was agricultural policies that forced the highlanders to sell products at low prices to the government and then buy necessities at high prices. They saw these policies as, in essence, a "highly regressive tax," almost a form of tribute, that was rapidly transferring wealth from them to Nicaragua's less needy Pacific region and especially to its cities.

Those interviewed also frequently mentioned two other causes. One was the Sandinistas' assignment to the Segovias of thousands of Pacific "outsiders," who were appointed as the region's new leadership and security forces. The attitudes of these intruders generated severe ethnic tensions. The other was the series of 1979 and 1980 house-to-house arms sweeps staged by the Sandinistas, which the highlanders interpreted as evidence they had been singled out as a target. When juxtaposed with the above description of the highlanders and the causes they gave for rebelling, the Sandinistas' decision to try to "descampesinizar" and then "proletarianizar" the highland peasant masses—transform them from independent micro-bourgeois farmers into proletarian rural laborers—can be seen as a direct challenge to their basic drives and values and, in particular, a threat to their ability to meet "the basic human needs to sustain life itself, food, clothing, shelter."[5] When a group is threatened at this level and denied the option of flight, fighting is the only remaining option. According to Daly and Wilson, and Durham,[6] a threatened group will respond just as an individual will: fight or flee.

In this light, the Nicaraguan highlander rebellion was a classic violent group reaction. The highlanders' pre-Columbian Chibchan Indian languages might have been supplanted by regionally accented Spanish, but the other key attributes of an ethnic group remained: geographic concentration, a shared history, common cultural traits and above all, common self-identification as indios.[7] From the Sandinista perspective, the Revolution was a conscious exercise in cultural restructuring and nation-building that challenged this group's ability to survive. From the highlanders' perspective, it was an exercise in forced assimilation to an alien ideological/cultural model. The result was a conflict analogous to the ethnic, or nationalities issue in the former Soviet Union.

The highlander rebellion can also be seen from a second angle. In addition to being a nationalities issue, it also manifested a second disabling anomaly that had been seen in the former Soviet Union–Marxist inability to deal with an independent peasantry. Many observers have described the process by which a Marxist revolution creates specific threats to the survival and fitness of a group such as the highlanders when it embarks on policies intended to "revolutionize" family and community structures, land owner-ship and labor patterns, and belief systems. As Stephen Ryan puts it, "forced assimilation, sometimes termed cultural genocide or ethnocide or cultural colonialism, involves an attempt by a domi-nant ethnic group to destroy the culture of certain other ethnic groups and to force them to adopt the dominant culture. . . . One aspect of such assimilationist policies is that, in a very real sense, subordinate ethnic groups find that it is illegal for them to be 'themselves.'"[8] In sum, a revolutionary project that requires the destruction of pre-existing ethnic patterns by definition challenges the survival of the group it intends to transform.

In Nicaragua, the dominant group after 1979 was the urban "Spanish" Europeanate vanguard of the Sandinista Party. The groups to be transformed were ethnically distinct, mountain indio highlanders, Miskito, Sumu and Rama Indian tribespeople, south Atlantic campesinos and, to an extent, Black Creoles. These are precisely the groups that rebelled.

As the dominant group, the Sandinistas enjoyed a monopoly on the legitimate use of violence. The project they chose to pursue was alien to the traditional cultures of most of Nicaragua's people, creating all the conditions precedent to violent rebellion. Deutsch and Shichman describe the process in theoretical terms:

> The likelihood that a conflict will take a constructive or a des-tructive course depends on the nature of the issue: its size, its rigidity, its centrality, its relationship to other issues, and the level of consciousness of the issue. . . . The size of a conflict is increased if it is perceived in win-lose terms, involves prin-ciples and rights, will establish important precedents, involves discordant views, and is ill-defined. . . . [Most especially] when the parties perceive no alternative or substitutes for

their expected outcomes or for their methods of achieving them, the conflict becomes rigidly defined.[9]

Little doubt exists that the Revolution's challenge was massive, rigid, central to events, related to other issues, and uppermost in the consciousness of Nicaragua's body politic. Equally certain is that it presented the highlanders with a win-lose situation, involved principles and rights, attempted to establish important precedents, and involved discordant views. By such measurements, both the Revolution and the Resistance were well defined indeed. By this definition, war became inevitable when the Sandinistas initiated a proactive and intrusive revolutionary process.

Radical revolutionaries and dogmatic reformers are thus caught in a double bind. When they seek to make radical changes, the very radicalism of what they seek to accomplish becomes the major generator of dissonances that can cause them to fail. Further, the only tools available to them, especially at the national level, are precisely those least likely to lead to success. By substituting coercion for persuasion, "reformers" may be able to create a mask that presents an illusion of apparent success. This is often done with such skill that even a movement's propagandists and its leaders begin to believe their own propaganda, which puts their entire enterprise even more in jeopardy. When they employ the power of the state to manipulate information, in other words, engage in propaganda, they create, in postmodern language, a dominant hegemonic discourse. In doing so they may convince others and even themselves that they are succeeding. The Sandinistas appear to have done just that, or in 1990 they would have never submitted their revolution to a popular plebiscite. But as suggested by the collapse of the former Soviet Union, ethnic warfare from Ireland to the former Yugoslavia, and ethnic, racial, and societal tensions almost everywhere, coercion, short of genocide, cannot change fundamental cultural identities, nor can rhetoric permanently substitute for reality. "Genio y cultura hasta la sepultura."

Although this argument strongly suggests that truly radical revolutions can never succeed in the long run, non-dogmatic reformers need not despair. To succeed, however, they must be flexible and willing to compromise, two qualities that true radicals notoriously lack. Reform "projects" must be adapted to the survival imperatives of the individuals and groups at which they are directed, not the other way around. To succeed, they must also first and foremost respect the person and the culture of those they seek to change. When reformers ignore this rule, they cause their own causes to fail, often only after a great deal of avoidable suffering, destruction, and violence. Unfortunately, neither flexibility nor tolerance are in great supply among committed reformers, much less among radical revolutionaries.

REVOLUTION AND RESPONSE

Applying this schema to Nicaragua's Contra War proves interesting. In the words of a top Sandinista agrarian reformer of the revolutionary period, Lúis Serra, "The policies of the Sandinista government, and especially the actual or threatened nationalization of land were seen by the lower classes as frustrating their efforts to survive and as attacks on both their social structure and their culture."[10] Serra is speaking specifically of Nicaragua's campesino highlanders.

A keen observer of the Soviet case, Teresa Rakowska-Harmstone, writing on Lenin's policies in the revolutionary Soviet Union, says of Soviet Marxist policies that they:

> carried within them the seeds of their own destruction. . . . The initial costs of collectivization were staggering, especially for the peasant and nomad populations of the non-Russian areas where resistance was strongest. . . . The fires of ethnic hatred were fanned by the arrival in the countryside of workers' detachments from urban and industrial centers, most of them Russians, who came to help in the de-kulakization [in Spanish, *descampezinizar*, precisely the word the Sandinistas used to describe their own program] and the establishment of

rural cooperatives . . . centrally determined criteria resulted
in a division of labor and regional specialization, which led
to the repetition of the old colonial pattern of exploitation of
the periphery by the center.[11]

The Sandinistas clearly committed all these Soviet errors and went
them one better. In a historic sense, theirs was but the most recent
of a millennia-long series of efforts by the various Pacific coast
elites to conquer and subordinate the indios of the highlands, and
the objectives pursued and methodology employed were eerily
reminiscent of earlier attempts: instill a new ideology, establish
dominance from the center, change land ownership patterns, control
indio labor, collect tribute. Those they sent to create this new
Nicaragua were also outsiders. To paraphrase Rakowska-Harmstone,
the fires of latent ethnic hatreds were fanned by the arrival in the
countryside of detachments of urban Spanish and Pacific coastal
cadre sent to impose the Revolution's will.

For many if not most Sandinista leaders, the highlanders' reaction appears to have come as a surprise. Most apparently believed
not only Marxism but also what Gould had called the "myth of the
mestiza" and did not think of Nicaragua in terms of ethnicity. But
the highlanders did think of themselves in such terms, and for
them the Revolution did not promise a new and better future but
rather the destruction of their identity. To them, the Sandinistas
were new conquistadores, and survival was at stake. The intensity
and duration of the war of resistance that followed were the result
of massive flows of external arms and other resources to both sides,
but its roots were centuries deep.

CHAPTER EIGHTEEN

CONCLUSIONS

The questions initially posed in this book seemed simple and straightforward: Who and what were the Contras, and where, when, and why did their war begin? The answers uncovered were indeed straightforward. But they were also unexpected.

Who? The "Contras" turned out to have been just poor dirt-farming "hillbillies" from Nicaragua's version of Appalachia. Their combat leaders were mostly anti-Somoza Sandinistas, not former Guardia, and they were created and sustained in the field for eleven years not by the CIA, but by highland peasants from a marginalized indio people with a thousand-year history of resisting attempts to subdue, dominate, and convert them to new masters or new ways of life. These faceless people are the largest definable ethnohistorical group in Nicaragua, a reality masked during recent Nicaraguan history by dominant elite discourse and during the MILPAS and Contra wars by wartime rhetoric. The reality was revealed in 1996, when the highland indio peasantry emerged as the largest voting bloc in the country. The most profound result of the Sandinista Revolution and Contra War appears to have been the conversion of this once marginal people into a major force on the national political scene.

When? According to Comando participants and witnesses, the conflict first took root in May 1979, inside the Sandinista camp within a highland guerrilla peasant battalion, the People's Anti-Somoza Militia, or MILPA. By August 1979, these rebelling former anti-Somoza Milpistas had joined with Segovian highland peasant comarcas to create a resistance movement, complete with an armed wing called the People's Anti- Sandinista Militia, or MILPAS, which became the largest armed opposition to the Sandinista Revolution. Initially concentrated in two river valleys, the Coco and Bocay, it soon spread throughout the mountains.

For the first three years, the MILPAS war inside Nicaragua was fought by independent peasants. But by late 1981, they were stretching local resources to the limit and feeling the pressure of increasingly large and sophisticated Sandinista military and security forces. Concurrently, a set of exile paramilitary organizations had been organized and, unlike the Milpistas, had begun to receive some covert foreign government support. The largest, the Guardia-dominated Legión 15 de Septiembre, was offered help by the CIA through Argentine intermediaries starting in late 1979. But this help appears to have been somewhat limited, and these exile organizations did not engage in sustained combat operations inside Nicaragua. Large-scale American help, which began to appear in late 1981, a year after Ronald Reagan became president, transformed the MILPAS War into a Guardia-MILPAS alliance effort that came to be known as the Contra War, after Reagan authorized a major increase in paramilitary support for the successor to the Legión 15 de Septiembre, the FDN. As soon as the FDN received the promise of more arms, the Guardia began recruiting MILPAS to join them in an alliance. The result was a hybrid army, heavily Guardia at the general staff and special-unit levels, mixed but heavily MILPAS at the combat unit commander level, and almost purely highland peasant at the trooper level.

This suggests a set of time lines for the Contra War: (a) a 1977 to May 1979 prelude, during which a Sandinista united front, with minimal peasant participation but extensive foreign help, overthrew the last Somoza; (b) a May 1979 to mid-1982 MILPAS War that began before the fall of Somoza when Milpista guerrillas of the Sandinista's Carlos Fonseca Front began to rebel; (c) a 1982–88

Contra War fought by a MILPAS/Guardia alliance brought together by American promises of large-scale aid; (d) a 1988–90 return by the Resistance to its MILPAS roots; (e) a 1990–96 continuing conflict in the highlands; and (f) the 1996 emergence of the Resistance, with the highland peasantry and Comandos as major political players on the Nicaraguan national scene.

Where? The geography and history of the highlander Resistance movement and its Comando army demonstrate that it was regional in origin and centered in historically resistant Chibchan-mestizo indio rural areas. The war was fought almost exclusively in the Segovian highlands before spreading southward through the rest of the highlands.

Why? For the highland peasants the alternatives were both stark and simple: flight or fight. To flee meant to lose the remainder of their millennia-old identities, their independence, their freedoms, their farms, and their traditions. Faced with a revolutionary on-slaught of political ideology and armed coercion, they chose instead to fight.

THE BLACK LEGEND: IMAGE OVER REALITY

One real puzzle is how the image of the Contras could have devi-ated so far from reality. The MILPAS and Contra Wars were clearly highland peasant phenomena. But their public image was almost entirely a product of an externally generated and highly negative discourse. How did this work? The wartime example of a Spanish Roman Catholic Bishop, Pedro Casaldáliga, may suggest an expla-nation. It is a classic case of words over evidence.

In 1986, Casaldáliga took a Sandinista-organized Potemkin village-style tour of the Segovian highlands and then provided the narrative for a book that told what he had "learned." One of his points was that "there is no civil war in Nicaragua. To say or think such a thing would reflect a stupidity or a perverse complicity, . . . the reality of death and destruction taking place in Nicaragua is a result of the war of aggression that the government of the United

States has declared." Casaldáliga also "learned" that the Contras were all, without exception, former Somoza Guardia mercenaries hired by the CIA, and "real madmen . . . always inhuman and besides they are usually on drugs." He did hear some peasant complaints but rejected these out of hand by reminding himself "how hard it is for a revolution to be accepted by all the people." When a Catholic lay preacher tried to tell him that the peasants were suffering at the hands of the Sandinistas, the bishop condemned the preacher, not the Sandinistas, as a man "heavily under reactionary influence [and who] obviously does not have an overall view of politics, of society, of what Nicaragua used to be." Based on his short visit, the bishop felt fully qualified to reach definitive conclusions. "The [highland] peasants experience the Sandinista revolution as if it were their own. And . . . experience the Contras—those 'champions of freedom' that Reagan canonized and maintains—as a daily threat, a mystery of iniquity that had no justification."[1]

Casaldáliga had uncritically memorized the Black Legend of the Contras, which had become the dominant external hegemonic discourse on the subject, but he was not the only one to be misled. Even Reagan's State Department and CIA point men largely subscribed to the idea. Had either Reagan or Casaldáliga heard Abuelito say that they were actually "just a whole bunch of *really* pissed off peasants," neither would have believed him. For them, image *was* reality—a reality that they could not believe.

In reality it was the Sandinistas, not the Contras, who never had much peasant support, even against Somoza. According to a study dedicated precisely to this question, during the war against Somoza, peasants had made up only 4.5 percent of the Sandinistas' combatants, and most of these were Pacific coast rural farm proletarians, not highlanders. Over 95 percent of the Sandinistas were urban students, workers, tradesmen, or mid-level technicians.[2] In contrast, the only large group of highland peasant guerrillas to fight alongside the Sandinistas against Somoza had been the MILPA, and this organization's members had become sufficiently alienated by May 1979 to begin taking up arms against the Sandinistas even before Somoza fell.

From the highland peasants' perspective as reflected by the Comandos I interviewed, the 1979–90 Revolution was the problem, not the solution. It impoverished them, threatened their land and their freedom, and sought to convert them from independent microbourgeois into dependent proletarian laborers on state farms. It was a Pacific coast urban-centered and urban-led assault that put their lives and well-being in jeopardy, attacked their way of life, endangered their families, and threatened their survival.

The highland peasants may have been poor and unschooled, but they were comfortable with their own traditions and way of life and libertarian in their attitudes, all stances that were anathema to the revolutionary Sandinistas. The highlanders' struggle became a war of resistance led mostly by former anti-Somoza Sandinista Milpistas, not former Guardia, and fought by peasants. By the time the first Guardia-led Contra units entered into combat in 1982, they had been at war for almost three years. The Guardia then became the public face of the movement. But, from beginning to end, the real Contra army was Milpista and peasant.

GEOGRAPHY, HISTORY, SOCIETY

My review of the history and geography of the highlands turned up previously unnoted phenomena that explains why the main Contra War happened where it did. First, the geography of the Resistance movement coincides with the pre-Columbian homeland of Chibchan Indians of South American origin. Second, the comarcas that rebelled coincide with places where Indian-Spanish battles had occurred from 1526 to as recently as 1923. The Contra War can thus be viewed as simply a modern manifestation of a centuries-old pattern of resistance with deep if latent ethnic roots.

This interpretation certainty fits the actual evidence much more convincingly than does the Black Legend version of what happened between 1979 and 1990. Put simply, the Sandinistas triggered an ethnic war. By employing Pacific coast urban students and outsider ideologues who were openly ethnocentric, intolerant, and unwilling to treat the peasants with respect, they made impossible what would already have been extremely difficult. The consequences were fatal for the Revolution.

HOW TO DESTROY YOUR OWN REVOLUTION

The Contra War was caused by the Sandinistas themselves. The consequence was what Plutarco Hernández labels "history's shortest revolution," because the conflict kept the Sandinistas from consolidating and led to the Revolution's failure. This changed the course of Nicaraguan history. Since the Spanish Conquest, the highlanders had lost much of their separate identity, in particular their native languages. This, combined with the "myth of mestizaje," had, in turn, masked their group cohesiveness. But the events of the Sandinista Revolution, the 1979–90 MILPAS and "Contra" wars, and the 1990–96 period of post-Revolution conflict appear to have reversed this process of deracination. Of all the events in Nicaragua of the past two decades, the most important may well turn out to have been the re-emergence under external pressure of the highlanders' "indio" identity, which has transformed both their self-image and their role in Nicaraguan society.

When their resistance movement began, Nicaragua's highland peasants were faceless, marginalized, and traditionally acted upon by Nicaragua's elites and vanguards but not themselves actors, often objects, but never subjects. By the end of the war, they had become something quite different, in many ways a still unamalgamated people, but with a shared common recent history, a new sense of self, and an awakened political consciousness. Although this was not immediately clear after the 1979–90 war, it became quite apparent in 1996, when, in a reasonably free democratic election, their ballots counted and they emerged as Nicaragua's largest voting bloc when Liberal presidential candidate Alemán was buoyed to victory on a tide of highland peasant votes. In the new Nicaraguan world of one-man-one-vote, the highlanders appear to have been transformed into a potentially decisive political group.

Far from being just Reagan's ragtag few, the Contra Comandos and the Resistance movement that produced them turned out to represent a people who will be of great importance to the future of a democratic Nicaragua.

QUESTIONS THAT LINGER

Yet even as answers to who, what, when, where, and why emerge, more questions arise. One important one is why, unlike Pacific Nicaragua or its Atlantic Indian littoral, the Central Nicaraguan mountains and their indio inhabitants constitute an academic black hole. With only rare exceptions, no anthropological, sociological, historical, political, or even economic studies of the region have been done, even though its population constitutes approximately 52 percent of the entire population of Nicaragua. Why have both Nicaraguan and foreign academics and scholars all but ignored a people who comprise most of Nicaragua's population? The tentative answer seems to be that nineteenth-century efforts by Nicaragua's traditional oligarchy to define the country's Indians out of existence by inventing a dominant hegemonic discourse of exclusion have succeeded. This issue merits renewed attention.

A second important question is just what the real objectives were of the United States in Nicaragua between 1977 and 1990. The evidence is overwhelming that the United States knowingly looked the other way while Castro shipped thousands of tons of arms in a massive airlift directly from Cuba to the Sandinista Front in 1978 and 1979. Costa Rican investigative files documenting this airlift and confirm that the United States knew of it seem irrefutable, as does the evidence of former Costa Rican minister Johnny Echeverria, who directed the flow. In fact, Echeverria went even further, both in a sworn statement to the Costa Rican legislature in 1980 and during a videotaped interview with the author, by asserting that not only had the Carter administration known about the airlift, it had encouraged it and, toward the end, even shipped the Sandinistas additional arms itself. This too was confirmed separately by numerous former Sandinista, Costa Rican, and other officials.[3]

Yet an enormous amount of evidence, everything short of a smoking gun, shows that just a few months later the Carter administration had reversed its position completely and that the CIA had initiated clandestine contact with exiled former Guardia for the purpose of helping their paramilitary efforts against the Sandinistas. The idea that, and completely contrary to the published history of events, it was Carter rather than Reagan who first involved the United States in a covert program to provide paramilitary help to the Contras seemed at first startling and incredible to me. But as participant after participant and observer after observer repeated the story in different countries at different times and in response to different questions, it developed for me overwhelming credibility. Might it have been that in 1977–79 the United States was actually making common cause with Nicaragua's traditional oligarchy in efforts to use the Sandinista guerrillas to rid themselves of the third Somoza but that the process got out of hand after Somoza fell? This line of inquiry, which also lies well beyond the scope of this book, most assuredly merits additional consideration, since the political implications are considerable.

Several other lines of inquiry suggested by my research but beyond the scope of this book concern the relationship between Nicaragua's traditional Conservative aristocracy and the Sandinistas; the role, or lack thereof, of Nicaragua's Liberals in either the war against Somoza or the Sandinista Revolution, and the real relationship between the first two Somozas and Nicaragua's elite. Clearly, all three Somozas were strongmen. But the extent to which they had symbiotic relationships with the country's traditional oligarchy merits further investigation, as does the reason why, in 1976, the Conservative faction of the elite suddenly turned against the third Somoza and made common cause with their radical cousins in the Sandinista guerrilla movement. Harry Strachan's study of Nicaragua's major family groups seems to suggest that the reason may have been linked less to stolen relief funds after Managua's disastrous 1974 earthquake, the standard explanation, than to Somoza family group economic competition with the two traditional dominate family groups—a process that created a third major bank to compete with the Pella's Bank of America and the Montealegre's Wells Fargo.[4] Other explanations may exist, but the topic merits rethinking.

Because the highland war did not stop in 1990 but continued at least through 1996, a third set of questions arises. Why, despite the 1990 defeat at the polls of the Sandinistas, did Conservative Violeta Chamorro decide to abandon those who elected her in favor of cogoverning with the Sandinistas? One plausible explanation, which also fits within Strachan's family group thesis, may be that the Sandinistas and Conservatives are really just two cliques of Nicaragua's traditional oligarchy. Neither clique really welcomes the competition for power and spoils inherent in the selection of governments by the people in one-person-one-vote elections.

THE CONTRA WAR'S AFTERSHOCKS

Since 1990, dozens of observers, from Sandinista comandantes to Marxist ideologues to Liberals, have begun to suggest that the Sandinista Revolution was less a popular consensus movement than a manifestation of the sort of intraelite rivalries for power, prestige, and fortune that have been the bane of Nicaragua since the sixteenth century.[5] If true, then it was, as Marxist dialectician Carlos Vilas has since said, less a revolution than a changing of the palace guard.[6]

This, in turn, makes an alternative interpretation of recent Nicaraguan history possible, one based on the nature and consequences of the MILPAS and the Contra War. In this new interpretation, Nicaragua's first real revolution may have just begun. It is neither radical nor reactionary, but rather the consequence of the emergence of once-marginalized peoples, especially the peasants of the highlands, into positions of influence in a newly democratized Nicaragua. Betrayed in 1979, and denied effective suffrage in 1990, they emerged in 1996 as a decisive voting bloc that has to be

wooed by anyone wanting to be elected to national office, a fundamental shift in Nicaragua's power structure.

During the 1996 presidential campaign, even the Sandinistas'
candidate, former President Daniel Ortega, recognized that real
revolutionary changes had taken place between 1990 and 1996. In
1989, Ortega was ordering the Sandinista army to hunt down and
kill every Contra it could find. From 1990 to 1995, thinly disguised
Sandinista death squads systematically tried to kill off the leadership of the highland peasantry, and efforts were made to disenfranchise them. But by 1996, he was seeking re-election by
promising the highlanders that, if elected, he would make a former
Guardia Contra his minister of government.

History does not end, and the denouement of this story is yet
to be written. But the final victory in Nicaragua's recent Contra
War appears to be going neither to the revolutionaries of the
Sandinista Front, nor to their national and international sympathizers, but to some simple dirt farmers. From a country that, until
now, has always been governed by and for the few, Nicaragua is
being transformed into one governed by the many, thanks neither
to Jimmy Carter nor Ronald Reagan, nor even to those who
grabbed power in the name of Augusto César Sandino, but to tens
of thousands of highlander peasants who were willing to lay down
their lives to remain free. And that, by historical Nicaraguan standards, is truly revolutionary. From 1996 forward, the success of
freedom and democracy in Nicaragua will be the true measure of
who won the Contra War. As of today, the Comandos of the comarcas and the highland peasants look like the ultimate winners.

PERSONNEL REPORT

Handwritten personnel report, Legión de Septiembre/FDN, 20 December 1981. Sixty-two Legionnaires are reported to have already graduated from training courses in Argentina and 16 in Guatemala. Note midway down, the report indicates fifteen Legionnaires were in Miami, "10 in US, 5 in 'projects.'" Note also that the estimated numbers of available combatants in both the Segovias and the Mosquitia is 3,000-3,500 in exile plus 5,500 already identified inside Nicaragua (*entrenandos internamente*), or 8,500-9,000 total.

62- L-15 Graduados en Argentina   "S-1"
16-   . ' C.   '   ' '   Guatemala
                                         Dic— 20- 81
tot 68

Actualmente : Fenix-(8-L-15) Emisora — (1-L15)
               Cebra-(2-L15) Sggitario - (3-L15)
               Pino (2-L15)   Ariel — (4-L15)
               Secc II (3-L15) Secc III — (2-L15)
               Secc V (1-L15) JEM — (1-L15)
               Guate (4-L15)   Total = 31 L-5

Potencial { Oficiales - en Miami
Pacifico {   10 en EU y 6 en proyectos = 16
          { Tropa - gran potencial 3000 á 3,500
          { actual — 238 Dist. ver Aoja. "R".

Potencia 1 { Oficiales- entrenados y Graduados en campamento
ATlanTico {   31 y 24 en proceso
           { Sub of II = 10 -Sub of III 17 (Misurasata)
           { tropa — 233
             (F.Interno)
           143 — infilTrados en grupos no mayores de
                5 Dirigidos por (1)of ó subof. asistido por(1)n,

Entrenados internamente
IN — 46 — — — — — — 80
Central — 26 —   —   — — 70
R.coco - 36 — —   — — 75
Mineral — 10 — — — — 20
Z.Sur — 12 — — — — 30
Total   130   D = 2600 L   275 = 5,500

SAMPLE FDN COMANDO PERSONNEL FILE

Sample FDN Comando individual personnel file for Marvin Gerónimo Centeno Zeledón, nom de guerre "Otoñiel." A nineteen-year-old peasant farmer from Barrio Germán Pomares in Jinotega, Otoñiel became a member of the COE, or Comando de Operaciones Especialies (Special Forces). His file is annotated "killed in Las Piedras, 5/11/85, mine field."

muerto en los Predios 5/11/85 / campamiento COE

F-001

FUERZA DEMOCRATICA NICARAGUENSE

"F. D. N."

CONTROL DE PERSONAL
DATOS GENERALES

FECHA: ....11 DE FEBRERO DE 1985

.....CENTENO...........ZELEDON.......MARVIN..........GERONIMO......

01.—Primer Apellido   Segundo Apellido   Primer Nombre   Segundo Nombre

02.—Edad 19 AÑOS Estatura 5.8 PIES.....Peso .150 LBS........ Color ...MORENO....

Ojos CAFE......... Boca PEQUENA.....Complexión ...DELGADA.........

03.—Señales Particulares ....NINGUNA..

04.—Fecha y lugar de nacimiento ...5 DE MARZO DE 1965...............
   ...DPTO DE JINOTEGA...

05.—Estado civil ....SOLTERO...

06.—Impedimentos físicos ....NINGUNO.................................

07.—Tipo de Sangre ....NO SABE.....................................

08.—Alias ......#~~ORNEL~~#....OTONIEL.................................

09.—Nombre del cónyuge ....Vive: SI NO

   Dirección: ....
   ....Tel. ....

10.—Nombre del padre: ...GERONIMO CENTENO RAMIRES............Vive: SÍ NO

   Dirección: ..BARRIO GERMAN POMARES. JINOTEGA.................
   ....Tel. ....

11.—Nombre de la Madre: ...BLANCA NIEVES ZELEDON HUVDA.......Vive: SÍ NO

   Dirección: ....LA MISMA.................................
   ....Tel. ....

12.—Pariente más cercano ...RODOLFO RODRIGUES...............Vive: SÍ NO

   •Dirección: ....LA MISMA..................................
   ....Tel. ....

13.—NOMBRE DE HIJOS:

A.—)... Edad .... Sexo ....

Dirección: ....

B.—)... Edad .... Sexo ....

Dirección: ....

C.—)... Edad .... Sexo ....

Dirección: ....

D.—)... Edad .... Sexo ....

Dirección: ....

E.—)... Edad .... Sexo ....

Dirección: ....

F.—)... Edad .... Sexo ....

Dirección: ....

14.—NOMBRE DE HERMANOS:

A.—)..YLY.DEL.ROSARIO...CENTENO.ZELEDON Edad 18 ANOS Sexo FEMENINO...

Dirección: .BARRIO..GERMAN.POMARES.JINOTEGA............................

B.—)...JOSE IVAN CENTENO ZELEDON.... Edad 17 ANOS Sexo MASCULINO

Dirección: ....LA MISMA...................

C.—)....BEATRIZ GREGORIA CENTENO ZELEDON 16 ANOS Sexo FEMENINO

Dirección: ...........LA.MISMA...........................

D.—)....MARTHA..AUXILIADORA...CENTENO.ZELEDON.15.ANOS Sexo FEMENINO...

Dirección: ....LA MISMA......................

E.—)...FELIX PEDRO CENTENO ZELEDON... Edad 1T4 ANOS Sexo MASCULINO

Dirección: ...........LA.MISMA........................

F.—)...MARCOS.OMAR.CENTENO.ZELEDON... Edad 12 ANOS Sexo MASCULINO

Dirección: ..........LA..MISMA............................

15.—En caso de emergencia avisar a: ...GERONIMO.CENTENO..RAMIRES.............

Dirección: ...BARRIO.GERMAN POM ARES JINOTEGA...................

16.-- Trabajo actual del legionario F. D. N.....PERTENECIENTE.A.COMANDOS.ESPECIALES...C.O.E

17.-- Dirección actual del legionario F. D. N. ....LEPA.......................

....

18.—Pasaporte No. .... Extendido en .... Fecha ....

Fecha de vencimiento .... Visas actuales p/viajar a ....

....

19.- Familiares en el actual gobierno de Nicaragua y clase de empleo .... NINGUNO ....

A.—) ....

       Militancia política .... Disponibilidad ....

B.—) ....

       Militancia política .... Disponibilidad ....

C.—) ....

       Militancia política .... Disponibilidad ....

20.—Educación General (civil o militar) ...... 3ER GRADO DE PRIMARIA ....

....

....

....

21..—Especialidad en la vida civil .... AGRICULTURA ....

22.—Especialidad militar .... ENMINAS KEEYMORE ,RPG—7 ,LOW ....

....

23.—Armas que conoce ... RPG—7, LOW, FAL, A.KA.47, ...

....

....

24.—En caso sea civil, conocimiento de armas ... PISTOLAS: 22, 38, 45,9MM, ...
.... RIFLES 22 Y ESCOPETAS ,44,410, ...

25 - Experiencias en combate [ciudad o montaña] ...... MONTANA .... 13 COMBATES ....
...... 15 MESES ....

....

26.- Zona de Nicaragua que más conoce [poblados o montañas] .... POBADOS: JINOTEGA ,SAN RAFAEL,
CEBACO, ...

....

....

27.- Rango-número y último lugar de servicio en Nicaragua _____ NINGUNO _____

28.- Si es civil su profesión u oficio _____ CIVIL _____

29.- Apto. militarmente

A.--) _____
B.--) _____
C.--) _____

P. I.

P. D.

MARVIN GERONIMO CENTENO ZELEDON

_____ TESTIGO

_____ JEFE DE PERSONAL

APPENDIX C

SAMPLES FROM CHRONOLOGICAL MESSAGE FILES

Sample pages from chronological message files kept throughout the war that quote both FDN and intercepted Sandinista army messages. Those of 11 September 1984 include radio call messages from EPS originators Volcán and Charlie Golf (EPS), and Norteño, (FDN). These messages reported on a Sandinista anti-guerrilla battalion, the *Simón Bolívar*, just arrived in Estelí with Cuban, Soviet, and other foreign military advisers, one of nine mentions in that month's message traffic. Messages dated 10 September 1984 are by FDN commanders C-45 and K-1.

D-P-

M E N S A J E - 7 - 11-9-84

AL::::::JCE F.D.N..(CAPTADO)

#2691 Punto A: Bluefields de: La Cruz de Rio Grande.. Le informo que las dos
pangas que teníamos aquí se las llevó el río ,la tratamos de buscar pero fue
imposible ya que ya no teníamos gasolina,necesitamos que nos manden un motor
ya que yo tengo una panga pero sin motor y estamos sin medio para movilizar
nos, las dos pangas talvez esten en mano de los c.r. necesitamos gasolina pto
084311 Sept 84....

                              Volcán
OKProfe P
....

#133 Pto A: Wiwilí de Movil (Yanta) necesito un tubo de mortero 82mm,
para mortear a los c.r. ya que ellos se encuentran en las coord- (13-60)
y van entrando en la coord (23-62) necesito un medio para sacar unos heridos
que tengo espero respuesta inmediata pto 093011 ept 84..

                          Charlie Golfo.
....

A: X-1 INF. WZ IV.
NRG(54).A los mensajes nro (5) 0750 03-09-84. de WZ Y mensaje nro(321) de
IV zona operacional esta super despejada y necesito ese equipo que yo estaba
listo. Acuse recibo PTO. 0926 09 septiembre 84.

                              X-15
OK:Quito/5 pino
0940 110984.

....
#2692 A WAMBLAN, BOCAY,PLAN DE GRAMA, EL CARMEN,(31)BI Y MOVILES.DE WIWILI.
La contra seña para el día de hoy es "cama-pino" PTO.0900 11 septiembre 84.

                            VOLCAN
....
#2693 A JEFE EM BI EN WIWILI DE JEFE (31)BI.
Se hace necesario que para seguir avanzando se nos apoye con la artilleria
ya que el enemigo se retira hacia la profundidad,el enemigo se mantiene
fuerte y en caso que nos apoyen se hace necesario que la tropa del (36-33)
y la del (36-34)y la (31)BI regresar a Plan de Grama o ya sea a Bocay para
planificar bien un nuevo operativo,nosotros nos encontramos en coordenada
(17-57/3)y el enemigo en la coordenada (18-60) y van avanzando hacia la
coordenada (23-62) el jefe c/r es el Tigrillo y sus otros,propongo salir
a Bocay la (31) BI y la tropa del (36-34) y la tropa del (36-33)saldra
   a Plan de Grama, ademas necesitamos sacar unos heridos, si regresamos seria
bueno ya pasariamos resolviendo una situacion o sea el enemigo que quede
atrás y asi planificariamos con usted en Bocay un nuevo operativo necesito
repuesta PTO 0915 11 septiembre 84.
                            VOLCAN
....

D-P

M E N S A J E   11 SEPTIEMBRE 84

A::JCE...FDN.(CAPTADOS).
#2694 A JEFE (31)BI DE JEFE EM BI WIWILI.
Por el momento no se les puede apoyar por lo tanto ejecute el regreso de usted
y la tropa del (36-34) a Bocay y la tropa del (36-33)a Plan de Grama,yo llegare
a Bocay para planificar nuevamente, traiga preparado el informe concreto del
enemigo,evacuaremos los heridos y en Bocay hay morteros solicitelos,el dia de
ayer envie municion a Bocay PTO. 0925 11 septiembre 84.

                              VOLCAN

2695 A PAIWAS DE MATIGUAS.
El grupo c/r que se dirigia hacia comarca los Mollejones se encuentra nuevamente
en el cerro el Gavilán coordenada (11-63) este grupo es el que cruzo el rio el
dia de ayer PTO.1000 11 septiembre 84.

                              VOLCAN

#2696 A NORMAN MATIGUAS DE RIO BLANCO.
Necesitamos informacion del enemigo,maniobrar con (30) firifale al P/3 (30)
de correr c/r,pasarlos a los de Muy Muy y Pacansan PTO 1015 11 septiembre 84.

                              VOLCAN

#134 Pto A. Portu al de méxico .. Aquí no se ha hecho nada, el trabajo esta
parado por la situación y disposición del gobierno pto 105011 Sept 84...

                           Charlie Golfo.

#135 Pto A. Portugal de México estamos en cuestión de la defensa y en este
sentido movilizamos 40 cros pto 105711 Sept 84...

                           Charlie Golfo.

#136 Pto A: Jicote de Diriangén...el delegado del Minint que iba para El Cuá no
aceptó ir, dijo que era peligrosa esa zona pto 1103 1 Sept 84.

                           Charlie Golfo.

A:::::JCE F.D.N..
#23 Punto En Estelí acampamenta el Bli Simón Bolivar, número de hombres 150
armas de apoyo (2) obuses (23) (2) antiaéreas(2) cañones(75) (3) ametralladoras
(50) (4) cañones (4) 120 y (3) 82 hasta ahora desta descubierto mision reforzar
Jalapa hasta de internacionalistas cubanos, rusos,en Estelí, en próxima infor
macion pasaré dirección cantidad y ubicación de ésta punto 090011 Sept 84

                           Norteño
OK103511 Sept 84
Langosta/FV

#2697 Punto A: La Dalia. de: Rancho Grande.. La tropa que metimos a operar con
tra el enemigo en dirección a Las Carpas chocó,aún no tenemos resultados,infor
maré cuando tenga informe concreto pto 103011 Sept 84...

                           Volcán
OKSB.

D-P

N ___ A J __ 10-9-84

A: : JCE F.D.N.

NR.5 Punto informo que el día 8 sept 84 el comandante _olando tomo por -
sorpresa al E.P.S. Alejándro Gonzalez quien openiéndose a los comandos die
ron muerte recuperándole un fusil a: 47 número 0870 dicho enemigo tenía
tres años de servicio . un revólver cal 38 punto 143610 Sept 84...

C-45

0K164510
EMI/Cairo.

•••

▪2483 A: (_URSNTE) _E B I SANTOS LÓPEZ.
LA(2) COMPAÑIA __ _ JUERZA __ C ORDENA (65-04) DONDE ERA EL P.M.
LA (3) C MPAÑIA __ NJUENTRA EN COORD NADA (95-01) DON_ FUE EL COMBATE
Y ESTAN REALIZANDO UN RASTREO, EL RE_TO D: LA T OPA SE ENCUENTRA RECONCENTRADA
EN EL P.M. E_ EL VEHICULO _UE SALIO DE AQUI __ FU_ ON (2) PA UE__ D: MUNICI_N
PE LA_ _UE U_A LA _ TR__ PAPITA _ JUAN_ SALGA ALGUN VEHICULO ME L_ _A__A
_IC A MUNI_ION. 17:15 10 septiembre 84.

VOL_ N

▪2684 A: JEFE DE O_ERACI N_S (562) SI LA _ALIA __ JCP _ N (36-22)RANCHO GRANDE
_ N _O_ __ GRU O C.R. NO DETERMINADO DE LA _ONA DE LA __CAR_A CON EL OBJETIVO
D_ ATACAR Y _ESPRUIR EL PUENTE _E LAS CARPA Y OBTACULI_AR LA VIA. (50) CROS
AL MANDO DE ERN__TO _A_IERON EN R_A DIRECCION.
FRATERNO: HORA. 17:50 10 septiembre 84.

VOLCAN

A: X+1 _ 6
INFORMO _UE _E MANTIENE B J_ CONTROL _O_A LAS _ARRET_RA_ _E L _ LUGARE_
DE POTRERILLO, MANCOTAL, LA _O_RITAS, ASTURIA, EL MOJON, _ERRODE AGUA
_SAN ISIDRO,LOS C___,_ JUAN_ TUMA, LA_ CUCHILLA_ LA _AVU_IA, LO_ ROBLES,
_ LA CO_ONIA, 18 :15 10 _E_TIEMBRE 84.

K..E.M.I./5 PINO   C-45
 18:10 HR_
•••

_ 19   A__X-1
ACUSE _E_I_O _ _U _O 6,19,28 de 10 _EP_I_MBR_ 84 __EAT_S PROCEDIENDO
SOLICIT__S ADELANT_DE AMETRALLA OHA R. _D. FUE ENVIADA A ESTORN_ _ON EL
PA_A O 17 DE AGO __ SON EL _HOPE, JON_OH. ESTOY PI_IEND_ (3) A PINO_ LA
LOGI_TICA _E _E_EM_RE _E ESPERA _RO_IMAMENTE PRO_IMA_ (48) HORA_. 18:15
10 _eptiembre 84.

K-1

0K.._-1_/ _ __
19:00 HR_.
                        (ADELántale).

SAMPLE FDN STATUS OF FORCES REPORT

Sample FDN Status of Forces Report on troop strength. FDN archives contain such reports from 1980 through 1990.

CUARTEL GRAL. GRAL. JEFATURA DEL NUEVO EJERCITO DE LA RESISTENCIA NICARAGUENSE
ESTADO MAYOR
SECCION DE PERSONAL

15 de marzo de 1990

I.- PERSONAL ADMINISTRATIVO EN YAMALES

UNIDAD	APTOS.	NO APTOS.	TOTAL
Pers. del Estado Mayor	112	203	315
Pers. del S.C.S. C/#1	105	-	105
Pers. del S.C.S. C/#4	32	33	65
Pers. Ayuda Humanitaria	32	21	53
Pers. de Transporte	56	29	85
Pers. del FRA DELTA	-	22	22
Hosp. Dr. y Cmdte. Aureliano	99	72	171
Pers. de Seg. del E.M.	68	59	127
Clinica Dental	43	30	73
Fuerza Aerea	19	15	34
Ofic. de Derechos Humanos	-	4	4
T O T A L	566	488	1,054

II.- PERSONAL TROPA EN LA BRUJA Y YAMALES

	UNIDAD	APTOS LA BRUJA	APTOS YAMALES	NO APTOS. YAMALES	TOTAL
UNID. INDEP.	BTN. Freddy Vilches	-	79	39	118
	BTN. Apoyo Auxiliar	-	303	-	303
	Personal del Estado Mayor	33	-	-	33
	G.O.E.	-	84	5	89
	Unidad de Artilleria	-	60	2	62
	C.I.M.	682	69	4	755
	Pers. del C.C. Admitiva.	-	-	121	121
	Pers. de Esc. de P/M.	-	117	13	130
	Personal de Inteligencia	220	-	-	220
	T O T A L	935	712	184	1,831
1er. C P.	Personal del CO.OP.	7	46	7	60
	BTN. Santiago Meza	179	146	31	356
	BTN. 15 de Septiembre	114	182	21	317
	BTN. Segovia	143	174	78	395
	BTN. Andres Castro	-	246	9	255
	T O T A L	443	794	146	1,383
2do. CO	Personal del CO.OP.	-	55	-	55
	BTN. Trinidad Poveda L.	-	348	37	385
	BTN. G.O.T.	-	358	26	384
	BTN. Salvador Pérez	-	500	28	528
	BTN. Basilio Garmendia	-	359	20	379
	T O T A L	-	1,620	111	1,731
3er. C P.	Personal del CO.OP.	-	72	-	72
	BTN. Pedro J. Gonsales	254	-	26	280
	BTN. San Jacinto	-	61	5	66
	BTN. Domingo Rivera	267	-	13	280
	BTN. Manuel Almengray	177	-	12	189
	T O T A L	698	133	56	887
4to. P.	Personal del CO.OP.	-	44	2	46
	BTN. Jorge Salazar #5	-	240	-	240
	BTN. Esteban Rise Moran	-	233	9	242
	BTN. Ismael Castillo U.	-	270	-	270
	BTN. Jorge Salazar #4	-	235	5	240
	T O T A L	-	1,022	16	1,038
5to. CO	Personal del CO.OP.	-	41	-	41
	BTN. Jorge Salazar #1	-	215	2-	217
	BTN. Jorge Salazar #2	-	142	11	153
	BTN. Jorge Salazar #3	-	206	6	212
	T O T A L	-	604	19	623
	TOTAL EN SANT. (TROPA).......	2,076	4,885	532	7,493

2

III.-   PERSONAL ADMINISTRATIVO EN S.A.B. "MEJAPA"

U N I D A D	APTOS.	NO APTOS.	TOTAL
Puesto de Mando del E.M.	82	107	189
Personal del S.C.S.	63	36	99
Clinica La Pelona	36	19	55
T O T A L	181	162	343

IV.-   PERSONAL TROPA EN S.A.B.

BTN. San Jacinto....................	206	47	253

V.-   PERSONAL EN LA LODOSA

BTN. Segovia....................	35	3	38

VI.-   PERSONAL ESPECIAL.................................... 20

VII.-   PERSONAL EN TEGUCIGALPA

U N I D A D	C A N T I D A D
Centro de Suministros	95
Oficina de Inteligencia	2
Radio 15 de Septiembre	3
Comunicaciones	8
Oficina de Finanzas	15
Clinica El Jardin	35
Clinica Danli	13
Rancho Grande	248
Oficina del Cuerpo Medico	17
Oficina de Transmisiones	6
Casa del Combatiente	65
Fuerza Aerea	26
Ayuda Humanitaria	20
Casa Politica	14
Fiscalia Militar	8
T O T A L	516

VIII.-   PERSONAL EN COCIGUINA

Personal del BTN. Freddy Vilches B.	28
Personal del S.C.S.	10 (3)
T O T A L	38

IX.-   PERSONAL EN CORINTO..................... (5)

PERSONAL EN TERRITORIO AMIGO DEL SUR "COSTA RICA"

BTN. Jorge Salazar #2................................ 60

3

PERSONAL EN NICARAGUA

U N I D A D	C A N T I D A D
1er. Comando Operacional..........................	12
BTN. Santiago Meza...........................	259
BTN. 15 de Septiembre	455
BTN. Segovia	253
BTN. Andres Castro	183
2do. Comando Operacional.....................	7
BTN. Trinidad Poveda L.	232
BTN. C.O.T.	249
BTN. Salvador Péres	61
BTN. Basilio Carmandia G.	100
3er. Comando Operacional	23
BTN. Pedro J. Gonzales	248
BTN. Domingo Rivera	223
BTN. Manuel Almugaray	199
BTN. San Jacinto	179
4to. Comando Operacional......................	23
BTN. Jorge Salazar #5	528
BTN. Esteban Riso Moran	450
BTN. Ismael Castillo U.	409
BTN. Jorge Salazar #4	513
5to. Comando Operacional......................	29
BTN. Jorge Salazar #1	444
BTN. Jorge Salazar #2	285
BTN. Jorge Salazar #3	305
UNID. INDEP. DE LOS CO.OP.	
BTN. Apoyo Auxiliar	372
C.O.E.	1
Personal Especial	21
Personal de Inteligencia	13
Unidad de Artilleria	39
T O T A L 6.115	

RESUMEN GENERAL DEL ESTADO DE FUERZA DEL E.R.

I.-	Personal Administrativo en Yamales............	1,054
II.-	Personal Tropa en Yamales y La Bruja.........	7,493
III.-	Personal Administrativo en S.A.B. Nejapa....	343
IV.-	Personal Tropa en S.A.B.....................	253
V.-	Personal en La Lodosa......................	38
VI.-	Personal Especial.........................	20
VII.-	Personal en Tegucigalpa...................	516
VIII.-	Personal en Cooigaina.....................	38
IX.-	Personal en Corinto.......................	(5)

TOTAL DEL PERS. EN TERRITORIO AMIGO (NORTE). 9,760

TOTAL DEL PERS. EN TERRITORIO AMIGO (SUR).. 60

PERSONAL EN NICARAGUA......................6.115

TOTAL GENERAL DEL E.F. DEL M.E.R.N......15.935

Cmdte. Denis

4

MUJERES Y NIÑOS QUE NO ESTAN EN E.F. GRAL.PERO ESTAN EN BTN. YAMALES

UNIDAD	APTAS YA REUN. YAMALES	NO APTAS YAMALES	NIÑOS YAMALES	TOTAL
Ctel Gral. E.M.	8	-	16	20	44
Transporte	-	-	11	14	25
S.C.S. C/#1	-	-	14	14	28
S.C.S. C/#4	-	-	4	7	11
PRA DELTA	-	-	2	5	7
Fuerza Aerea	-	-	18	7	17
Seg. del Estado Mayor	-	5	3	10	18
Hosp. Dr. y Cadte. Aureliano	-	6	41	51	98
Clinica Dental	-	3	33	35	71
BTN. Freddy Vilches B.	-	-	10	15	25
BTN. Apoyo Auxiliar	-	-	10	6	16
C.O.E.	-	-	6	6	12
Unidad de Artilleria	-	-	11	13	24
Esc. de Para Medico	-	-	9	10	19
C.I.M.	-	-	12	14	26
Centro de Cap. Admitiva.	-	-	21	9	30
Ayuda Humanitaria	-	-	3	-	3
T O T A L	8	14	216	236	474
1er. CO.OP.	-	-	6	8	14
BTN. Santiago Meza	8	6	49	73	136
BTN. 15 de Septiembre	8	-	7	55	70
BTN. Segovia	11	-	71	73	155
BTN. Andres Castro	-	7	16	40	63
T O T A L	27	13	149	249	438
2do. CO.OP.	-	-	4	-	4
BTN. Trinidad Poveda L.	-	-	57	75	132
BTN. G.O.T.	-	19	26	63	108
BTN. Salvador Pérez	-	-	30	51	81
BTN. Basilio Garmendia G.	-	-	35	64	99
T O T A L	-	19	152	253	424
3er. CO.OP.	-	-	8	-	8
BTN. Pedro J. Gonzales	-	-	32	57	89
BTN. San Jacinto	-	-	3	-	3
BTN. Domingo Rivera R.	-	-	41	53	94
BTN. Manuel Almuzorav	-	-	26	50	76
T O T A L	-	-	110	160	270
4to. CO.OP.	-	-	11	6	17
BTN. Jorge Salazar #5	-	3	3	4	10
BTN. Esteban Rizo Moran	-	-	19	16	35
BTN. Ismael Castillo U.	-	-	15	6	21
BTN. Jorge Salazar #4	-	3	9	9	21
T O T A L	-	6	57	41	104
5to. CO.OP.	-	7	-	-	7
BTN. Jorge Salazar #1	-	9	4	12	25
BTN. Jorge Salazar #2	-	4	10	16	30
BTN. Jorge Salazar #3	-	8	19	22	49
T O T A L	-	28	33	50	111
TOTAL GRAL. DE MUJ. Y NIÑOS........	35	80	717	989	1821

D. INDEP.

. CO.OP.

. CO.OP.

. CO.OP.

. CO.OP.

. CO.OP.

MUJERES Y NIÑOS QUE ESTAN EN B.A.R. Y NO ESTA EN E.F. GRAL.

UNIDAD	MUJERES.	NIÑOS .	TOTAL
Puesto de Mando del B.M.	31	28	59
S.C.S.	26	23	49
BTN. San Jacinto	38	58	96
Clinica La Pelona	17	11	28
T O T A L	112	120	232

STOCK DE PACIENTES EN HOSP. Y CLINICAS

Hosp. Dr. Aureliano.....(130), Clin. Danli.....(30) + (7) Niños, El Jardin (75)
Clin. Dental........(30), La Pelona ......(20), Niños en Rancho Grande ...(29) niños.

EPS ARMS INVENTORY
AND REQUEST

EPS inventory of armaments on hand or already in the pipeline as of 3 October 1987 (lines 1–5). Line 6 lists additional arms on request from the Soviet Union in accordance with two bilateral agreements, Project Diriangen I for 1989–90 and Project Diriangen II for 1990–95. The new arms approved as part of Diriangen I and II would have allowed the EPS roughly to double its size, for example by adding to its arsenal 21,481 Makarov pistols, 118,851 AK-47s, 44 tanks, and so forth.

This inventory was brought out of Nicaragua by Maj. Roger Miranda, personal aide to EPS commanding general Humberto Ortega at the time Miranda defected. Courtesy of the Hoover Institution, Stanford University.

EJERCITO POPULAR SANDINISTA

CAP. VII PEDIDO COMPLEMENTARIO DE ARMAMENTO, TECNICA Y ASEGURAMIENTO TECNICO MATERIAL PARA EL PERIODO 1988 - 1990 (DIRIANGEN - II)

CAP. VIII PEDIDO PRELIMINAR DE ARMAMENTO Y TECNICA PARA EL QUINQUENIO 1991 - 1995 (DIRIANGEN - III)

FORMA-03

EJERCITO POPULAR SANDINISTA
ARMAMENTO Y TECNICA
PEDIDO DE ARMAMENTO Y TECNICA PARA DIRIANGEN 1

Fecha : 10/03/87
Pagina : 2

N/O	CODIGO	DESCRIPCION	UNIDAD DE MED	LLEVA EPS ACTUAL	EXISTENCIA	PENDIENTE x RECIBIR	EXISTENCIA TOTAL	PEDIDO
1	01-0001	PISTOLA MAKAROV 9 MM	PZA.	40,557	11,576	7,500	19,076	21,481
2	01-0002	FUSIL AKM (AKMS) 7.62MM. M43	PZA.	371,570	252,719	0	252,719	118,851
3	01-0005	FUS.FRANCOT. SVD 7.62MM M1908	PZA.	888	740	0	740	148
6	01-0008	AMET.LIVIANA RPK 7.62mm M43	PZA.	9,394	4,342	0	4,342	5,052
	01-0013	LANZA COHETE RPG-7V	PZA.	7,927	3,500	792	4,292	3,635
7	01-0015	LANZA GRANADA AGS-17	PZA.	519	247	0	247	272
	01-0018	MORTERO BM 82MM	PZA.	978	578	58	636	342
	01-0018	CAÑON AT 57MM M-43 ZIS-2	PZA.	360	345	6	351	9
13	01-0021	SPG-9	PZA.	351	0	100	100	251
17	01-0025	LANZA COHETES GRAD-1P	PZA.	568	215	204	420	148
20	01-0028	AMET. A.A. ZGU-1 14.5 MM	PZA.	351	263	6	269	82
21	01-0029	AMET. A.A. ZPU-2 14.5MM	PZA.	106	100	0	100	6
	01-0031	CAÑON A.A. ZU-23-2 23MM	PZA.	378	252	0	252	126
	01-0034	CAÑON A.A DE 85mm (100mm)	PZA	24	0	0	0	24
	01-0035	C.A.A.P. C-2M (9PS8)	PZA.	346	325	4	329	17
29	01-0037	C.A.A.P. C-3M (9PS8M)	PZA.	637	166	0	166	471
30	01-0038	C.A.A.P. IGLA-1M (9PS19-2)	PZA.	273	54	0	54	219
31	01-0039	SIST. COHETERIL A.A C-125	GPO.	4	0	0	0	4

*262,719 - 20,000 Mak.h Weis 232,719/1K

* incluye 20,000 Mak. h Weis - nos entregó 20 no debe - no entregó 5,006 3, 4,500 V2 3,550 M-23-26
Y 5,000 PPSH

** incluye corresde referencia (2) de 20,100/1K

*** Mas referencia (6)

EJERCITO POPULAR SANDINISTA
ARMAMENTO Y TECNICA
PEDIDO DE ARMAMENTO Y TECNICA PARA DIRIANGEN I

Fecha: 10/03/87   Pagina: 3

CODIGO	DESCRIPCION	UNIDAD DE MED	LLEVA EPS ACTUAL	EXISTENCIA	PENDIENTE x RECIBIR	EXISTENCIA TOTAL	PEDIDO
01-0040	DISPARO 152mm C-U 152mm D-20	PIEZA	25,200	22,455	0	22,455	2,745
01-0042	PROYECTIL REACT. 122mm M-21 OF	PIEZA	25,920	24,280	0	24,280	1,640
01-0043	PROYECTIL REACT. 122mm 9M 22M	PIEZA	30,240	10,200	16,271	26,471	3,769
01-0044	DIS. TARG. 100MM D-10 T25 C100	PIEZA	42,390	41,282	0	41,282	1,108
01-0045	DISP. 82mm MORTERO BM	PIEZA	636,000	422,217	60,000	482,217	153,783
01-0046	DISP. 82mm ILUMINACION BM	PIEZA	5,000	2,500	0	2,500	2,500
01-0049	DISP 75mm TAR. PT-76 C-76 ZIS-3	PIEZA	51,520	28,768	0	28,768	22,752
01-0050	DISPARO VOG-17 30mm	PIEZA	451,269	350,791	80,000	430,791	20,478
01-0051	DISPARO PG-7VM	PIEZA	343,360	188,964	150,000	338,964	4,396
01-0052	CART. REACT. SEÑAL 30mm	PIEZA	40,000	8,000	12,000	20,000	20,000
01-0053	CARTUCHO ILUM. 30mm	PIEZA	50,000	10,000	15,000	25,000	25,000
01-0054	CARTUCHO 14.5 MM	MIL	7,586	4,939	0	4,939	2,647
01-0058	CART. FUSIL 7.62MM M1908 SALVA	MILES	4,000	500	1,500	2,000	2,000
01-0059	CART. 7.62mm M43	MILES	540,405	260,692	59,100	319,792	220,613
01-0060	CART. 7.62mm M43 TIRO SALVA	MILES	8,000	1,000	3,000	4,000	4,000
01-0061	CARTUCHO 23 MM INSTAL. ZU-23-2	MIL	4,706	2,256	870	3,126	1,580
01-0064	CARTUCHO 100MM, CAÑON KS-19	PZA.	8,640	5,724	0	5,724	2,916
01-0065	COHETE 9M32M	PZA.	3,290	1,519	0	1,519	1,771
01-0066	COHETE 9M-36-1	PZA.	1,660	654	0	654	995
01-0067	COHETE 9M319-1	PZA.	540	270	0	270	270

Modelo el Ejercito = 75 millones de Cartuchos

Modelo del Cohete = 3.00 Cohetes

FORMA-03
N/O CODIGO

EJERCITO POPULAR SANDINISTA — ARMAMENTO Y TECNICA
PEDIDO DE ARMAMENTO Y TECNICA PARA DIRIANGEN

Fecha: 10/03/87 Pagina:

N/O	CODIGO	DESCRIPCION	UNIDAD DE MED	LLEVA EPS ACTUAL	EXISTENCIA EPS	PENDIENTE x RECIBIR	EXISTENCIA TOTAL	PEDIDO
106	02-0005	KAMAZ-4310 MILITAR	PIEZA	125	50	0	50	76
107	02-0006	KAMAZ-54112 TRACTOR-CABEZAL	PIEZA	135	0	0	0	135
108	02-0007	KAMAZ-53212 PLATAFORMA	PIEZA	55	0	0	0	55
110	02-0009	URAL-4320 MILITAR	PIEZA	240	40	0	40	200
111	02-0010	ZIL-131 MILITAR	PIEZA	2,251	1,023	515	1,538	713
115	02-0014	UAZ-31512 JEEP	PIEZA	1,615	1,065	150	1,215	400
116	02-0015	UR-57 URAL-MOTO	PIEZA	309	19		19	290
117	02-0016	TANQUES T-55	PIEZA	89	85	0	85	4
120	02-0019	BTR 60-PB TRANSPORTE BLINDADO	PIEZA	22	19	0	19	3
122	02-0022	BROM-2 EXPLORADOR BLINDADO	PIEZA	79	77	0	77	2
123	02-0023	MTO-BO/ZIL-131 TALL MT TANQUE	PIEZA	13	6	0	6	7
125	02-0024	MTD-AT-70/ZIL-131 TALL MT TPTE	PIEZA	37	12	0	12	25
126	02-0025	EGSN/ZIL-131 TALL SOLD CHAPIS	PIEZA	14	4	0		10
128	02-0027	SRZ-A/ZIL-131 TALL BATERIA	PIEZA	14	11	0	11	3
129	02-0028	TRM-A-70/ZIL-131 TALL REP TANQ	PIEZA	11	1	0	1	1
130	02-0029	TRM-B/ZIL-131 TALL MAQUINADO	JUEGO	11		0		11
131	02-0030	PARM-1 TALL RM TO Y TPTE	JUEGO	3	2	0	2	1
132	02-0031	MRM-M1/ZIL-131 TALL MECANICA	JUEGO	6	5	0	5	1
133	02-0032	UAT-452 A AMBULANCIA	PIEZA	145	66	30	96	50
134	02-0033	MAZ-5205A-SEMI REMOLQUE	PIEZA	75	0	0	0	75
135	02-0034	CHMZAP-5208 TRANSPORTADOR	PIEZA	24	10	0	10	14
136	02-0035	CHMZAP-5523 TRANSPORTADOR	PIEZA	12	12	0		12
138	02-0037	ATS-5-53TD AUTO-ABAST /URAL	PIEZA	38	18	0	18	20
139	02-0038	AC-8-53-4 AUTO-CISTERNA/MAZ	PIEZA	108	48	30	78	30
140	02-0039	MAZ-500 AUTO-ABAST /MAZ	PIEZA	40	20	0	20	20
141	02-0040	MAZ-500 LUBRICO - ENGRASADOR	PIEZA	2	2	0	0	2
143	02-0042	IZH 27151 CAMIONETA	PIEZA	300	15	0	15	285
144	02-0044	MAZ 5337-07 CHASIS	PIEZA	21	8	0	6	15
145	02-0045	MAZ 5429 TRACTOR CABEZAL	PIEZA	8	2	0	2	6
146	02-0047	KAMAZ-5511 VOLQUETE	PIEZA	151	0	0	0	151
147	02-0048	BTR-70PB TRANSPORTE BLINDADO	PIEZA	44	0	0	0	44
149	02-0050	KAMAZ Cisterna Combustible	PIEZA	35	0	0	0	35

Bou de P7-76
Total 28
Queda 22 far fu 6 in utilizaras fera banco de repuesto /ara 22
* Total de Taufas P.P. 133 — 287-55 + 45T-54 — Se pedir 4/00 fara al compilar 3/ara completar la flanilla
Y NO repuesses
Bou de Tau/13, P.P. 23 (2x6)+ el 4/0/46

COSTA RICAN PASSPORT OF
ALEJANDRO MARTÍNEZ

Pages 2, 17, and 40 from Costa Rican passport 8-043-357 of Alejandro Martínez confirming he traveled to Washington, D.C., late in the Carter presidency. Martínez says he was invited there by the CIA to discuss paramilitary aid to the Contras. On 13 January 1981, the American Consul in San José, Costa Rica, initially refused Martínez's visa, and to alert other Consuls to his decision, inserted a special handwritten note to that effect on page 40 of the passport. The American Ambassador immediately intervened at the urging of the CIA Station Chief, and the Consul reversed his decision that same day, issuing Martínez a most unusual three-month one-entry B-1 visa valid for business travel only (visa 00464, page 17). (Tourists receive B-2 visas; most business travelers receive dual B-1/B2s.) Martínez traveled immediately and was admitted to the United States on 15 January. His business-only status is confirmed by Immigration Service admission stamp 060 MIA 26 (also page 17).

Ronald Reagan was inaugurated as president on 20 January 1981 and did not issue his first (now declassified) Presidential Finding authorizing covert paramilitary aid to the Contras until December 24, eleven months after his inauguration. Because by law such a Finding authorizing engagement in covert operations must be signed in advance by the president with formal notifications made to select committees of Congress, it is clear that Martínez's trip must have taken place pursuant to an earlier but still secret Finding by President Carter. (Passport photographs courtesy of Alejandro Martínez.)

No. DEL PASAPORTE 8-043-357.

Nombre del portador
Bearer's name *Alejandro Cesar Martinez Sáenz*

Nacionalidad
Nationality *Costarricense*

Estatura
Height

Domicilio
Address *Limon*

Fecha de Nacimiento
Date of birth *13 Febrero 1928*

Profesión u Oficio
Profession or occupation *Fee Higaecola*

Cédula de Identidad No.
Identification card *8-043-357*

Estado civil
Married or single *Casado* Color *Blanco*

Peculiaridades físicas
Physical scars and marks

Dado en
Given at } SAN JOSE, COSTA RICA

a los *18* días del més de *Febrero*
The of

de 19 *76*
of

Valido hasta *18 - Feb. 1978.*
Valid until

Pudiendo ser renovado a su vencimiento
hasta cumplir diez años

Director General de Migración

PERSONAS INCLUIDAS EN ESTE PASAPORTE
PERSONS INCLUDED IN THIS PASSPORT

1. Nombre de la esposa
   Wife's name *8-043-357*

   Cédula de identidad
   Identification card

2. Nombre del niño
   Child's name

   Fecha de nacimiento
   Date of birth

3. Nombre del niño
   Child's name

   Fecha de nacimiento
   Date of birth

4. Nombre del niño
   Child's name

   Fecha de nacimiento
   Date of birth

FOTOGRAFIA
Photograph

Firma del Portador
Bearer's Signature

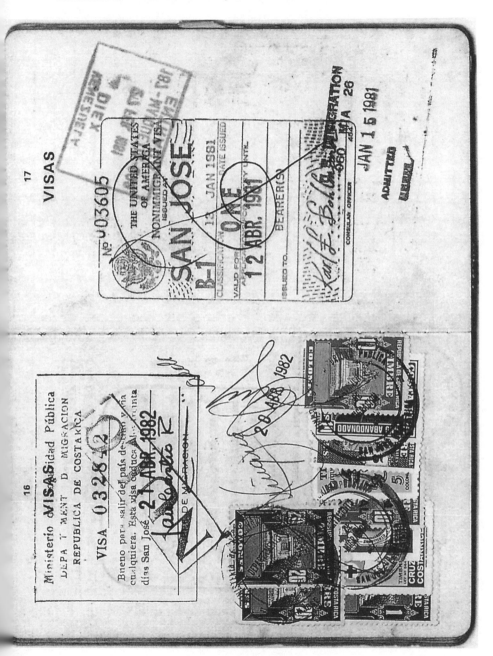

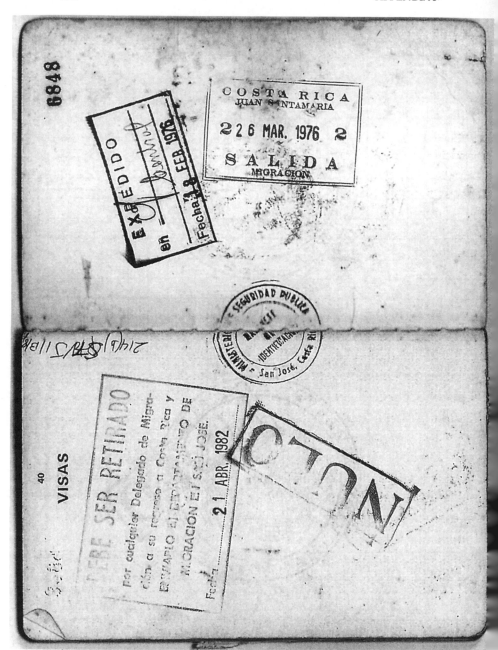

NOTES

PREFACE

1. Later, under CIA pressure, it was relabeled the Ejército de Resistencia Nicaragüense, or ERN. But among themselves the Comandos ignored the new name.

2. Oral history, Hernández Sancho, Plutarco Elías ("Comandante Marcial"). In the standard *Who's Who* of Nicaragua the entry on Hernández is longer than those on either Daniel or Humberto Ortega (Jirón, *Quien es Quíen*, 206–11). After attending Patrice Lumumba University in Moscow, Hernández received almost two years of training as a guerrilla leader in Cuba and North Korea and then spent fifteen years as a Marxist guerrilla in the field. From 1965 through 1977 he was a principal architect of Sandinista clandestine operation inside Nicaragua. In 1999 he was Costa Rican ambassador in Moscow. Hernández is the nephew of one former Costa Rican president, Calderón Guardia, and first cousin of another, Calderón Fornier. He is also the first cousin of the military commander of El Salvador's Faribundo Marti Liberation Front, Eduardo Sancho Castañeda, "Fermán Cienfuegos." Both Hernández and Cienfuegos told me their stories in extended oral history interviews and also wrote essays that are included in my companion book to this one (Brown, ed., *AK-47s*).

3. The other 20 percent were from other Contra armies that had been active in Nicaragua's Atlantic lowlands under separate commands.

4. Sergio Caramagna, "Peacemaking in Nicaragua," in Brown, ed., *AK-47s*.

5. For discussion of the prolongation of the Contra War, see Brown, *Causes of Continuing Conflict in Nicaragua*.

CHAPTER 1

1. Kagan, *A Twilight Struggle*, xvi, 180, 200.

2. Clarridge, *A Spy for All Seasons*, 208, 200, 190, 245.

3. *Contra* is a pejorative. Resistance fighters called themselves *Comandos*, the term generally used in this book.

4. The Comandos' postwar organization, the Asociación Cívica Resistencia Nicaragüense (ACRN), made available to me original records of the Fuerza Democratica Nicaragüense (FDN) and Ejército de Resistencia Nicaragüense (ERN), some dating back to 1979 and 1980, including more than 28,000 individual personnel folders. I identified some 276 living veterans of the 1979–81 period and held more than 200 interviews with them and with other informed individuals. These interviews included 42 oral histories provided by a randomly selected sampling of the earliest combatants.

5. In addition to the ACRN archives, I obtained and reviewed about 18,000 U.S. government documents through the Freedom of Information and Privacy Act (FOIA) from the Departments of State and Defense, the CIA, and the Agency for International Development (AID) and more than 3,000 pages of investigative records from the archives of the Costa Rican Congress in San José. In addition, I reviewed several thousand pages of other documents in private collections in Nicaragua, Honduras, Costa Rica and the United States.

6. Abuelito, interview, location withheld, ca. November 1989, and video (author's collection), ca. 1983. *Un aterro:* Nicaraguan slang for "a whole lot of." *Enchacimba'os:* slang for infuriated, or *"really* pissed-off." Unless otherwise noted, all translations in this book are by the author.

7. Pérez Bustamante, oral history. This oral history was conducted in El Zúngano, Nicaragua, on 4 February 1998. El Zúngano lies between the mountain towns of Quilalí and Wiwilí just opposite El Chipote, where Sandino had his headquarters. A combatant with Sandino before his war with the U.S. Marines, and a Sandino agent during that conflict, Pérez tells his story in his own words in Brown, ed., *When the AK-47s Fall Silent*.

8. Kagan dates their entry into combat at late spring and early summer of 1982. Kagan, *Twilight*, 221.

9. The Sandinista Ministry of the Interior claims that all together 130 rebels and Sandinistas were killed in combat during 1979–81. Nuñez, ed., *La Guerra*, 272–73. Former Contra Chief of Staff "Rubén" said the actual

number may have been twice as high. Rubén, interview, Managua, 9 June 1996.

10. Bernard Nietschmann, a specialist in Nicaragua's Miskito Indians, called the choice a particularly strong indicator because of the high social costs involved. Personal communication, 12 April 1997.

CHAPTER 2

1. Las Segovias include the Departments (provinces) of Nueva Segovia, Madríz, Estelí, and Jinotega. The broader highlands also include Matagalpa, Boaco, Chontales, and parts of Zelaya, Rio San Juan, and León.

2. Carlos Luís Fonseca Amador is usually considered the father of the FSLN but was actually its second leader after Noel Guerrero Santiago.

3. The word *comarca* is used in this book as the highland campesinos use it informally: to denote the rural settlement valley or other area they call home. In formal terms, a comarca is also a division of local government.

4. Dimas, Tigrillo, Jimmy Leo, Pirata, and Marina, oral histories. Two other former Comandos, serving at the time with Sandinista forces, also dated their knowledge of the existence of early MILPAS groups to August or September 1979. Segovia and Jhonson, oral histories.

5. Pryor, interview, Managua, 6 June 1996. In my interview with Pryor, he described the battle as it was recounted to him by his half-brother. At the time of the battle, Pryor was himself in the Sandinista army but was secretly helping the new anti-Sandinista guerrillas.

6. Most Nicaraguan highland campesinos, or peasants, are independent small farmers, not rural laborers (petit bourgeois, not rural proletarians). In this book the terms *campesino* and *peasant* refer only to this group and are used interchangeably.

7. Comandos used noms de guerre for security. Often more than one Comando used the same one, or one Comando would take the nom de guerre of a fallen Comando. I have used real names when they are known and can be published. The real names of these two Comandos are not known, and even the noms de guerre of the other three have been lost.

8. Cáliz's real name was Oscar Rodríguez Lisiano. Pryor's real name, Juan Rodríguez Campos, indicates that he and Cáliz had a different mother but the same father. Pryor, oral history.

9. Chapters 3–5 describe several of them.

10. His real name was Salvador Pérez. A major Resistance combat unit was later named for him.

11. Pryor, oral history. El Danto, whose death served as a catalyst of MILPA disaffection, is discussed in chapter 3.

12. Nicaraguan highland peasants usually live in isolated farmsteads in settlement areas (comarcas) without fixed nuclei. Place-names in this book are those used by the Comandos. Many are not listed in U.S. Department of Defense, *Gazetteer of Nicaragua.*

13. Correos and clandestine comarca committees were the backbone of the highlander rebellion. Chapter 9 is devoted to describing them and the larger popular support base on which they in turn depended. As a rule, there were from fifteen to twenty active correos, committee members, and popular-base supporters for every Comando.

14. *Cacique:* Indian Chief.

15. The first Sandinista agrarian reform decree, Decreto 3, was issued in July 1979. Wheelock, *La verdad sobre la Piñata,* 9.

16. Later renamed the Ejército Popular Sandinista (EPS), the Sandinista People's Army.

17. Pryor, oral history. This incident took place before the official establishment of the Sandinistas' militia system.

18. Ibid.

19. Tigre, oral history.

20. *Olla Fuerte:* Hearty Stew. Olla in this case is short for *olla de carne,* or beef stew. An *olla* is a clay cooking pot.

21. Tigre, oral history.

22. *El Norteño:* The Northerner. *Gato Brunés:* Dark Cat. *Pocoyo* is a Maya-Quiche name for a mythical feathered forest animal found in the *Popol-Vuh.* Mantica, *El Habla Nicaragüense,* 242. Pocoyo and Jimmy Leo are discussed in chapter 5.

23. Oscar Kilo, interview, Managua, 8 June 1996. The Galeano clan is discussed in chapter 5. The term *clan* is used advisedly. Although Nicaraguan mountain clans do not trace their origins back to a single apical founder as do Scottish clans, they are composed of kith and kin who do share agricultural properties, recognize their group in an "us-vs.-them" sense, and have internal authority patterns that, while loose in normal times, tighten during times of troubles. After reviewing alternative terms (*kinship group, kindred, extended family, descent group*), *clan* seemed to be the term that fit best. For definitions, see Kottack, *Anthropology,* 315–22.

24. Oscar Kilo, interview.

25. Ibid.

26. A peasant farmer from near San Sebastian de Yalí, Tirso Ramón Moreno Aguilar had been a correo for El Danto during the war against Somoza before becoming an anti-Sandinista Milpista. U.S. Department of State, *Nicaraguan Biographies,* 52. In 1996, he was an unsuccessful candidate for vice president of Nicaragua on the Partido de Unidad Liberal ticket.

27. Rubén, interview, Managua, 9 June 1996. Irene Calderón and his group are discussed in chapter 4.

28. Tigre, oral history.

29. Rubén, interview, Managua, July 1996. Rubén's own group, Las Culebras, is described in chapter 5. He was to go on to become the last chief of staff of the Contras' main army. In 1991–92 Sobalvarro was vice minister for the reinsertion and retraining of former Comandos in Nicaragua's postrevolution government.

30. Ibid.

31. Ibid.

32. Fidel Castro, 23 July speech in Estelí, Havana, Domestic Television Services, 24 July 1980. FBIS (Foreign Broadcast Information Service) VI, 25 July 1980, p. 9, Central America, FL241452.

33. "Public Security Chief on 'War' against Counter-revolutionaries," Agence France Presse, 26 July 1980. FBIS VI, 1 August 1980, p. 12, Central America, PA261444.

34. Barricada newspaper, 29 July 1980, p. 8. As reported by La Prensa newspaper 30 July 1980, pp. 1, 12. FBIS VI, 30 July 1980, p. 16, Central America, PA060367.

35. Radio Sandino, Managua, 28 July 1980. FBIS VI, 30 July 1980, p. 8, Central America, PA281826.

CHAPTER 3

1. Interview, Marina, Quilalí, 1994.

2. Variations on the nom de guerre "Dimas" were later used by several other Comandos, including Adán Ernesto González Rodríguez, "Dimas" (not known to have been related, U.S. Department of State, Nicaraguan Biographies, 48) and Tomás Laguna Rayo, "Dimas" (State, Biographies, 50). There was also a "Dimas Tigrillo" (Francisco Baldivia, State, Biographies, 45), a "Dimas Negro," and a "Dimas Sagitario" (State, Biographies, 54).

3. Dimas's personal history was reconstructed primarily from information provided by his common-law wife Andrea Pinell, "Marina," during an interview at her home in Quilalí in 1994. Her own oral history, cited separately, was recorded at the same time. Others who had known Dimas also contributed.

4. Pomáres, El Danto, 16.

5. The four peasants rejected along with Pomáres were Narciso Zepeda, Dolores Diaz, Manuel Guevara, and Raul Sandoval. The group they tried to join eventually attacked Guardia Nacional bases in Jinotega and Diriamba on 11 November 1960. Ibid., 20–22.

6. World War II vintage military weapons.

7. A report that he then participated in the 1959 Olama y Mojellones incursion (U.S. Department of State, *Nicaraguan Biographies*, 14) is not mentioned in Pomáres, *El Danto*, nor is he mentioned as a participant in Mendieta Alfaro, *Olama y Mojellones*. I was unable to resolve this discrepancy.

8. El Danto was in and out of Cuba, Honduras, Costa Rica, and various Eastern Bloc countries on numerous occasions. Pomáres, *El Danto*, 55, 72, 76, 78, 92, 111.

9. Hernández Sancho told the story in detail during a September 1998 oral history. He also discusses it in his book *El FSLN por Dentro*.

10. Abel Cespedes, "Cyro," and Ricardo "Chino Lau" Lau, interviews, location withheld, 1995. Pomáres's autobiography confirms he was in custody twice. Pomáres, *El Danto*, 35, 99–111.

11. Martínez, a Conservative, had been active as an anti-Somoza guerrilla since 1948 and as a member of the Frente Revolucionario Sandino, a pre-Sandinista Liberation Front movement. Although a political prisoner and then an internal exile in Cuba from 1960 to 1972 (due to secret denunciations by Marxists from within the nascent Sandinista movement), he was later released and went on to become a Sandinista field commander against Somoza from 1974 to 1979, only to rebel again against the 1979–80 Sandinista social revolution and become a top leader of the Southern Front of the Contra movement. In 1980, the CIA attempted unsuccessfully to recruit him to lead their Contra project. In 1999, Martínez was an auxiliary colonel in the Costa Rican Guardia Civil. He tells his own story in Brown, ed., *When the AK-47s Fall Silent*.

12. Hernández Sancho, interview, San José, July 1996.

13. Dimas Tigrillo, oral history. At the time, Dimas Tigrillo, who had become an anti-Somoza guerrilla in 1977, was a platoon leader with a different nom de guerre. He became Dimas Tigrillo after joining the MILPAS in honor of Pedro Joaquín González. The name "Tigrillo" was for his brother, Encarnación Baldivia. Sometimes he was also known as "Dimas de Tigrillo." U.S. Department of State, *Nicaraguan Biographies*, 45.

14. Oral histories, Marina, Jimmy Leo, and Bruce Lee.

15. Confirmed during a visit by the author to Jinotega in 1995.

16. Confidential source, Matagalpa, Nicaragua, 1995.

17. Pomáres, *El Danto*, 159.

18. "Pepe" Puente's home in Mexico City was the Sandinistas' principal safe house from 1960 to 1979. In 1956–58 he and his father had been close collaborators of Castro and the other 26th of July Movement leaders, including Ché Guevara, during their sojourn in Mexico preparatory to the Cuban Revolution. His father, who as a youth in the 1920s had worked for Sandino when Sandino was in Mexico, financed much of Castro's stay

in Mexico from 1956 to 1958, and in 1959 became one of Castro's top labor advisors in Havana. Pepe, who had carried the funds from his father to Castro, was also close to Castro and his group. During Central America's cold war revolutions, in addition to his work with the Sandinistas, Pepe was a liaison agent between the Cuban and Soviet embassies in Mexico City and revolutionaries in El Salvador, Guatemala, and Honduras. He tells his own story for the first time in Brown, ed., *When the AK-47s Fall Silent*.

19. Oral History, Marina.

20. "La ideologia de Pomáres no era la ideologia de los Sandinistas. Cuando cayo Pomáres era cuando todo ya lo tergiversaron." Marina, interview.

21. Ibid.

22. Ibid.

23. Marina, oral history.

24. Dimas was still a senior Sandinista officer, so it seems unlikely Marina was suspected of anything other than prior association with her first husband.

25. Her descriptions of her duties as a correo are referenced in chapter 9.

26. Marina, oral history. Marina and others described a colorful but inaccurate version from Arturo Cruz, Jr., of how Dimas became an insurgent after a fight with General Humberto Ortega at the very beginning of the Revolution. Cruz, Jr., *Memoirs of a Counter-Revolutionary*, 88–89.

27. The towns and locales in the ensuing discussion are not widely known outside Nicaragua. All are in the Rio Coco basin in the heart of the Segovian highlands.

28. Pirata, oral history. Pirata went on to found his own MILPAS group and lead his own Resistance combat unit, the Grupo Pirata, discussed below, the only formation of its kind listed in Resistance status of forces reports.

29. Francisco Rivera Herrera, "Cadejo." U.S. Department of State, *Nicaraguan Biographies*, 55. El Cadejo is a legendary ferocious black dog that attacks unwary victims at night and the principal figure in one of Central America's best known folk stories.

30. Freddy Gadea Zeledon, "Coral," was a campesino from Quilalí who had "fought with the Sandinistas against Somoza from 1977–79 in the Nueva Segovia mountains" before joining the MILPAS in 1979. Anroyce Zelaya Zeledon, "Douglas," was a campesino from Quilalí who served with Dimas and El Danto against Somoza before "rejoining Pedro Joaquín González against the Sandinistas in late 1979 and early 1980." U.S. Department of State, *Nicaraguan Biographies*, 47, 57. Neither La Iguana (The Iguana), Mono (Monkey), nor Gallo (Rooster) are listed in *Biographies*.

31. Oscar Kilo, oral history.

32. Ibid.

33. According to another Milpista. Jimmy Leo, oral history. "Jimmy" was Altamirano's nickname. He was born under the zodiac sign of Leo.

34. Contemporary photographs of Dimas as a Sandinista Milpista fit this description. Author's collection.

35. Hernández Sancho, interview.

36. Rubén, interview. A postwar study by Centro de Investigaciones y Estudios (CIERA), *La Guerra Imperialista: Organización y Participación Popular en el Campo*, vol. 1, states that Dimas's Band was made up of 237 ex-Guardia but then presents data on the social origins of 253 of his Milpistas that demonstrate the opposite by showing that at most three of Dimas's group *may* have been former Guardia. The text does not conform with my findings for this study; the data do. See also Nuñez, ed., *La Guerra*, 237, 253.

37. Hombrito, oral history. The name *Hombrito* (Little Man) refers to his youth and stature.

38. Then still Civil Defense Committees, or CDCs.

39. Hombrito, oral history.

40. Ibid.

41. Name reserved, oral history, Segovian Highlands, December 1994. This former Comando requested anonymity for reasons of personal security. When I interviewed him, he showed me a copy of a "death list" with his name on it and explained that two attempts had already been made on his life.

42. Ibid.

43. The data on which this calculation is based are given in chapter 9.

44. A Nicaraguan pejorative for peasant is *botas de hule*, a joke about the rubber boots peasants wear when working in the mud of their farms.

45. Oscar Kilo, oral history.

46. Marina, oral history.

47. This detachment appears to have made the first MILPAS contact with Argentines, Americans, and exile Guardia. See chapter 7.

48. Oscar Kilo, oral history.

49. Tegucigalpa, Radio America. FBIS VI, 25 July 1980, p. 1, Central America, PA250128.

50. Also known as the Segovia and as the Wangki. Among its tributaries are the Pantasma, Cuá, Chachagua and Wamblan. Most of the places mentioned in connection with the MILPAS war, such as Quilalí, Wiwilí, El Cuá, Kilambé, and El Chipote are in the Rio Coco watershed. The Coco becomes the Nicaragua-Honduras border just north of Wamblan.

51. U.S. Department of State, *Nicaraguan Biographies*, 35.

52. Junta de Reconstrucción de Matagalpa, "Las Milicias en Acción" (author's translation), 14–18. Original version available in the library of the University of California, Berkeley. The Junta no longer exists; therefore, written permission to use the quotation was not obtained.

53. Marina, oral history; Fuerza Democratica Nicaragüense, "Historia de Fuerza Democratica Nicaragüense," 5; and Nuñez, ed., *La Guerra*, 249. Nuñez identifies Herrera by his Sandinista nom de guerre Elias. In U.S. Department of State, *Nicaraguan Biographies*, 35, he is identified as Mamerto Torrera.

54. Marina, oral history.

55. "Muertos del ERN/FDN, diferentes unidades, 1979–90." ACRN archives.

CHAPTER 4

1. Irene. Pronounced *Ee-ray-neh.* In this case a male, not female, first name.

2. Bruce Lee, oral history. Bruce Lee took his nom de guerre from the popular Chinese martial arts film star.

3. That sympathizer's name was given as Sr. Aquila. No further information about his identity was offered.

4. Tigre, oral history.

5. Wiwilí, sometimes spelled *Güigüili.*

6. Tigre, oral history.

7. Discussed in chapter 9.

8. La Chaparra, oral history. *Chaparra* is slang for "Shorty." La Chaparra, whose real name is Elisa María Galeano, is a member of the Galeano clan. About 7 percent of the Resistance Comandos, more than 3,000 combatants, were women, and more than 1,000 were killed. Their role is discussed in Chapter 10.

9. *Chilote:* Green Ear of Corn.

10. Tiro al Blanco, Johnny and Irma are discussed in U.S. Department of State, *Nicaraguan Biographies*, 45.

11. Israel Galeano Cornejo, "Franklyn," another early Milpista. Sometimes spelled "Franklin." Also known as "Franklyn-16." Franklyn was chief of staff of the main Contra army after 1988–89. He died in a suspicious "one-car" accident in 1995.

12. La Chaparra, oral history. She later became a comandante de grupo and instructor at the FDN's Centro de Instrucción Militar (CIM).

13. Oscar Kilo, oral history.

14. Dimas Tigrillo, oral history. U.S. Department of State, *Nicaraguan Biographies*, 45.

15. Jimmy Leo, oral history.
16. Bruce Lee, oral history.
17. Tigre, interview, Managua, 11 June 1996.

CHAPTER 5

1. Encarnación Baldivia. *Tigrillo:* Wild Cat. Tigrillo and Dimas Tigrillo, oral histories.

2. Dimas Tigrillo, oral history.

3. Ibid.

4. Quilalí and Wiwilí lie on either side of the same mountain deep in the Segovian mountains. The suffix *lí,* Chibchan Matagalpan Indian for "beside the stream," is widely encountered among place-names in the Segovias and nearby, such as Quilalí, Wiwilí, Yali, and Danli in nearby Honduras. Incer, *Toponimias Indigenas de Nicaragua.* A ratio of 40:1 non-Guardia to Guardia is consistent with data on the MILPAS in the ACRN archives and also with data published later. See Nuñez, ed., *La Guerra,* 253.

5. Johnny, oral history. Tigrillo went on to command the Rafael Herrera Regional Command, a four-task force formation of some one thousand Comandos. U.S. Department of State, *Nicaraguan Biographies,* 45. He also tells his own story in Brown, ed., *When the AK-47s Fall Silent.*

6. Jimmy Leo, oral history.

7. Ibid.

8. "Creo que si hubiera sido nosotros de la Guardia no se podria haber llevado a cabo un proselitismo tan exitoso. Exito existía porque eramos gente de la montaña, de la zona, y ellos lo podrían ver con sus proprios ojos." Ibid.

9. Ibid.

10. Pirata, oral history.

11. He did not know which language, but Pirata had some knowledge of Sumu and Miskito and said it was neither of those. Wiwilí is within the pre-Columbian Matagalpan, or Misumalpan Chibchan language area. Pirata was born in 1963. Ibid. To remember that his grandfather spoke Matagalpan or another Chibchan language would date its use into the 1970s, suggesting that reports that Chibchan languages in Nicaragua had become extinct by the 1920s may have been premature. Constenla, *Las Lenguas del Area Intermedia,* 17.

12. *Walakitan,* from Kitan, stream; *Walas,* devil or dark. Probably Chibchan Misumalpan, although today the place-name *Walakitan* occurs in an area inhabited by Sumu Indians. The name appears three times in Jinotega. Instituto de Estudios Territoriales (INETER), *Reporte de Toponimos*

Departamentales. There is also a Walakitan Creek in the RAAN that is tributary to the Coco River. Incer, *Toponimia*, 244. The origin of the name
Walakitan is not known, but nouns beginning with the consonant w appear
in Carlos Mantica, *El habla Nicaraguense*, only in Chibchan, not in Nahua
or Spanish.

13. In Nicaragua, *vos* means *you* but is informal. Pirata's description of
the intensely Indian nature of his comarca was particularly detailed.

14. Pirata, oral history. Another instance of a militia unit being created
before the Sandinistas' official militia program was established.

15. Ibid.

16. Ibid.

17. The Grupo Pirata had 43 Comandos as of 28 April 1988. Twelve were
in San Andrés de Bocay, 23 in Yamales, and 10 inside Nicaragua. "Estado
de Fuerza Semanal," Cuartel General Ejercito de la Resistencia, Comando
Estrategico, Seccion de Personal, 28 April 1988, pp. 1, 4. ACRN archives.

18. Pirata, oral history.

19. *Farolín:* Little Lamp. *Paloma:* Dove or Pigeon.

20. Segovia, oral history.

21. Ibid.

22. Five of Segovia's brothers, a sister, and his father eventually became
Comandos.

23. Rufo César Zeledón Castil-Blanco. U.S. Department of State,
Nicaraguan Biographies, 57.

24. Formerly a luxurious Somoza beach hideaway.

25. "Escoja. O tu madre o tu Revolucion." Segovia, oral history.

26. Ibid. Segovia's time of entry into the Resistance is given as April
1981 in U.S. Department of State, *Nicaraguan Biographies*, 56. But this was
when he joined the FDN, not the MILPAS. By April 1981 he had been a
Milpista for almost a year.

27. Segovia, oral history.

28. Segovia went on to serve as a Resistance commander for almost a
decade, becoming a senior comandante of the Segovias Regional Command.
U.S. Department of State, *Nicaraguan Biographies*, 55.

29. Rubén, oral history. Sobalvarro first took the nom de guerre
"Culebra," or Snake, changing it later to "Rubén" in honor of Nicaragua's
premier poet, Rubén Dario.

30. "Esto me molesto mucho." Probably an understatement.

31. *Chilindrín:* Rattle.

32. Made popular by the U.S. Marines during their expeditions to
Nicaragua in the early 1900s, baseball is now Nicaragua's national sport.

33. "Culebra" was to prove a durable nom de guerre. As late as February 1997, three different highland Re-Contra guerrilla groups were being

led by commanders with the pseudonym "Culebra." One was active near El Cuá Bocay, Jinotega. A second was near Matiguás, Matagalpa. A third, with about twenty-five members, was operational near Bocana de Paiwas, RAAS, and led by Denis Rodas Galeano, a member of the Galeano clan. All were part of a new organization known as the Frente Norte 3-80, named after former Contra commander Enrique Bermúdez, "Comandante 3-80."

34. *Calambrito:* Little Cramp.

35. "Porque no? Pues de por si ya eran simpatizantes nuestros." Rubén, oral history.

36. Ibid.

37. A Swiss-German *solidarista,* or Sandinista sympathizer, reached the same conclusion at the same time and place from the opposite side of the process. Keller, *Wiwilí 1980,* 264–66.

38. An example of how campesinos designated targets for the Comandos, rather than the other way around. "New Militias to Protect Literacy Guerrilla," Managua, Domestic Service, 9 April 1980. FBIS VI, 10 April 1980, p. 6, Central America, PA092009.

39. "Officials Discuss Literacy Crusade Problems," Radio Sandino, 9 April 1980. FBIS VI, 11 Apr 80, p. 14, Central America, PS101306.

40. Rubén, oral history.

41. This occurred during a postrevolution wave of killings of former Comando leaders. Due to "uncertainties," his name, like that of Enrique Bermúdez (who was killed in Managua with a professional assassin's pistol), is not among the 708 listed by the OAS as victims of homicides. CIAV, "Denuncias Junio'90/Diciembre'96." Confidential sources. Bermúdez's case was reopened in April of 1997. "Procuraduría ordena reactivar investigacíon de caso Bermúdez," Managua, *La Tribuna,* 25 April 1997.

42. Johnny, oral history, and Resistance personnel files. The U.S. Department of State's *Nicaraguan Biographies* lists five Galeanos, including Johnny, among the "top fighters" of the Resistance. U.S. Department of State, *Nicaraguan Biographies,* 48.

43. Johnny, oral history.

44. La Chaparra and Johnny, oral histories.

45. Johnny, oral history.

46. *La Perrera:* The Dog Kennel.

47. La Chaparra, oral history.

48. Johnny, oral history.

49. In this usage *Don* is an honorific title, not a first name.

50. José Danilo Galeano Rodas, another Galeano clansman. U.S. Department of State, *Nicaraguan Biographies,* 48. A first cousin, Denis Rodas Galeano, was still fighting as a Re-Contra in March 1997 under the nom de guerre "Culebra." Private source.

51. *Relámpago:* Lightning.

52. Ibid.

53. *Tiro al Blanco:* Marksman. A first cousin.

54. U.S. Department of State, *Nicaraguan Biographies,* 88–91.

55. The real name of this "Fernando" is not known, but he was not the Diogenes Hernández Membreño, "Fernando," listed in U.S. Department of State, *Nicaraguan Biographies,* 50.

56. "L-20" would have been a later nom de guerre, indicating that its bearer was one of the earliest Comandos to join the Legión 15 de Septiembre as Legionnaire No. 20.

57. Rio Blanco later became a hotbed of rebellion.

58. Chino-4, oral history.

59. Neither is listed in U.S. Department of Defense, *Gazetteer of Nicaragua.*

60. Johnny, oral history. A different "Aureliano," Manuel Adan Rugama Acevedo, a medical doctor, joined the Resistance in 1981. U.S. Department of State, *Nicaraguan Biographies,* 55.

61. Jhonson, oral history.

62. Jhonson, oral history. He found it amusing to spell his name differently from the more conventional "Johnson."

63. *Juan:23:* John:23, as in the Bible. *El Sordo:* The Deaf One.

64. Dillon, *Comandos: The CIA and Nicaragua's Contra Rebels,* cites Jhonson as a key source.

65. Jhonson, oral history.

66. The three tendencias were known as the Insurrecional, Guerra Popular Prolongada, and Tercerista. It was widely claimed that the Nine Comandantes who came to lead the three tendencias were chosen by their comrades from below, but José "Pepe" Puente claims this is false. He insists that he personally received a telephone call at his Mexico City home from Castro, who was disturbed by continuing dissension and in-fighting among the three tendencias and directed him to select three leaders from each and send them to Havana. Castro intended to require unity as the price of continued Cuban assistance to their movement. The more experienced FSLN leaders were almost all fully engaged in the struggle and could not go. So Puente chose the Nine, rented an airplane, and sent them to Cuba. He says he was shocked when Castro appointed them as the FSLN's new directorate. Puente tells this story in Brown, ed., *When the AK-47s Fall Silent.*

67. Jhonson, oral history.

68. Ibid.

69. CIERA, *La Reforma Agraria en Nicaragua,* 233.

70. Ibid., 233.

71. Raul, interview, Miami, 1993.

72. Confidential source, oral history. The EEBI was actually an elite infantry battalion, not an *escuela*, or school, that was commanded by President Anastacio "Tacho" Somoza's son, also named Anastacio but nicknamed "El Chigüin."

73. Ibid.

74. Pirata, oral history. The "Kaliman," Simeon Aguirrez Torrez, identified in U.S. Department of State, *Nicaraguan Biographies*, 44, is not the same person.

75. *Frijol:* Bean. *Rafaga:* Burst (of automatic weapons fire).

76. *El Cuervo:* The Crow.

77. Tinoco Zeledón and Mike Lima, *Agenda Perpetua*, unpublished manuscript, Segovian Highlands, 1980–1982, author's collection.

78. Tinoco Zeledón and Mike Lima, *Agenda Perpetua*, 14, 49.

79. Ibid., 40.

80. Two of the pistols' serial numbers were WS#7277 and WS#3251. Ibid., 44.

81. This sighting took place on 21 November 1981. It suggests that by then some modern military arms were reaching the MILPAS.

82. Tinoco Zeledón and Mike Lima, *Agenda Perpetua*, 34, 36, 49.

83. FBIS, October 1979–December 1981. It should be noted that FBIS normally reports only on topics that analysts have determined are of policy interest to the United States government. This determination appears to have been made by October 1979. See also International Press Service for Latin America (ISLA).

84. Wheelock, *La verdad sobre la piñata*, 9–21.

CHAPTER 6

1. Chino Lau, oral history. The nickname "Chino" is often given to anyone with a noticeable epicanthic eye fold regardless of ancestry, but in this case Chino Lau is half-Chinese, the son of a Cantonese Chinese diplomat father and Nicaraguan mother.

2. The others were Atenas Ariel and Sagitario. "Informe a Vd. Detalladamente el Estado de Fuerza Reportado por los Proyectos," Jefe de Personal, FDN, 19 January 1982. ACRN archives.

3. "Zebras," unedited document, dated 22 July 1979. Author's collection.

4. ACRN, personnel files, 1981.

5. Johnny II, oral history. Called here "Johnny II" to differentiate him from Denis Galeano Cornejo, whose nom de guerre was also "Johnny."

6. Ibid.

7. Jimmy Leo and Rubén, oral histories.

8. Rubén, interview.

9. "Guerrillas Give Details of Plans of Somoza Gangs," Managua Domestic Service. FBIS VI, 11 April 1980, pp. 13–14, Central America, PA100439.

10. La Castilla, oral history. She had served with Comandante Bravo and withdrew with him from San Juan del Sur, Nicaragua, to La Unión, El Salvador. See also *La Estrella de Nicaragua*, Miami, Florida, 1–15 May 1994, 1A, 7A–8A; 16–31 May, 1994, 1A, 5A, 7B.

11. Reportedly with the knowledge of the Honduran armed forces. La Castilla, oral history. Morales was among those who traveled between Honduras and El Salvador escorting arms shipments. Confirmed by former Honduran military officers. Confidential sources.

12. For an account of the event, see "Asi Mataron al Comandante Bravo," *La Estrella de Nicaragua*, Miami, Florida, 16–31 May 1994, 1A–7A. It is widely believed that senior Sandinista Security Chief Lenin Cerna was present.

13. Chino Lau, oral history.

14. Fighter was one of two graduates of France's St. Cyr Military Academy who were senior Contra officers. The other was Abel Cespedes, "Cyro." At the time, Gomez was in exile. He later commanded Resistance air operations during the war.

15. The identities of those present raise questions beyond the scope of this work. Chester Y. Williams classified the 1978 Guardia as "a medium-deference" institution able to confront Somoza (Williams, "Presidential Leadership in Nicaragua," 135–54), and the officers who formed the Legión were from a group of known dissenters. According to senior American and Nicaraguan officers well informed at the time, Bermúdez had been exiled to Washington by Somoza. Clarridge also says this in *A Spy for All Seasons*, 216. Former Guardia officers explained that the Guardia was divided between nonpolitical officers and Somoza's personal coterie known as the ALAS, for Anastacio, Luis, Anastacio, Somoza. ALAS was a play on words since in Spanish *alas* also means wings that sustain a bird in flight, or in this case a Somoza in power.

16. Fuerza Democratia Nicaragüense, "Historia de Fuerza Democratica Nicaragüense."

17. 4-2, oral history.

18. Ibid.

19. Ibid.

20. In January 1997, Chino-85, under his real name Carlos Garcia, was vice minister of Nicaragua's Ministry of Natural Resources and the

Environment (MARENA), with special responsibilities for the highlands and the Atlantic coast. Chino-85, interview, Managua, 10 March 1997.

21. Chino 85, oral history.

22. Third-country support to the Legión is discussed in chapter 7.

23. Johnny II, oral history.

24. Fuerza Democratia Nicaragüense, "Historia de Fuerza Democratica Nicaragüense," 1.

25. "Clandestine Anti-Sandinista Radio Station Reported Operating," ACAN, Panama City, FBIS VI, 13 May 1980, p. 13, Central America, PA131726.

26. Chino 85, oral history. Clarridge, *A Spy for All Seasons*, 200–201, identifies the Honduran officers providing protection as then Police (FUSEP) Commander Colonel Gustavo Alvarez with the approval of Army Commander General Policarpo Paz. This was confirmed for me by three confidential sources. Alvarez was later Honduran commander in chief.

27. Walter Calderón Lopez, "Comandante Toño." U.S. Department of State, *Nicaraguan Biographies*, 46.

28. The roles played by Argentina and the United States are discussed in more detail in the next chapter on the MILPAS-Guardia alliance.

29. Johnny II, oral history.

30. At the time of this operation in Costa Rica, Pastóra was still a minister in the Sandinista government. Unlike the highlander Resistance, both Southern Fronts were made up of Pacific lowlanders, their combatants being mostly rural peasants or urban workers of Pacific lowland origins. While some came directly to the Southern Fronts from rural areas around the major Pacific lowland cities, most were peasants who had been moved in the 1930s to the region of Nueva Guinea in the Atlantic lowlands from the area of Chinandega as part of an agrarian reform program of the first Somoza. The leaders of these fronts were urban middle– and upper–middle-class politicians or intellectuals, often leftists but not Marxists, from Pacific cities. Pastóra, for example, although a Sandinista leader since the 1960s, was a graduate of Nicaragua's most exclusive upper-class high school, the Jesuit Colegio Centroamericano of Granada. Despite numerous attempts by Pastóra to take overall command and by the leaders of the FDN to establish a single overall headquarters operation, and constant pressure from the CIA to unite, the ethnic, historical, geographic, and social differences between the FDN and the second Southern Front were simply too deep to be bridged. They fought under entirely separate commands throughout the war, the FDN in the central highlands (their homeland), the second Southern Front in the Atlantic lowlands (the home of their peasant supporters). Similar and even deeper differences lay

within the unwillingness of the third large Contra army, the YATAMA Indian force, which operated in the northern and central Atlantic, and two smaller forces, the Indian Sumus de Las Montañas from the rain-forest region of Bocay along the River Coco between the homelands of the FDN and YATAMA, and the Black Creole Floyd Wilson Task Force that was mainly active along the Atlantic littoral from Bluefields north to Prinzapolka and inland along the Rama and Rio Grande de Matagalpa Rivers. Once the United States began providing them with assistance, these forces did receive and use standardized equipment, have largely compatible communications systems, and on occasion even coordinate operations; none, however, ever agreed to a unitary command structure, whether under Pastóra or the FDN. These divisions plagued the Contras throughout the war.

31. "Newsman Reports Troop Deployment to Rivas," Agence France Presse, 31 March 1980. FBIS VI, 31 March 1980, p. 12, Central America, PA310231. "Attacks on Military Posts Reported in West, South," Agence France Presse. FBIS VI, 29 May 1980, p. 12, Central America, PA281225.

32. This is the only instance uncovered of an important Resistance force made up of Pacific lowland campesinos. The later Southern Front was also made up of campesinos of Pacific origin, but most had moved to the Atlantic region during pre-Sandinista agrarian reform efforts.

33. Name withheld, oral history, 5 December 1994. This respondent suddenly came under an extreme threat after the first version of this book was completed in 1997.

34. Name withheld and Johnny II, oral histories.

35. LAW: Light Anti-tank Weapon.

36. Name withheld, oral history.

37. Untitled, handwritten personnel report, ACRN archives, 20 December 1981, S-1. This report also indicates that the Legión was active by then in the United States and Guatemala.

CHAPTER 7

1. See for example, Christian, *Nicaragua: Revolution in the Family*, 24.

2. See for example, Williams, "Presidential Leadership in Nicaragua"; Walter, *The Regime of Anastacio Somoza 1936–1956*; and Strachan, *Family and Other Business Groups*.

3. General Raudáles had been an officer with Gen. Augusto Sandino. He was accompanied by thirty men. Martino, oral history.

4. Mendieta Alfaro, *Olama*, 53–56; Gamboa, *Como fue que no hicimos la revolucion*, 9; Hernández, *El FSLN por Dentro*, 21–22.

5. Gamboa, *Como Fue que no hicimos las revolucion*, 3.

6. Confidential source.

7. Comisión de Asuntos Especiales, *Informe Sobre el Trafico de Armas*, San José, National Congress, 14 May 1981, 7 vols.

8. Suñol, *Insurrección en Nicaragua*, 141.

9. Much of this was detailed by the Department of State in a series of reports. See also Kasten, "Extent and Nature of the Soviet Presence in Nicaragua." Messages quoted verbatim in daily FDN electronic intelligence reports routinely mention the presence of Cuban, Soviet and Eastern Bloc military advisors and even combatants with Sandinista army units in combat zones. An example is at appendix C.

10. "The Soviet Militarization of Nicaragua," *Human Events*, 2 September 1989.

11. "Equipo Militar Suministrado a Nicaragua Hasta la Fecha (Octubre de 1987)" and "Informe de la FAS-DAA para la Reunión Tripartita 1987," Managua, Ejército Popular Sandinista. Classified *Muy Secreto*, or Top Secret. Annexes V, VII and VIII. "Tripartita" refers to Nicaragua, Cuba, and the Soviet Union. Hoover Institution, Stanford University.

12. According to *Fermán Cienfuegos*, the former commander of El Salvador's Frente Faribundo Martí de Liberación Nacional (FMLN), who was responsible for the arsenal, about eighty-three thousand of the Cuban supplied weapons were shipped by the Sandinistas to his forces during the 1980s, several thousand of which were then sent by them to other guerrilla groups. Fermán Cienfuegos, oral history.

13. Alejandro Martínez Saenz, oral history. A chapter by Martínez is also included in Brown, ed., *When the AK-47s Fall Silent*.

14. Chino Lau and 4-2, oral histories.

15. Numerous private sources of three nationalities in four countries. The CIA ignored that portion of a 1992 FOIA request seeking documents on this period.

16. Costa Rican officials confirmed that Montonero guerrillas were active with the Sandinistas' forces in Costa Rica during the 1978–79 war. Confidential sources.

17. The story was told by former Costa Rican Minister of Public Security Juan José "Johnny" Echeverria Brealey who, as a guest of honor of the Sandinistas, witnessed the event and then talked with the Argentine ambassadors to Nicaragua and Costa Rica. Echeverria had been the key Costa Rican in charge of facilitating arms deliveries and other support to the Sandinista Front during the war against Somoza. "Johnny" Echeverria Brealey, interviews, 11, 15 November 1994.

18. Clarridge, *A Spy for All Seasons*, 202.

19. Sworn statements by four Alvarengas describe the family's active support for the rebels, beginning with the MILPAS in early 1980. ACRN archives.

20. Including a former Milpista and another Resistance activist, both of whom asked not to be identified.

21. Argentina was known by the CIA as early as 1979 to be unhappy with the Sandinistas. Clarridge, *A Spy for All Seasons*, 202.

22. Adolfo Calero, interview, 12 March 1997. At the time Calero was the president of the Conservative Party.

23. Doctor Javier, interview, Managua, 11 March 1997.

CHAPTER 8

1. Clarridge, *A Spy for all Seasons*, 208.

2. "Reseña Historica del Surgimiento de la Organización C/R. F.D.N.," Managua, EPS, Dirección de Inteligencia Militar, 1987, 1–3. Classified Muy Secreto. According to the previous chief of personnel (GN-1) of the Guardia, Col. Aurelio Somarriba, in July 1979 total Guardia strength was about 11,000, but only 5,500 to 6,000 were combat troops. The remainder were on the rolls but were actually security guards, administrative personnel, or servants of Guardia officers or government officials. Colonels Federico Mejia and Aurelio Somarriba, telephone interviews, Miami, 14 February 1997. Mejia replaced General Somoza as Guardia commander in July of 1979.

3. Woodward, *Central America*, 263, supports seven thousand, but both numbers appear high.

4. According to officially published data, in 1985 the seven highland departments had a population of 951,341, of whom about 70 percent (665,000) were comarca peasants. INEC, *Anuario Estadístico de Nicaragua 1985*, 9. A second 1996 census suggests the pool was closer to 1.2 million. *Encuesta a Municipios y Comunidades S/Recursos Sociodem. Disponibles* (Ministries of Social Welfare, Education and Health, Managua, 6 April 1996), Project NIC/92 P01 FNUAP/OIM. See also United Nations, *Diagnostico Basico de las Municipalidades* (INFOM, Managua, July 1994), 8 vols.

5. 4-2, oral history.

6. Ibid.

7. They appear to have been successful. A well-informed former senior Sandinista leader said that Dimas had just returned from training in Argentina when he was killed in August 1981. If so, he would have gone to Argentina in June, suggesting he was among the first Milpistas to rally

to the FDN. Confidential source. Confirmed by one other confidential source.

8. Jimmy Leo, Segovia, Pirata, Dimas Tigrillo, and Bruce Lee, oral histories.

9. Abel Cespedes, "Cyro," interview, Managua, 9 June 1996. Cespedes was a Liberal Party official during the 1996 presidential elections and became a senior official in Managua's municipal government in 1997.

10. Juan Ramón Rivas Romero, a former sergeant from Boaco. U.S. Department of State, *Nicaraguan Biographies*, 55. Whether this was by accident or design could not be determined.

CHAPTER 9

1. Angel Sosa, "Emiliano," interview, Managua, 18 November 1994. Sosa is discussed in U.S. Department of State, *Nicaraguan Biographies*, 56.

2. Not included in Status of Forces reports, giving the FDN more combatants than were ever reported.

3. "Handwritten Memoranda on Troop Strengths, 820812." ACRN archives. 820812 stands for 12 August 1982.

4. "Informe de Estado de Fuerzas de FDN al dia 20 de Octubre de 1983," Cuartel General General Fuerza Democratica Nicaragüense, Jefatura de Personal, 20 October 1983. ACRN archives.

5. "Estado de Fuersa [sic] . . . ," Comando Regional Gorge [sic] Salazar NRO (1), FDN, 22 May 1997. ACRN archives.

6. "Estado de Fuerza," Sección de Personal, Cuartel General General de la Resistencia, Estado Mayor, 13 July 1988. ACRN archives.

7. For example, "Volcan, 0940260984, A: Jefe Puerto Cabezas, De: Jefe La Tronquera." The number 0940260984 is a chronological message number assigned by Sandinista army communications. It means that the message was transmitted at 0940 hours (9:40 A.M.) local time, on 26 September 1984. ACRN archives. This possibly unique series contains verbatim message texts in chronological order of both FDN communications and decrypted intercepts of Sandinista army regional headquarters messages. A sample is in appendix A.

8. "Mensajes Recibidos—Venado: Mes Septiembre," ACRN archives. This particular folder contains several thousand copies of FDN radio messages and Sandinista army messages intercepted by FDN communications intelligence.

9. To protect those who were involved from possible reprisals the names, exact numbers, and precise locations, although given in the two messages, are not repeated.

10. "Organización del Apoyo Auxiliar a Fuerzas Clandestinas: Fuerzas Clandestinas," undated but probably, from the context in which it was found, sometime in mid-1982. ACRN archives.

11. "Informe Area Insureccional Nueva Segovia, Nic., A: Jefe de Estado Mayor, De: Cmdte Base Operacional Nicarao," 7 October 1982. ACRN archives.

12. In a region between Estelí and Jinotega.

13. Comandos infiltrating into Nicaragua usually carried from 80 to 90 pounds of supplies on their backs both for their own use and for delivery to Comandos inside. Once inside they became dependent for food, water, and shelter on locally available sources. Captured weapons, munitions, and military materials and equipment were used when possible, since the only other alternative was to depend on rare and often undependable air drops.

14. Throughout the conflict, Comando units regularly reported on the seizure of military materials, especially weapons and munitions. For example, during the month of September 1984, thirty-four messages from Resistance units reported the capture of 268 AK-47 assault rifles and 189,700 rounds of ammunition for FAL rifles, a reminder that captured ammunition is not always useful, nor are nonstandard weapons necessarily easily assimilated into the table of equipment of a unit. "Mensajes Recibidos: Mes: Septiembre-Venado," September 1984. ACRN archives.

15. The following description of highland campesino life emerged from discussions with the Comandos and other active participants and from several visits to the region during 1993–98. It was also discussed at length with Sergio Caramagna, director of CIAV/OAS, and his staff. CIAV/OAS, a protective international agency, had worked in the highlands for seven years directly with the Resistance, especially in the most remote comarcas. He and his staff agreed with the analysis.

16. What psychologists would call both cognitive and affective dissonance.

17. For an extensive discussion of highland kinship patterns see Keller, *Wiwilí*, 88–93.

18. *Guaro:* a locally made alcoholic drink, usually very potent.

19. Miranda and Ratliff, *The Civil War in Nicaragua*, and Jaime Morales Carazo, *La Contra.*

20. Miranda, *Civil War*, 243.

21. "Status of Forces," Cuartel General General Ejército de la Resistencia Nicaragüense, Estado Mayor, Sección de Personal, 6 de Septiembre de 1988. ACRN archives.

22. Exceptions existed in special cases such as Special Forces, medical and air operations, logistics, and the like. Some recommendations or even

interim appointments might be made at the Headquarters level, but these were then normally subject to troop ratification.

23. Colonels Abel Cespedes, Cyro, and Ricardo Lau, Chino Lau, stressed repeatedly that in almost all instances Strategic Headquarters only suggested operations to field units. It did not issue orders for them.

CHAPTER 10

1. "Datos Generales (Personnel File), Juan José Martínez Tercero, no. 332, Legión 15 de Septiembre, Control de Personal," n.d., circa 1983. ACRN archives.

2. Message "Toro, 103005 Sept 84, OK 113505, S20/Marilac, Mensajes recibidos." ACRN archives.

3. Angelica María, oral history and interviews, 1995, 1997.

4. *Jefe de Grupo:* roughly equivalent to a platoon leader or lieutenant.

5. "Historial de los Nombres Que Llevan las Fuerzas de Tarea del Comando Regional 'Salvador Perez'," 6 April 1985. ACRN archives.

6. A Resistance wag once said that some Americans must have thought them strange indeed. Besides size 3 combat boots and child-sized camouflage combat uniforms, they regularly asked for enough panty hose, sanitary napkins, Avon Skin-So-Soft body lotion, and women's underwear to supply their entire army. Some supplies were for women Comandos, but most had broader uses. I was once asked by an officer of TFHA who was new to the project and processing supply requisitions whether the FDN was an army of dwarf transvestites. I assured him they were not and explained that panty hose kept leeches off in swamps, Skin-So-Soft was an excellent insect repellent, women's underwear did not chaff the crotch and also washed and dried quickly, and sanitary napkins dressed battle wounds better than bandages.

7. "Listas de Mujeres que hay a agregar en el estado de fuerzas del comando estrategico," Cuartel General General Ejército de la Resistencia Estado Mayor, 16 April 1989, Cdte Rubén, G-5, Estado Mayor. ACRN archives.

8. "Estado de Fuerza de Mujeres y Niños Que No Estan en el E.F. General del E.R. en San Andres de Bocay," Status of Forces Report, Cuartel General General, Ejército de la Resistencia, Estado Mayor, 6 September 1988; and "Estado de Fuerzas," Cuartel General General Ejército de la Resistencia Nicaragüense, Sección de Personal, 6 September 1988. ACRN archives.

9. Comandos normally joined a unit with which they then perma- nently identified, and parent Regional and Task Forces operating inside

Nicaragua kept behind a detachment in Yamales, Bocay, or another sanctuary area. In addition to maintenance personnel and Comandos on detached assignments, these rear-guard formations usually included the unit's women and children, as well as its wounded and disabled.

10. Author's collection.

CHAPTER 11

1. Chamorro was president from 1990 through 1996.The widow of Pedro Joaquín Chamorro, a martyr of the Somoza period, she was herself descended from eight presidents. A former Sandinista junta member, she had children in both the Resistance and Sandinista camps.

2. Senior Resistance comandantes knew the agreement was distinctly not in their interests and for a while even planned to launch a last-ditch independent offensive out of sheer frustration. Rubén and Emiliano, interviews, Managua, 1994.

3. FDN, YATAMA, Southern Front, and a postwar Central Front. CIAV/OAS, *Numero de Desmovilizados por Lugar de Nacimiento*, Managua, 25 June 1993.

4. The Spanish acronym for UN observers in Central America. ONUCA also had responsibilities in El Salvador and Guatemala.

5. Confidential interviews.

6. Tegucigalpa 08456, 15 May 15 1988, CONFIDENTIAL EXDIS CONTRA.

7. The FDN's estimate. Many former senior comandantes said that hundreds of other FDN deaths-in-action were never officially reported. The other two fronts, YATAMA and the second Southern Front, lost between 1,500 and 2,000.

8. Together with YATAMA, Southern Front, separate Sumu Indian, Internal Front, and Black Creole Contra forces, perhaps 55,000 to 60,000 were Nicaraguan Resistance combatants at one time or another.

9. The Sandinistas' literacy campaign does not appear to have reached the campesinos of the Comandos' home comarcas. Telegram, State 078645, 14 May 1989, CONFIDENTIAL.

10. This profile applies only to Comandos. Data are not available on supporters.

11. CENPAP, *Informe Evaluativo de las Actividades Realizadas por el CENPAP: Septiembre 1990–Septiembre 1992*, Managua, November 1992, 1.

12. Computer run. CIAV/OAS, December 1994.

13. Fifteen of the seventeen had centuries-old histories of violent resistance to outside domination attempts. This is discussed in chapter 12.

14. Personnel dossiers. ACRN archives.

15. The earliest were created by the Legión 15 de Septiembre. A sample dossier is in appendix B.

16. Rushdie, *The Jaguar Smiles.*

17. These Chibchas are not to be confused with the Atlantic lowland Miskitos.

18. The "Linea de la Frontera Espanola" is discussed in chapter 12.

19. CIAV/OAS was kind enough to perform a special computer run for this purpose.

20. Two examples are discussed in chapter 12.

21. Self-identification as an *indio* puts one squarely on the indigenous side of Nicaragua's principal ethnic abyss and also constitutes conscious and informed rejection of the label *mestizo.*

CHAPTER 12

1. *Nahua* is used here for groups from Mexico. *Chibcha* is used for those of South American extraction. Tribal or city-state names are used only when they clarify more than confuse.

2. Leon-Portillo, *Religion de los Nicaraos,* 24–34, including an excellent map showing their route to Nicaragua on page 29.

3. About 4,500 years, according to glotochronology. Constenla, *Las Lenguas.* Microbiologists are also closing in on the identity and timing of the Chibchan presence in Nicaragua. Barrantes, *Evolución en el tropico* and "Mitochondrial DNA 'clock'." Some anthropological studies are also under way.

4. The Pacific lowlands of modern Chiapas, Mexico.

5. See Newson, *Indian Survival,* 88, and two works by Denevan, (ed.) *Native Population* and *Upland Pine Forests.* Other estimates vary. Newson and Denevan both wrote their Ph.D. dissertations on Nicaragua. Newson concentrated on the early Spanish Conquest period. Denevan studied the Segovian highlands. When I consulted with them, both agreed that the Chibchan highlanders largely survived the Conquest but that the Mexica lowlanders did not.

6. Archaeological excavations near the eastern skirt of the Laguna de Tiscapa in central Managua were under way in 1996 under the supervision of Dr. William Lange of the University of Colorado Museum. He was kind enough to give me a guided tour of the excavation and said that what was being uncovered appeared to show that in pre-Columbian times Managua was an extensive line city-village with a population of several tens of thousands distributed, as is modern Managua, along the eastern shore of lake

Xolotlan (Managua). See Guerrero and Soriano, *Managua en sus 40 siglos*, for a history of the city.

7. The Spanish colonial city of Granada was founded next to Jalteba. Nicaragua's other major colonial city, León, was planted in the middle of Imabite.

8. Newson, *Indian Survival*, 48–49.

9. Six key chronicles from the Gil Gonzalez expedition, three from that of Francisco Hernandez de Cordoba, and three on early explorations, can be found in Incer, *Cronicos de Viajeros*.

10. Fowler, "Ethnohistoric Sources on the Pipil-Nicarao of Central America," is a useful critique of the early chronicles.

11. Fowler, *The Cultural Evolution of Ancient Nahua Civilizations*, is an especially rich study of Mexica-Nahua culture and peoples, including of those who inhabited Nicaragua.

12. For discussion see Garcia Bresso's essay "Los Nicarao." There is a schematic of Nicarao society on page 14 of that essay.

13. Radell, *Historical Geography*, 48.

14. Human porters. The use of tamemes was continued by the Spanish for several decades but in a manner that resulted in massive abuse. Sherman, *Forced Native Labor*, 111–28, 220–32. Sherman agrees that Nicaragua was densely populated but puts the total much lower than do Newson and Denevan.

15. Constenla, *Las Lenguas*, 6–8.

16. At least one Chibchan group had stayed in the mountains of the Cosigüina Peninsula. Incer, *Viajes*, 68. Radell identifies them by their Nahua name—*Nahuatlato*. Radell, *Historical Geography*, 37.

17. Incer, *Viajes*, 63, 95.

18. Newson, *Indian Survival*, 64.

19. The route ran through a region known as Taguzgalpa in the highlands from present-day Nicaragua to present-day Honduras through the locales of the modern-day towns of Teotecacinte, Jalapa, Ciudad Nueva, Jinotega, and Nueva Segovia, Nicaragua. Guillen de Herrera, *Nueva Segovia*, 75–76.

20. Newson, *Indian Survival*, 88; Denevan, *Upland Pine Forests*, 283.

21. The Chontales were Chibchas, the Chorotegas Nahua-Mexica.

22. Incer, *Viajes*, 95.

23. Jicaques or Xicaques, Lencas, Kiribíes, and dozens of other groups were among the Chibcha. Especially confusing is early use of the names *Caribes* or *Caribises* to designate the north-central mountain groups and later use of the same names for the related but separate Miskito, Sumu, and Rama. *Indios bravos* or *indios de las montañas* are also used by some for either or even both.

24. See Wheelock, *Raices indigenas de la lucha anti-colonialista;* Guerrero and Soriano's series on the various departments (provinces) of Nicaragua; Romero Vargas, *Persistencia indigena en Nicaragua;* Guillen de Herrera, *Nueva Segovia;* Incer, *Nueva Geografia, Viajes,* and *Toponimias Indigenas de Nicaragua;* and Mantica, *El Habla Nicaragüense.* For primary sources, most chronicles can be found in the seventeen-volume *Colección Somoza: Documentos Para la Historia de Nicaragua,* edited by Andrés Vega Bolaños, and *Nicaragua en los cronistas de la Indias,* edited and annotated by Jorge E. Arellano.

25. Incer, *Viajes,* 19.

26. Cuadra devotes a chapter to this theme, entitled "El Indio que llevamos adentro: Herencias de nuestras dos culturas indigenas madres" ("The Indian-ness We Carry Within: The Heritage of Our Two Indigenous Mother Cultures"). Cuadra, *El Nicaragüense,* 105–10.

27. Bartolome De Las Casas, in Arellano, ed., *Nicaragua el las cronistas de las Indias,* vol. 1, 71.

28. Incer, *Viajes,* 62.

29. Howell, ed., *Prescott: The Conquest of Peru, The Conquest of Mexico, and Other Selections,* 247–48.

30. One of the first FDN bases was Base Nicarao. A Comando Regional Nicarao was later a major resistance unit. "Informe del Estado de Fuerzas," BOP, FDN, 13 September 1982, and "Estado de Fuerzas," Cuartel General General Ejercito de Resistencia Nicaragüense (ERN), 6 September 1987. ACRN archives.

31. Incer, *Viajes,* 47.

32. Diriangen was to be the name of a second early FDN base and another major Comando Regional. "Informe de Fuerzas" and "Estado de Fuerzas," op. cit. The EPS also used the name. For example, its 1987 project to request additional arms was known by the code name Diriangen I-Diriangen II, "Informe de la FAS-DAA . . ." For a discussion of the original Chief Diriangen, see Guerrero and Soriano, *Caciques Heroicos,* 45–53.

33. Incer, *Viajes,* 53–54, 68.

34. Newson, *Indian Survival,* 120.

35. Ibid., 117. Elsewhere Newson adjudges this number as "fairly accurate, since the 'oidor' [a sort of Inspector General sent by the Crown or a Viceroy] was familiar with the area at the time, and it is also fairly consistent with the numbers of tributary Indians registered in the Tasaciones tribute books made for the greater part of Western Nicaragua in 1548." Newson, *Indian Survival,* 86.

36. Ibid., 110. Each tributary Indian represented a household. Using a generous multiplier of four, Managua had been reduced from 40,000 to

slightly over 1,000 and Jalteba from 8,000 to about 800. The drop from 1 million to 30,000 represented a reduction of 97 percent.

37. Newson, *Indian Survival*. See also chap. 4, "Native Depopulation and the Slave Trade, 1527–1578," in Radell, *Historical Geography*. Sherman, *Forced Native Labor*, is dedicated in large part to discussion of this same issue.

38. Newson, *Indian Survival*, 101–107.

39. Sherman, *Forced Native Labor*, 22.

40. Ibid., 21.

41. MacLeod, *Spanish Central America*, 49.

42. Ibid., 51.

43. For a fascinating tour d'horizon of Central America's modern ruling class and its genetic Spanish roots, see Samuel Z[emmuray] Stone, *The Heritage of the Conquistadores: Ruling Classes in Central America from the Conquistadores to the Sandinistas*. Stone provides genealogical tables, especially lines of common descent from Conquistadors. Ten Nicaraguan and 24 Costa Rican presidents are descendants of Juan Vasquez de Coronado. One Guatemalan, 2 Salvadoran, 1 Honduran, 1 Panamanian, 7 Nicaraguan, and 32 Costa Rican presidents are related via Jorge de Alvarado. Twenty-seven leading Sandinistas and 10 Nicaraguan presidents are in the Lacayo family tree. Eighteen are Cuadras. Postwar President Chamorro had 8 in her tree.

44. Newson, *Indian Survival*, 12.

45. There was a small exception around the gold mining area of Nueva Segovia.

46. MacLeod, *Spanish Central America*, 206.

47. The population of Nicaragua did not recuperate to its 1520s levels until about 1950, and Nicaragua still has labor shortages at harvest time.

48. Those interested in pursuing this issue are referred especially to studies by MacLeod, Newson, and Sherman.

49. Newson, *Indian Survival*, 92.

50. Incer, *Viajes*, 68.

51. See Gould, "La Raza Rebelde," 69–117.

52. Cuadra, in *El Nicaragüense*, reviews this process.

53. Gould estimates that as recently as 1920, 15 to 20 percent of the population of Nicaragua, or 125,000 people, mostly in the highlands, retained their indigenous ethnic consciousness and Indian (not "indio") identities. His is a narrower definition than the one used in this book. Gould, "¡Vana Ilusion!", 3.

54. Ibarra, "Los Matagalpa a principios del siglo XVI," 233.

55. Protestantism has been making inroads. Martínez, *Las sectas en Nicaragua*, 63–65.

56. Oral Histories, *Pirata* and *Name Withheld*.

57. *Indios bravos:* Wild Indians.

58. The line of the Spanish frontier. Guerrero's Chontal-Chorotega line appears accurately to delineate the Mexica-Chibcha divide. Guerrero and Soriano, *Los 9 tribus*, 43. Incer's version follows the commercial road between Nicaragua and Honduras described earlier, but Chibcha also dominated in the mountains to its west. Incer, *Viajes*, 6.

59. Incer mentions major early Spanish-Chibchan confrontations in 1524, 1527, 1547, 1560, 1597, 1603, 1608, 1610, 1611, 1623, 1674, 1703, 1713, 1741, 1743, and 1780. Incer, *Viajes*, 83, 252–334. In their monograph on Matagalpa, Guerrero and Soriano dedicate twelve pages to short synopses of numerous clashes and other Indian problems in that province during the 1600s, 1700s and 1800s. Their monographs, *Nueva Segovia, Jinotega, Boaco, Chontales, Estelí*, and *Madríz* include similar lists. Wheelock, in *Raíces*, mentions clashes through 1881. Gould, in "!Vana Ilusion!" lists nineteenth- and twentieth-century incidents as recent as 1954.

60. The town and department of Nueva Segovia should not be confused. The town is now Ciudad Antigua. The department remains Nueva Segovia. Guillen, *Nueva Segovia*, 36–40.

61. United Nations Development Program, *Diagnóstico Básico de las Municipalidades: I Region "Las Segovias,"* vol. 2. For chronicles of the travails of early colonial Nueva Segovia, see Guerrero and Soriano, *Monografia de Nueva Segovia*, and Guillen de Herrera, *Nueva Segovia*, 37–44.

62. Guillen de Herrera, *Nueva Segovia*.

63. Mentioned several times earlier in connection with MILPAS activities in 1979–81.

64. Guillen de Herrera, *Nueva Segovia*, 256. Jicaques and Lencas were Chibchan tribes.

65. Ibid. See also Guillen de Herrera, *Nueva Segovia* and Guerrero and Soriano, various monographs.

66. Cuá, also know as Cuá Bocay. *Wiwilí* is sometimes spelled *Güigüili*. This list correlates closely both with the comarcas in which the MILPAS rebellion started and the locales to which the highest number of Comandos returned in 1990.

67. Since the nineteenth century, the term *Zambo* has not been in general usage. However, it implies a mixture of African black and Miskito Indian that has not disappeared. One top commander of YATAMA was a Black Creole/Miskito known as Comandante Samba (his real name was Carlos Kennard Hodgson Moody). U.S. Department of State, *Nicaraguan Biographies*, 50.

68. Incer, *Viajes*, 327–401.

69. Burns, *Patriarch and Folk*, 31.

70. Ibid., 31.

71. Ibid., 34.

72. Ibid., 34, 156.

73. Ibid., 157.

74. The elite united in 1977–79 to rid itself of descendants of Bernabé Somoza. In that instance the death of another patriarch, Pedro Joaquín Chamorro, played a key role in uniting them.

75. Guerrero and Soriano, *Caciques Heroicos*, 87.

76. Ibid., 92–93.

77. Ibid., 95.

78. Catholic lay brotherhoods of indios. They have served the indios for centuries as one of a few socially accepted institutions through which their indio identity and values could be transmitted from generation to generation.

79. Gould, "!Vana Illusion!". See also his "La Raza Rebelde" and *To Lead as Equals*.

80. Gould, "!Vana Illusion!", 403

81. Ibid., 402–409.

82. Ibid., 24.

83. Ibid., 393–94. Emphasis in the original.

84. Ibid., 397.

85. Ibid., 4.

86. Emphasis added.

87. Schroeder, "Patriots, Peasants, and Process."

88. On his mother's side.

89. In English, Wheelock's title would be *The Indigenous Roots of the Anti-Colonial Struggle in Nicaragua from Gil Gonzalez to Joaquin Zavala (1523–1881)*. This places Wheelock squarely within the tradition of elite hegemonic discourse as described by Gould.

90. Eugenia Ibarra, interview, San José, 1994.

CHAPTER 13

1. The upper class of this study. Adams, *Cultural Surveys*, 195.

2. Ibid., 195.

3. Strachan, *Family and Other Business Groups*, 9, 16.

4. Stone, *Heritage*, 45.

5. Burns, *Patriarch and Folk*, 31.

6. Joaquín Cuadra Lacayo, commanding general of the Nicaraguan army in 1997, is an excellent example. A linear descendant on both sides

of Spanish conquistadores and Nicaraguan presidents, his father, Joaquín Cuadra Chamorro, is known as The Prince of Calle Atravesada. (Calle Atravesada is a grand avenue that marks the heart of Granada's aristocracy.) Jirón, *Quien es Quien*, 122–25. Cuadra was named commanding general of the army by his first cousin, President Violeta Chamorro. He was supported by six Sandinista "Spanish" senior officers popularly known as "Los Cheles," the White Guys.

7. Radell, *Historical Geography*, 264, 240.

8. Strachan, *Family and Other Business Groups*, 9.

9. In 1986, Alfredo F. Pellas was reportedly still "one of the richest men in Central America." Jirón, *Quien es Quién*, 308–12. His mother and wife are Chamorros.

10. Strachan, *Family and Other Business Groups*, 10.

11. He was with the Harvard Business School's Instituto Centroamericano de Administracion de Empresas (INCAE). INCAE has since been moved to Costa Rica.

12. For discussion in greater depth, see Brown, *Causes of Continuing Conflict in Nicaragua*, 19–23.

13. Adams, *Cultural Surveys*, 197.

14. Squier, *Waikna;* Conzemius, *Ethnographic Survey of the Miskito and Sumu Indians;* Nietzchmann, *Between Land and Water* and *Caribbean Edge*.

15. Pataky, *Nicaragua desconocida*. Pataky was for many years a senior official of Somoza's intelligence services. He is named repeatedly as a source in Stephen Kinzer's *Blood of Brothers*.

16. It is interesting that those demanding independence are mostly former Sandinistas. Confidential source, June 1996.

17. Escobar, Valverde and Rojas, "Situacion de los habitantes de la zona del Caribe de Nicaragua."

18. Southern Indigenous Creole Community of Nicaragua (SICC), *The Origins and Development of the African-Ancestry Ethnic Groups of the Atlantic Coast of Nicaragua*. Author's collection.

19. United Nations Development Program (UNDP), *Nicaragua: Poblacion Absoluta y Relativa*, 12–13.

20. Data were drawn from a wide variety of sources, including scattered documents, references and interviews. The most extensive published sources used were Jirón, *Quien es Quién;* Samuel Stone, *Heritage;* U.S. Department of State, *Nicaraguan Biographies;* and David Nolan, *FSLN*, especially appendix 2, 137–54.

21. It might be argued that petit bourgeois like the Ortegas were less prominent in the Sandinista hierarchy than aristocrats, but they were certainly not proletarians or peasants.

CHAPTER 14

1. "Possible Sandinista Killing Blow into Honduras," Memorandum, ARA, Elliott Abrams to the Secretary of State, SECRET/SENSITIVE, Action Memorandum, 7 March 1988.

2. A videotape I made during the battle shows me visiting Bermúdez at headquarters and then visiting the front lines with him. Author's collection.

3. "Sitrep: Situation at Bocay as of 1000 Hours Local March 18," telegram, Embassy Tegucigalpa 04637, March 1990, SECRET EXDIS CONTRA.

4. "Resistance Forces Depend on Peasants: Sandinistas Enhance Military Position," Embassy Managua 03356, May 1988, CONFIDENTIAL, paragraphs 12, 16, 17, 20.

5. Ibid., paragraph 23.

6. Author's collection.

7. "Nicaragua Resistance—Snapshot of the NR (ERN/North) on March 8, 1988 Visit to San Andrés de Bocay," Embassy Tegucigalpa 04046, SECRET EXDIS CONTRA. Message sent from my Special Liaison Office (SLO) just before the 10 March attack on Bocay.

8. "Resistance: Interview with Jorge Salazar II Commander," Embassy Tegucigalpa 14415, August 1990, SECRET EXDIS CONTRA. SLO message.

9. The lack of medical attention inside resulted in unusually high death rates among the wounded.

10. Confidential source, 1995.

11. At a public presentation by him and Carter National Security Council (NSC) advisor Robert Pastor during the February 1992 conference of the Latin American Studies Association (LASA) in Los Angeles. The author was present. The State Department later claimed that no verbatim text exists.

12. U.S. Department of State, *Nicaraguan Biographies*, 55.

13. Confidential sources.

14. "Resistance Prospects: The View from Yamales," Embassy Tegucigalpa 17132, September 1990, SECRET EXDIS CONTRA. SLO message.

CHAPTER 15

1. "A Visit to Contra Country," telegram, Embassy Managua 05371, August 5 1990, CONFIDENTIAL.

2. Ibid.

3. Cardinal Miguel Obando y Bravo, interview, Managua, 10 December 1994.

4. Brown, *Causes of Continuing Conflict*, 24–25.

5. General Joaquín Cuadra Lacayo, chief of staff of the Nicaraguan army, reported it had been reduced from 90,000 to 14,500. "Gral. Cuadra promete lealtad al nuevo gobierno," *La Prensa*, Managua, 19 October 1996, A10.

6. About $900 million in bilateral aid, the remainder arrived via international programs, bank loans (Interamerican Development Bank [IDB], International Bank for Reconstruction and Development [IBRD, better known as the World Bank], and others), multilateral programs, and American budget support for programs of the UN, OAS, and others.

7. *Nicaragua—Economic Fact Sheet*, Managua, U.S. Embassy, March 1997, 1.

8. Brown, *Causes of Continuing Conflict*, 31–32.

9. See CIAV/OAS, "Denuncias por organización del autor de los hechos—Desmovilizados de la RN y familiares—Junio'90/Diciembre '96," and *Nicaragua: La Frontera del Conflicto*, for in-depth studies of the situation.

10. Confidential sources, interviews, Managua, June 1996.

11. Asociación Nicaragüense Pro-Derechos Humanos (ANPDH), interview, Managua, 6 June 1996.

12. *Compa* was slang for *companero, comrade*, or *compadre*, the opposite of *Comando*. The pejorative opposite of Contra was *piri* or *piricuaque*, Miskito Indian for rabid dog.

13. *Revueltos:* scrambled, mixed together.

14. OAS, *La Frontera*, 3.

15. Underlining in the OAS original. The OAS's 3-in-10 estimate is close to the 37 percent of Nicaragua's population living in the 26 rural Segovian Resistance municipios (counties) that were almost disenfranchised in 1996 (see chapter 6).

16. OAS, *La Frontera*, 5.

17. Some of the shading also touches the second Southern Front. No YATAMA area is marked.

18. A comparable problem existed in the Indian Atlantic but was not addressed by the process.

19. International Republican Institute (IRI), *Nicaragua: Ad Hoc Voter Registration Observation Report, June/July 1996*.

20. Roberto Mayorga-Cortes, "Nicaragua pide elecciones libres, garantizadas y transparentes," *Diario Las Americas*, Miami, 19 October 1996, A4. Mayorga-Cortes was Nicaraguan ambassador to the United States at that time.

21. Multiple private conversations with observers from several delegations in Managua during the process.

22. Former two-term Democratic governor of Nevada "Mike" O'Callaghan, who has observed dozens of difficult elections from Israel to Kurdistan, as well as Nicaragua's 1990 election as a Carter Center observer.

23. Chontales, Boaco, Matagalpa, Jinotega, Estelí, Madríz, Nueva Segovia, Rio San Juan, and the Region Autonoma del Atlantico Sur (RAAS). *Población por Departamentos, Censos 1971 y 1995*, Managua, Ministerio de Accion Social, June 1996.

24. An official of one of the ministries explained that unlike partisan elected officials, providers of government health, education, and welfare must base their programs on real numbers rather than on "politically useful estimates." Confidential source, Managua, June 1996.

25. "Cuadro 2. Encuesta a Municipio/Comun," Managua, Ministerio de Acción Social, April 1996. This is an abstract from the full second census, which was done under UN auspices, Proyecto NIC/92/PO1-FNUAP/OIM, 1995–96, with USAID support. The record of the second census that, as of March 1997 was still not public, runs about 2,000 computer print-out pages. The author was given a sample of 97 pages. As of the October 1996 national elections, the UN had still not shared it with the OAS, even though the latter was responsible for monitoring the elections, nor had AID shared it with the American Embassy in Managua.

26. For example, the government's Instituto de Estudios Territoriales (INETER) was in the process of creating a new gazetteer of Nicaragua place-names to replace the one destroyed by the Sandinistas when they left office. The second census contains the most complete list of place names available in Nicaragua, but INETER was denied access to it. Confidential sources.

27. "Cuadro 9. Población de 15 años y mas segun sexo, por Departamento y Municipio en los Censos de 1971 y 1995," Managua, Ministerio de Acción Social, April 1996. The voting age is fifteen.

28. Three well-informed sources—a former Sandinista leader, an American academic, and a third-country intelligence operative—each described the plan to observers several months before this was to take place. It was these warnings that generated demand for an ad hoc registration process under international scrutiny. Confidential sources.

29. Brown, "Who Will Keep Nicaragua's October Elections Honest?", *Wall Street Journal*, 6 October 1997, A15.

30. As the results of informal polling done in connection with this study had indicated would happen.

CHAPTER 16

1. For a synopsis of pressures exerted by the Sandinistas during the 1990 process, see Asociación Nicaragüense Pro-Derechos Humanos (ANDPH), *Foreign Observers in the Labyrinth of Nicaraguan Elections*,

Managua, 15 February 1990. The ACRN archive also contains hundreds of reports from units inside Nicaragua on incidents taking place.

2. Ministro de Gobernación. There is no precise equivalent in the American system.

3. Although the case against him was dubious and his separation generated considerable bitterness. Confidential source.

4. Confidential sources.

5. The stories are told by Morales in his 1989 book *La Contra*, which focuses on the early Comandos.

6. U.S. Department of State, *Nicaraguan Biographies*, 40.

7. Fernando Avellano.

8. Walter Calderón Lopez, "Comandante Toño." U.S. Department of State, *Nicaraguan Biographies*, 46.

9. U.S. Department of State, *Nicaraguan Biographies*, 55.

10. Adolfo Calero, interview, Managua, 12 March 1997.

11. Confidential conversations, Managua, March 1997.

CHAPTER 17

1. Guevara, *The Bolivian Diary of Ernesto Che Guevara.*

2. Alarcón Ramírez, *Memorias de un soldado Cubano*, 82–93.

3. *Operation Zapata*, 4.

4. Kornbluh, ed., *The Secret CIA Report*, 117.

5. Hersey and Blanchard, *Management of Organizational Behavior*, 9–14, 23.

6. Daly, *Sex, Evolution and Behavior*, and Daly and Wilson, *Homicide.*

7. Jackson, "Ethnicity," in Ryan, ed., *Ethnic Conflict and International Relations*, 205–33.

8. Ryan, ed., *Ethnic Conflict and International Relations*, 6–7.

9. Deutsch and Shichman, "Conflict: A Social Psychological Perspective," in Herman, *Political Psychology*, 221–22.

10. Serra, *El Movimiento Campesino*, 258–59.

11. Rakowska–Harmstone, "Chickens Coming Home to Roost," 523–29.

CHAPTER 18

1. Pisani, *Prophets*, 13, 20, 38, 70–71, 76, 90.

2. Le Blanc, "Workers and Revolution," table 9, "Occupation of Participants in Nicaraguan Revolution," 295.

3. Echeverria Brealey, interviews.

4. Strachan, *Family and Other Business Groups.*
5. Vilas, "Family Affairs."
6. Ibid.

GLOSSARY: TERMS AND ABBREVIATIONS

ACRN: Asociación Cívica Resistencia Nicaragüense (Nicaraguan Resistance Civic Association). Veterans association of former Comandos and their families.

ANPDH: Asociación Nicaragüense Pro-Derechos Humanos (Nicaraguan Association for Human Rights).

BLC: Batallón de Lucha Irregular (Unconventional Warfare Battalion).

Chibcha: Indian group that occupied Nicaragua east of the lakes before, during, and after the Spanish conquest.

Chilotes: Peasant slang for the combatants of the MILPAS Anti-Sandinista People's Militias. A milpista guerrilla of the MILPAS.

CIAV, CIAV/OEA, CIAV/OAS: Comisión Internacional de Apoyo y Verificación (International Commission for Verification and Support, Organization of American States).

CIM: Centro de Instrucción Military, of the FDN.

Comandante: In the Resistance, commander of a Comando Regional (CR) or Fuerza de Tarea (TF), senior staff officer, Member of Council of Commanders. In the FSLN and the EPS, a guerrilla commander during the anti-Somoza war or senior military member of political hierarchy.

Comando: Resistance combatant, Contra. Sometimes written C/R or c/r. C/R is also sometimes used to mean Comando Regional (see below). Meaning can often only be distinguished by context.

Comando Regional (CR) (Regional Command): Resistance unit comparable to a regiment. Sometimes written C/R. Can often be distinguished from C/R used to mean Comando only by context.

Comarca: The mountain *indio* term for home or community, usually a settlement area without a nucleus. Also a mountain valley. The smallest unit of local government.

Compa: Combatant of the Sandinista armed forces. Short for *compañero* or *comadre;* or for *compadre,* godfather or close companion. See also Piri.

Consejo de Comandantes Regionales: Council of Regional Commanders. FDN's ultimate authority.

Contra Army: Popular collective term for the five armed Nicaraguan Resistance armies: FDN, YATAMA, Frente Sur, Sumos de Las Montañas, and Floyd Wilson TF. Most often applied to the largest, the FDN.

Contra War: 1979–90 armed rebellion against the Sandinista Revolution.

Contra Counterrevolutionary: Pejorative for Comando. Sometimes written C/R or c/r.

Correo(s): Intelligence runners, guides.

EPS: Ejército Popular Sandinista (Sandinista People's Army).

ERN: Ejército de Resistencia Nicaragüense (Nicaraguan Resistance Army). Official 1986–90 name of the FDN.

FDN: Fuerza Democratica Nicaragüense (Nicaraguan Democratic Force). Largest Resistance army.

Frente Revolucionario Sandino (ERS): 1948–58 anti-Somoza guerrilla movement.

FSLN: Frente Sandinista de Liberacíon Nacional (Sandinista National Liberation Front).

Fuerza de Tarea (FT, F/T): Task force. Company-sized Resistance unit.

Guardia Nacional (GN): National Guard. The Nicaraguan army during the Somoza period.

HAF: Honduran Armed Forces.

Indio: Term used in this book for mostly Indian mestizos of highland Nicaragua.

Legión 15 de Septiembre: 15th of September Legion. Exile paramilitary organization created in December 1980. Became the FDN in August 1981.

Mestizo: Of mixed Spanish-Indian genetic origins.

MILPA: Milicias Populares Anti-Somocistas (People's Anti-Somoza Militia). A Sandinista Segovian highland guerrilla battalion that fought as part of the Sandinista northern Carlos Fonseca Front against the Somoza regime. Its combatants were called *milpistas.* Also a play on words, as a *milpa* is also an indio cornfield.

MILPAS: Milicias Populares Anti-Sandinistas (People's Anti-Sandinista Militia). The first armed Resistance group. A successor movement to the Sandinista MILPA, made up of Segovian highland peasants and led by former Sandinista guerrillas. Its combatants were also called *milpistas*.

Milpas War: May 1979–82 highland peasant rebellion.

Milpista(s): Combatant of the MILPA and/or MILPAS.

MININT: Ministry of the Interior. State security forces.

Miskito: Main Indian tribe of Atlantic Nicaragua.

Nahua: Main Indian group in pre-Columbian Pacific Nicaragua.

ONUCA: Observadores de las Naciones Unidas en Centroamerica (United Nations Observers in Central America). UN military disarmament and ceasefire observers.

Piri: Comando pejorative for Sandinista combatants. From *piricuaque,* Miskito Indian for rabid dog.

RN: Resistancia Nicaragüense, civilian political movement.

TF, T/F: Task Force.

TFHA/AID: Task Force for Humanitarian Assistance, U.S. Agency for International Development (AID).

YATAMA: Yapti Tasba Masraka Nani Asla Takanka (Main Indian Resistance Army). Successor of Miskitoa, Sumus Ramas United (MISURA), Miskitos, Sumos, Ramas, and Sandinistas United (MISURASATA), and United Indigenous Peoples of Nicaragua (KISAN).

BIBLIOGRAPHY

ARCHIVES

Archivo General del Gobierno de Guatemala, 1/1, 46–48, Francisco de Posada. *Relación Geográfica del Partido de Chontales y Sébaco, 1740.*

Asociación Civica Resistencia Nicaragüense (ACRN). Author's collection. Approx. 265,000 pages.

Comisión de Asuntos Especiales. *Informe Sobre el Trafico de Armas* [Report on Arms Trafficking]. Departamento Archivo, Investigaciones y Tramite, Archivado A 41 E 7677, Expediente 8768, 1/8 through 6/8. National Congress, San José, Costa Rica, 14 May 1981. Approx. 3,000 pages.

Instituto de Estudios Territoriales (INETER), Nicaragua. *Reporte de Toponimias Departamentales: Jinotega. Matagalpa, Nueva Segovia.* Computer run. Managua, 17 March 1997. Author's collection. Approx. 65 pages.

U.S. Agency for International Development. Task Force for Humanitarian Assistance (TFHA/AID). Freedom of Information and Privacy Act (FOIA) releases. Author's collection. Approx. 210,000 pages.

U.S. Defense Mapping Agency, map series. 1:50,000. Nicaragua and Honduras.

U.S. Department of State. Freedom of Information and Privacy Act (FOIA) releases. Approx. 30,000 pages.

PRINTED DOCUMENTS

Asociación Nicaragüense Pro-Derechos Humanos (ANPDH).
Los Cementerios Clandestinos en Nicaragua. Managua, September 1991.
Foreign Observers in the Labyrinth of Nicaraguan Elections. Managua, 15 February 1990.
Problematica del Norte. Managua, 1991.
Raices de la Recontra: Casos de Jalapa y Corinto Finca. Managua, September 1991.
Six-Month Report on Human Rights in the Nicaraguan Resistance. San José, Costa Rica, July 1987.
Second Six-Month Report on Human Rights in the Nicaraguan Resistance. San José, Costa Rica, January 1988.
Violaciones de Derechos Humanos Cometidas por el Gobierno de Nicaragua. Managua, January 1988.
Bermúdez Varela, Enrique. *Causas Psicosociales de la Subversión, Trabajo Individual.* Interamerican Defense College. Washington, D.C., April 1976.
Comisión Internacional de Apoyo y Verificación, Organization of American States (CIAV/OAS).
Cuadros estadisticos del proceso de Desmovilización y repatriación en Nicaragua. 27 January 1991.
Homicidios contra desmovilizados R.N. y sus familiares: Junio '90/Agosto '95. Managua, 4 Sepember 1995.
Informe estadistico de denuncias: Desmovilizados, de la Resistencia y sus Familiares: Junio '90/Noviembre '94. Managua, December 1994.
Informe estadistico de denuncias por homicidio: Demovilizados de la Resistencia y familiares (Junio '90/Marzo '96). Managua, April 1996.
List of Murders and Assassinations. Programa de Seguimiento y Verificación de Derechos y Garantias (PSV). Managua, 23 June 1993.
Nicaragua: La Frontera del Conflicto. Managua, September 1995.
Numero de desmovilizados por lugar de nacimiento. Computer run. Managua, June 1993.
Comisión Tripartita. *Primer informe de avance de la Comisión Tripartita.* Managua, 1992.
Consejo Supremo Electoral, Republica de Nicaragua. *Elecciones 1996.* Unbound advance copy, 357 pages.
Ejército de Resistencia Nicaragüense (ERN). *Six Month Report From the Legal Counsel and the Military Prosecuting Office of the Army of Nicaraguan Resistance.* In Sanctuary, Legal Counsel of the Army of the Nicaraguan Resistance, January 1988. Author's collection.

Fuerza Democratica Nicaragüense (FDN).
  Codigo de Conducta del FDN. In Sanctuary, FDN National Directorate,
  ca. 1985. Author's collection.
  El Libro Azul y Blanco. In Sanctuary, 1985. Author's collection.
International Republican Institute (IRI). *Ad Hoc Voter Registration Observa-
  tion Report June/July 1996*. Washington D.C., 5 August 1996.
MISURA. *Menorias étnicas denuncian genocidio, Nicaragua 1979–1984*.
  Lakia Tara, Honduras, Council of Elders (Mullins Tilleth, Wycliff
  Diego, Stedman Fagoth Muller, Tefilo Archibold, and Enrique López),
  ca. 1984.
RAND Corporation.
  *The Nicaraguan Resistance and U.S. Foreign Policy Report on a May 1987
  Conference*. R-3678-OSD/AF/A, Santa Monica, Calif., June 1989.
  Nicaraguan Security Policy, Trends and Directions, R-3532-PA&E. Santa
  Monica, Calif., January 1988.
Resistencia Nicaragüense.
  Refugiados, desarriagados y desplazados de guerra. San José, Costa Rica, 1988.
  La Resistencia Nicaragüense, 1987. n.p.
Southern Indigenous Creole Community of Nicaragua (SICC). *The Origins
  and Development of the African-Ancestry Ethnic Groups of the Atlantic Coast
  of Nicaragua and Their Experience under the Sandinista Revolution*. Miami,
  30 January 1987.
United Nations Development Program (UNDP). *Diagnostico Basico de las
  Municipalidades*. 8 vols. Managua: INIFOM, 1994.
U.S. Agency for International Development (AID).
  Nicaraguan Democratic Resistance. Tegucigalpa, 1989.
  Emphasis on Health. Managua, June 1993.
U.S. Department of State.
  *Comandante Bayardo Arce's Secret Speech Before the Nicaraguan Socialist
  Party (PSN)*. Pub. 9422, Interamerican Series 118, March 1985.
  *Crackdown on Freedom in Nicaragua and Profiles of Internal Opposition
  Leaders*. August 1986.
  *Documents on the Nicaraguan Resistance Leaders, Military Personnel, and
  Program*. Special Report No, 141, March, 1986.
  Nicaraguan Biographies: A Resource Book. 2d edition. Special Affairs
  Report 142, March 1986.
  Nicaraguan Contra Pamphlets. Mexico and Central America Social
  Ephemera, 1990.
U.S. General Accounting Office (GAO). *Central America: Humanitarian
  Assistance to the Nicaraguan Democratic Resistance*. Washington, D.C.:
  GAO/NSIAD-90-62, January 1990.

PRESS SERVICES

International Service for Latin America (ISLA). Select U.S. major press reports. Annual bound volumes. 1979–1982.

U.S. Foreign Broadcast Information Service (FBIS) VI. Central America. Daily summaries, selected articles, and broadcasts of the Latin American press. 1979–1981. Microfiche.

ORAL HISTORIES AND INTERVIEWS

Note: Oral histories and interviews were conducted by the author. Subjects are listed according to their noms de guerre, followed by their real names (in parentheses). Asterisks indicate subjects known primarily or exclusively by their real names.

Oral Histories

4-2 (Filemón Espinal), Managua, November 1994
Angelica María (Saris Peréz), Miami, Fla., March 1998
Blas (Salomón Osorno Coleman), Managua, March 1995
Britton (Israel Rocha Vásquez), Managua, November 1994
Bruce Lee (Ernán Úbeda), Managua, December 1994
Cairo (José Benito Cáceres), Managua, November 1994
Chino-4 (José Antonio Aguirre), Zamora, December 1994
Chino-85 (Carlos Garcia), Managua, November 1994
Chino Lau (Ricardo Lau Castillo), location withheld, January 1995
Dimas (Pedro Joaquín González), reconstructed from interviews, Nicaragua and Honduras, 1994–96
Dimas Tigrillo (Francisco "Chico" Baldivia), La Concordia, December 1994
Douglas (Anroyce Zelaya Zeledon), 1995
Emiliano (Angel Sosa), Managua, November 1995
Fermán Cienfuegos (Eduardo Sancho Castañeda), San Salvador, El Salvador, August 1998
Hernández Sancho, Plutarco Elías* (nom de guerre = Comandante Marcial), San José, Costa Rica, September 1997
Hombrito (Fanor Pérez Mejia), Jinotega, December 1994
Invisible (Rodolfo Ampie), Managua, December 1994
Isaac (Denis Díaz), Tegucigalpa, December 1994
Jackson (Julio César Sotelo), Managua, November, 1994
Jhonson (Luis Fley), Managua, November 1994

Jimmy Leo (Fremio Altamirano), Managua, November 1994
Johnny (Denis Galeano Cornejo), Managua, December 1994
Johnny II (Guillermo Yubank), Managua, November 1994
José (José Filadelfia Rivas), Managua, November 1994
La Castilla (Linda Morales), Miami, Fla., August 1995
La Chaparra (Elisa María Galeano Cornejo), Managua, November 1994
La China (Berta Chavez), Managua, November 1994
Marina (Andrea Pinell), Jinotega, December 1994
Martínez Saenz, Alejandro* (nom de guerre = Comandante Martínez), San
    José, Costa Rica, September 1998
Mike Lima (Luis Moreno Payán), Miami, Fla., August 1995
Pérez Bustamante, Alejandro,* El Súngano, 1998
Puente León, José Obidia,* Mexico City, March 1998
Oscar Kilo (Orlando Algava), Managua, November 1994
Pirata (José Noél Herrera), Estelí, November 1994
Pryor (Juan Rodríguez Campos), Managua, November 1994
Rubén (Oscar Sobalvarro), Managua, December 1995
Segovia (José María Rodriguez), location withheld, November 1994
Tigre (Oscar Calderon), Managua, November 1994
Tigrillo (Encarnación Baldivia Chavarria), Matagalpa, August 1998
Zúñiga Duran, Carlos Manuel,* San José, Costa Rica, September 1997
Ten others, identities and locations withheld.

Interviews

Abuelito, real name withheld, ca. November 1989
Angelica María (Saris Pérez), 1995, 1997
Bermúdez, Elsa Itali vda de,* 1990–99
Calero, Adolfo,* 1992, 1999
Capi Luque (Capt. Leonel Luque),* 1994
Caramagna, Sergio,* 1992–99
Chino-85 (Carlos Garcia), 1997
Chino Lau (Ricardo Lau Castillo), 1995
Coleman, Laura,* May 1998
Comandante Wilmer (Maximinimo Rodríguez), 1994.
Cyro (Abel Cespedes),* 1992–99
Doctor Javier, real name withheld, 1997
Douglas, Gen. Ian,* 1992–2000
Echeverria Brealey, Juan José ("Johnny"),* 1994
Emiliano (Angel Sosa), 1992–95
Gersony, Robert,* dates withheld
Guidi, Alejandro,* 1994–99

Hernández Sancho, Plutarco Elías,* 1994–99
Herrera Zúñiga, René,* 1992–98
Ibarra, Eugenia,* 1994
Lange, Frederick,* 1996
Marina (Andrea Pinell), 1994
Mejía, Col. Federico,* 1995
Morales Carazo, Jaime,* 1995–98
Obando y Bravo, Cardinal Miguel,* 1994
Oscar Kilo (Orlando Algava), 1994–98
Paz Garcia, Gen. Policarpo,* 1994
Pryor (Juan Rodríguez Campos), 1996
Rubén (Oscar Sobalvarro), 1992–99
Raul (Rodolfo Robles), 1993
Somarriba, Col. Aureliano,* telephone interview, 1997
Tigre (Oscar Calderón), 1996
Toño (Walter Calderón Lopez), 1995
(Numerous interviews were also held with participants who asked not to
     be named, many still engaged in public life in positions that made them
     prefer not to be identified.)

BOOKS, ARTICLES, AND DISSERTATIONS

Adams, Richard N. *Cultural Surveys of Panama, Nicaragua, Guatemala, El
     Salvador and Honduras.* Washington D.C.: Pan American Sanitary
     Bureau, 1957.
———. "The Dynamics of Societal Diversity: Notes from Nicaragua for a
     Sociology of Survival." *American Ethnologist* 8, no. 1 (1981), 272–340.
Alarcón Ramírez, "Benigno" Dariel. *Memorias de un Soldado Cubano: Vida
     y Muerte la Revolucion.* Edited and translated by Elizabeth Burgos.
     Barcelona, Spain: Tusquets Editores, 1997.
Alvarez Montalvan, Emilio. *Las Fuerzas Armadas en Nicaragua: Sinopsis
     histórico, 1821–1994.* Managua: Ediciones Jorge Eduardo Arellano,
     1994.
Amador A., Freddy Ambrogi, R. Rosario, and Gerardo Ribbink. *La Reforma
     Agraria en Nicaragua de Rojinegro a Violeta.* Managua: Universidad
     Nacional Autonoma de Nicaragua, 1991.
Americas Watch. *Human Rights in Nicaragua.* Washington, D.C., 1988.
Anders, Jon, and E. Bilbao. *Migration, War and Agrarian Reform: Peasant
     Settlements in Nicaragua.* Washington, D.C.: Georgetown University,
     1988.

Anderson, Leslie Elin. "From Quiescence to Rebellion: Peasant Political Activity in Costa Rica and Nicaragua." Ph.D. diss., University of Michigan, 1987.

Anderson, Thomas P. *The Two Revolutions: Nicaragua and Cuba: Similarities and Differences.* Washington, D.C.: Office of Long-Range Assessments and Research, U.S. Department of State, 1983.

Andrews, Christopher, and Vasili Mirokhin. *The Sword and the Shield: The Mitrokhin Archive and the Secret History of the KGB.* New York: Basic Books, 1999.

Anuario estadístico de Nicaragua, 1985. Managua: Instituto Nacional de Estadística y Censo, 1986.

Apuntes: Curso sobre la problemática nacional. Managua: Departamento de Ciencias Sociales, Universidad Autonoma de Nicaragua, 1980.

Arellano, Jorge E. *Nicaragua en los cronistas de Indias.* Managua: Banco de America, Serie cronistas, 1975.

Argüello Argüello, Alfonso. *Historia de León Viejo.* León, Nicaragua: Editorial Antorcha, 1969.

Arnson, Cynthia J. "Congress and Central America: The Search for Consensus." Ph.D. diss., Johns Hopkins University, 1988.

Ashby, Timothy. *The Bear in the Backyard: Moscow's Caribbean Strategy.* Lexington, Ky.: Lexington Books, 1987.

Aspaturain, Vernon V. "Nicaragua Between East and West: The Soviet Perspective." In *Conflict in Nicaragua,* edited by Jiri Valenta and Esperanza Duran. Boston: Allen and Unwin, 1987.

Atlas de la lucha de liberación nacional. Managua: Instituto Geográfico Nacional, 1980.

Bodan Shields, Harry. *Nicaragua: El Teatro de lo Absurdo.* Tibas, Costa Rica: Litografia y Imprenta LILA, 1988.

Bardini, Roberto. *Conexión en Tegucigalpa: El Somocismo en Honduras.* Puebla, Mexico: Editorial Mex-Sur, 1982.

———. *Edén Pastora: Un cero en la historia.* Mexico City: Mex-Sur Editorial, Universidad Nacional Autonoma de Mexico, 1984.

Barrantes, Ramíro. *Evolucíon en el tropico: Los Amerindios de Costa Rica y Panama.* San José, Costa Rica: Editorial de la Universidad de Costa Rica, 1993.

———. "Mitochondrial DNA 'Clock' for the Entry of Amerinds and Its Implications for Timing Their Entry into North America." *Proceedings of the National Academy of Sciences of the United States of America—Genetics* 91 (1994), 158–1162.

Barrantes, Ramíro, María Eugenia Bozzoli, and Patricia Gudino. "Memorias del Primer Simposio Cientifico Sobre Pueblos Indigenas de Costa Rica." San José, Costa Rica: Instituto Geográfico de Costa Rica, 1986.

Barriero, José. *The Disapearance of Raiti: A Human Rights Narrative, Interview with Dr. Kenneth Sarapio.* Highland Park, Md.: Indigenous People's Network, 1985.

Beal, Carleton. *Banana God.* Philadelphia: J.B. Lippincott, 1932.

Bell, Belden, ed. *Nicaragua: An Ally Under Siege.* Washington, D.C.: Council on American Affairs, 1978.

Bell, C. Napier. *Tangaweera: Life and Adventure Among Gentle Savages.* Austin: University of Texas Press, 1989.

Belli, Humberto. *Breaking Faith: The Sandinista Revolution and Its Impact on Freedom and Christian Faith in Nicaragua.* Westchester, Ill.: Puebla Institute, 1985.

———. "Christianity and Sandinismo." In *Voices Against the State: Nicaraguan Opposition to the FSLN,* edited by Steven Blakemore. Coral Gables, Fla.: University of Miami, 1986.

Bendaña, Alejandro. *Una tragedia campesina: Testimonios de la Resistencia.* Managua: Editora de Ante, 1991.

Bengoechea, Adolfo J. *Distrito minero del Noreste.* Managua: Servicio Geológico Nacional, 1963.

Bermúdez Varela, Enrique ("Comandante 3-80"). "The Contras' Valley Forge: How I View the Nicaragua Crisis." *Policy Review,* Summer 1998, no. 45 (1998), 56–62.

———. "The Nicaraguan Resistance at a Crossroads." *Strategic Review* 17, no. 2 (1989), 9–17.

Biderman, Jaime M. "Class Structure, The State and Capitalist Development in Nicaraguan Agriculture." Ph.D. diss., University of California, Berkeley, 1982.

Bilbao E., Jon Anders, Antonio Belli, Eduardo Rivas, and D. Cisneros. *Migration, War and Agrarian Reform: Peasant Settlements in Nicaragua.* Washington, D.C.: Georgetown University, 1988.

Billig, Michael. *Social Psychology and Intergroup Relations.* London: Academic Press, 1976.

Blakemore, Steven, ed. *Voices Against the State: Nicaraguan Opposition to the FSLN.* Coral Gables, Fla.: University of Miami, 1986.

Bloque Opositor del Sur (BOS). *Doce apuntes acerca del B.O.S.* Unpublished, n.d.

B'nai B'rith. *Bibliography of Anti-Semitism.* New York: B'nai B'rith, 1984.

———. *A White Paper on the Sandinistas and Jews.* New York: Anti-Defamation League, 1986.

Bolivar Juarez, Orient. *Causas de la Creacion, Supresion y Restablecimiento del Departamento de Esteli a fines del siglo XIX.* Managua: Centro de Investigaciones Históricas de Nicaragua, 1995.

Bonfill Batalla, Guillermo. *Mexico profundo: Una civilizacion negada.* Mexico City: Editorial Grijalbo, 1990.

Borge, Tomás. *The Patient Impatience.* East Haven, Conn.: Curbstone Press, 1992.

Borge Martinez, Tomás. *Carlos, the Dawn is No Longer Beyond Our Reach.* Vancouver, Can.: New Star Books, n.d.

Bourgois, Phillipe. "Class, Ethnicity, and the State Among the Miskitu Amerindians of Northeastern Nicaragua," *Latin American Perspectives* vol. 3, no. 2 (1981), 22–39.

Bovallius, Carl. *Nicaraguan Antiquities.* Stockholm, Sweden: P.A. Norstedt & Soner, Kongl. Boktryckeriet, 1886.

Brody, Reed. *Contra Terror in Nicaragua: Report of a Fact Finding Mission: Sept. 1984–Jan. 1985.* Boston: South End Press, 1985.

Brooks, David C. "U.S. Marines, Miskitos, and the Hunt for Sandino: The Rio Coco Patrol in 1928." *Journal of Latin American Studies* 21, no. 2 (1989), 311–43.

Brown, Timothy C. "Advice to Aleman: Don't Cuddle a Cobra." *Wall Street Journal,* 11 April 1997, A15.

———. *Causes of Continuing Conflict in Nicaragua: A View from the Radical Middle.* Stanford: Hoover Institution, Stanford University, 1995.

———. "Nahuas, Gachupines, Patriarchs and Piris: Nicaraguan History through Highlands Peasant Eyes." *Journal of American Culture* 2, no. 4 (1997), 97–111.

———. "Realist Revolutions: Free Trade, Open Economies, Participatory Democracy and Their Impact on Latin American Politics." *Policy Studies Review* 15, no. 2/3 (1998), 35–62.

———. "The United States and Nicaragua: Inside the Carter and Sandinista Administrations." *Journal of Interamerican Studies and World Affairs* 36, no. 2 (1994), 207–19.

———. "Who Will Keep Nicaragua's October Elections Honest?" *Wall Street Journal,* 11 October 1996, sec. A, p. 1.

———. "Women Unfit for Combat? Au Contraire!" *Wall Street Journal,* 30 September 1997, sec. A, p. 15.

———, ed. *When the AK-47s Fall Silent: Revolutionaries, Guerrillas and the Dangers of Peace.* Stanford: Hoover Institution Press, 2000.

Buciak, Elja A. "The Sandinista Revolution and the Poor: Basic Needs and Political Participation in Nicaragua." Ph.D. diss., University of Iowa, 1987.

———. *Sandinista Communism and Rural Nicaragua.* New York: Praeger, 1990.

Bulmer-Thomas, Victor. *The Political Economy of Central America Since 1920.* Cambridge: Cambridge University Press, 1987.

Burns, E. Bradford. *Patriarch and Folk: The Emergence of Nicaragua, 1798–1858*. Cambridge: Harvard University Press, 1991.

Buvollens, Hans Petter."The Miskitu-Sandinista Conflict: International Concerns and Outside Actors." In *Ethnic Conflicts in Human Rights*. Oslo: Norwegian University Press, 1987.

Cabesteros, Teofilo. *Blood of the Innocents: Victims of the Contra War in Nicaragua*. New York: Orbis Books, 1985.

Cabezas, Omar. *Fire from the Mountain*. New York: Crown Publishers, 1985.

Camacho Navarro, Enrique. *Los usos de Sandino*. Mexico City: Universidad Nacional Autonoma de Mexico, 1991.

Cardenal Chamorro, Roberto. *Lo que se quiso ocultar: 8 anos de censura Sandinista*. San José, Costa Rica: Editorial Libro Libre, 1989.

Carr, Archie. *High Jungles and Low*. Gainesville: University of Florida Press, 1953.

Carrera, Alvaro [Joaquin]. *Nicaragua Frente Sur: Diario de guerra*. Caracas, Venezuala: Editorial Carlos Aponte, 1980.

Carrión Montoya, Luís. *La ruta del Comandante Pancho*. Managua: Nueva Nicaragua, 1992.

Castellón, Hildebrando H. A. *Biografia de Bernabé Somoza*. Managua: Editorial San Enrique, 1963.

Castillo Rivas, Donald, ed. *Centroamerica mas alla de la crisis*. Mexico City.: Ediciones SIAP, 1983.

————. *Gringos, Contras y Sandinistas: Testimonio de la guerra civil en Nicaragua*. Bogota, Colombia: T/M Editores, 1993.

Central American Historical Institute. "Pentecostals in Nicaragua." *Update* vol. 6 (no. 8), Georgetown University Intercultural Center, March 1987.

Centro de Estudios Internacionales. *Hablan los demovilizados de guerra: Nicaragua, El Salvador y Mozambique*. Managua: CEI, 1995.

Centro de Investigaciones y Estudios para la Reforma Agraria (CIERA). *La guerra imperialista: Organizacion y participacion popular en el campo*. Managua: CIERA, 1989.

————. *La Mosquitia en la Revolucion*. Managua: CIERA, Coleccion Blas Real Espinola, 1981.

————. *La reforma agraria en Nicaragua: 1979–1989: Economia campesina*. Managua: CIERA, 1990.

Centro Nacional de Planificación de Apoyo de Desarrollo (CENPAP). *Informe evaluativo de las actividades realizadas por el CENPAP: Septiembre 1990–Septiembre 1992*. Managua: CENPAP, November 1992.

Chamorro, Edgar. *Packaging the Contras: A Case of CIA Disinformation*. New York: Institute for Media Analysis, Monograph Series No. 2, 1987.

Chamorro Cardenal, Jaime. *Frente a dos dictaduras: La lucha por la libertad de expresion*. San José, Costa Rica: Libro Libre, 1987.

Chamorro Cardenal, Pedro Joaquín. *Estirpe sangriente los Somoza.* Mexico City: Editorial Patria y Libertad, 1957.

―――. *La patria de Pedro: El pensamiento de Pedro Joaquín Chamorro.* Managua: La Prensa, 1987.

Chamorro Coronel, Edgardo. *Miami: Secretos de un exilio.* Managua: Editorial El Amanecer, 1988.

Chapman, Anne. "An Historical Analysis of the Tropical Forest Tribes on the Southern Border of Mesoamerica." Ph.D. diss., Columbia University, 1958.

Child, Jack, ed. *Conflict in Central America.* New York: St. Martin's Press, 1986.

Christian, Shirley. "Decade of Disasters." *The New Republic,* 29 August 1988, 44–49.

―――. *Nicaragua: Revolution in the Family.* New York: Random House, 1985.

Clarridge, Duane. *A Spy for All Seasons: My Life in the CIA.* New York: Scribners, 1997.

Close, David. *Nicaragua: Politics, Economics and Society.* London/New York: Pinter Books, 1985.

Colburn, Forrest D. *Post-Revolutionary Nicaragua: State, Class, and the Dilemmas of Agrarian Policy.* Berkeley: University of California Press, 1986.

Collins, Joseph. *Nicaragua: What Difference Could a Revolution Make?* 3d ed. New York: Grove Weidenfeld, 1986.

Comisión Nacional de Promoción y Protección de los Derechos Humanos. *Ataques contrarevolucionarios a la poblacion civil Nicaragüense.* Unpublished, Managua, 1988.

Constenla Umaña, Adolfo. "Rasgos caracterizadores de la cultura Guatusa tradicional." *Estudios Varios Sobre Las Lenguas Chibchas de Costa Rica.* San José: Editorial de la Universidad de Costa Rica, 1990.

―――. *Las lenguas del area intermedia: Introduccion a su estudio areal.* San José: Editorial de la Universidad de Costa Rica, 1991.

Conzemius, Eduardo. *Ethnographical Survey of the Miskito and Sumu Indians of Nicaragua and Honduras.* Washington, D.C.: Smithsonian Institution, 1921.

Cortéz y Lárraz, Pedro. *Descripcion geografico-moral de la Diocesis de Goathemala.* Vol. 1. Guatemala City: Sociedad Geografia y Historia, June 1958.

Cottam, Martha L. "The Carter Administration's Policy Towards Nicaragua: Images, Goals, and Tactics." *Political Science Quarterly* 42, no. 2 (spring 1992), 123–47.

Cox, Jack. *Requiem for the Tropics.* Evanston/New York/Miami: UCA Books, 1987.

Crawley, Eduardo. *Nicaragua in Perspective.* New York: St. Martin's Press, 1984.

Cruz, Arturo, Jr. *Memoirs of a Counter-Revolutionary.* New York, Doubleday, 1989.

Cruz Sequiero, Arturo J. *Nicaragua's Continuing Struggle.* New York: Freedom House, 1988.

Cuadra, Pablo Antonio. *El Nicaragüense.* 13th ed. San José, Costa Rica: EDUCA, 1976.

Daly, Martin. *Sex, Evolution and Behavior.* 2d ed. Boston: Willard Grant Press, 1983.

Daly, Martin, and Margo Wilson. *Homicide.* New York: Aldine de Gruyter Press, 1988.

Davies, James Chowning. *When Men Revolt—And Why: A Reader in Political Violence and Revolution.* New York: The Free Press, 1971.

Day, Peter. "Miskito Power: Back to the British Main." *Quadrant* (January/February 1988), 27–37.

Deighton, Jane, Rossana Horsley, Sarah Stewart, and Cathy Cain. *Sweet Ramparts: Women in Revolutionary Nicaragua.* London: War on Want, 1983.

Denevan, William M. *The Native Population of the Americas in 1492.* Madison: University of Wisconsin Press, 1992.

———, ed. *The Upland Pine Forest of Nicaragua: A Study in Cultural Plant Geography.* Berkley: University of California, 1961.

De Stephano, Gian Franco, and Jorge Jenkins Molieri. "Contributo per uno studio antropologico comparitivo delle popolazioni dei Nicaragua." Atti del XII Congresso Internazionali degli Americanisti, Geneva/Rome, 1972.

Diaz Briquet, Sergio. *Conflict in Central America: The Demographic Dimension.* Washington, D.C.: Population Reference Bureau, 1986.

Dickey, Christopher. *With the Contras: A Reporter in the Wilds of Nicaragua.* New York: Simon and Schuster, 1987.

Diederich, Bernard. *Somoza and the Legacy of U.S. Involvement in Central America.* New York: Elsevier-Dutton, 1981.

Dillon, Sam. *Comandos: The CIA and Nicaragua's Contra Rebels.* New York: Henry Holt, 1991.

Dixon, Marlene, ed. *Revolution and Intervention in Central America.* San Francisco: Synthesis Press, 1981.

Dixon, Marlene, and Susanne Jonas, eds. *Nicaragua under Siege.* San Francisco: Synthesis Press, 1983.

Dodson, Michael. *Nicaragua: The Struggle for the Church.* Chapel Hill: University of North Carolina Press, 1986.

Dodson, Michael, and Laura Nuzzi O'Shaughnessy. *Nicaragua's Other Revolution.* Chapel Hill: University of North Carolina Press, 1990.

Dozier, Craig L. *Nicaragua's Mosquito Shore.* Montgomery: University of Alabama Press, 1985.

Early, Stephen. *Arms and Politics in Nicaragua and Costa Rica.* Albuquerque: University of New Mexico, Research Paper, series no. 9, 1982.

Economic Commission on Latin America. *Human Resources of Central America, Panama and Mexico, 1950–80.* New York: United Nations (ECLA), 1960.

Eich, Deiter, and Carlos Rincon. *The Contras: Interviews with Anti-Sandinistas.* San Francisco: Synthesis Press, 1985.

Enriquez, Laura J. *Harvesting Change: Labor and Agrarian Reform in Nicaragua, 1979–90.* Chapel Hill: University of North Carolina Press, 1991.

Escobar, Lincoln, Olga Marta Valverde, and Oscar Mario Rojas. "Situacion de los habitantes de la zona del Caribe de Nicaragua: Antes y ahora." Master's thesis, Universidad de Costa Rica, 1983.

Esquivel Alfaro, José Enrique. *La participacion politica de Costa Rica en el derrocamiento de la dictadura Somocista en Nicaragua.* San José, Costa Rica: Libro Libre, 1992.

Farhi, Farideh. *States and Urban-Based Revolutions: Iran and Nicaragua.* Urbana: University of Illinois Press, 1990.

Findling, John E. *Close Neighbors, Distant Friends: United States–Central America Relations.* New York: Greenwood Press, 1987.

Facultad Centroamericana de Ciencias Sociales (FLACSO). *Centroamerica en Cifras.* San José, Costa Rica: Editorial IICA, 1991.

Fonseca Amador, Carlos Luís. *Un Nicaragüense en Moscu.* Managua: Publicaciones Unidad, 1958.

———. *Obras: Viva Sandino.* Vol. 2. Managua: Editorial Nueva Nicaragua, 1985.

Fowler, William R. *The Cultural Evolution of Ancient Nahua Civilizations: The Pipil-Nicarao of Central America.* Norman: University of Oklahoma Press, 1989.

———. "Ethnohistorical Sources on the Pipil-Nicarao of Central America: A Critical Essay." *Ethnohistory* 32, no. 1 (1985), 37–60.

Gamboa, Francisco. *Como fue que no hicimos la Revolucion.* San José, Costa Rica: Editorial Universidad Estatal a Distancia, 1991.

Gámez, José Dolores. *Historia de Nicaragua desde los tiempos prehistoricos.* Managua: Tipografia de El Pais, 1889.

García Bresso, Javier. "Los Nicarao: Una sociedad en los umbrales del estado". *Encuentro* (January–April 1987), 9–30.

Garcia Gutierrez, Terencio. *Habla un testigo de la lucha en Nicaragua.* Mexico City: Costa-Amic Editores, 1983.

Garvin, Glenn. *Everybody Had His Own Gringo: The CIA and the Contras.* Riverside, N.J.: Brassey's, 1992.

Goldwert, Marvin. "The Constabulary in the Dominican Republic and Nicaragua: Progeny and Legacy of United States Intervention." Ph.D. diss., University of Florida, 1962.

Gonzalez, Edward. *Reflections on Nicaragua and the Cuban Model.* Santa Monica, Calif.: RAND Corporation.

Gorman, Stephen M. *Social Change and Political Revolution: The Case of Nicaragua.* Albuquerque: University of New Mexico, 1984.

Gould, Jeffrey L. *To Die This Way: Nicaraguan Indians and the Myth of Mestisaje.* Chapel Hill: University of North Carolina Press, 1988.

————. *To Lead as Equals: Rural Protest and Political Consciousness in Chinandega, Nicaragua, 1912–1979.* Chapel Hill: University of North Carolina Press, 1990.

————. "La Raza Rebelde: Las luchas de la comunidad indigena de Subtiava, Nicaragua: 1900–1960." Revista de Historia. Universidad Nacional de Costa Rica, vol. 21/22, 1990.

————. "*!Vana Ilusion!* The Highlands Indians of Nicaragua and the Myth of Nicaraguan Mestiza, 1880–1925." *Hispanic American Historical Review* 73, no. 3 (1993), 393–430.

Government of Nicaragua, Instituto Nacional de Estadística y Censo [INEC]. *Anuario Estadístico de Nicaragua 1985.* Managua: INEC, 1985.

————. Ministerios de Bienestar Social, Educación, y Salud. *Encuesta a Municipios y comunidades S/Recursos Sociodem. Disponibles.* Project NIC/92 FNUAP/OIM, Managua, 6 April 1996.

"Gral. Cuadra promete lealtad al nuevo gobierno." *La Prensa* (Managua newspaper), 19 October 1996, sec. A, p. 10.

Guardia Nacional de Nicaragua. *Codigo Juridico-Militar de la Guardia Nacional de Nicaragua.* Managua: Cuartel General, Guardia Nacional de Nicaragua, Lomas de Tiscapa, 1948.

Guerrero Castillo, Julian N., and Lola Soriano de Guerrero. *Boaco: Estudio monografico.* Managua: Tipografia Alemana, 1957.

————. *Caciques heroicos de Centroamerica: Rebelión indigena en 1,881 y expulsion de los Jesuitas.* Boaco, Nicaragua: n.p., 1982.

————. *Chinandega: Monografia.* Managua: Coleccion Nicaragua, 1964.

————. *Managua en sus 40 siglos de existencia.* Managua: Tipografia Valdez, Valdez y Compania, 1994.

————. *Monografia del Departamento de Jinotega.* Managua: Ednaluf, 1966.

————. *Monografía de Chontales.* Managua: Colección Nicaragua, no. 11, 1969.

————. *Monografia de Rivas.* Managua: Banco Nacional, 1966.

————. *Monografia de Estelí.* Managua: Banco Nacional, 1967.

————. *Monografia de Madríz.* Managua: Banco Nacional, 1972.

————. *Monografia de Matagalpa.* Managua: Banco Nacional, 1967.

————. *Las 9 tribus indigenas de Nicaragua*. Managua: Banco Nacional, 1989.

————. *Nueva Segovia: Monografia*. Managua: Litografia y Editora Arte Gráfica, 1969.

————. *100 Biografias Centroamericanas*. Vols. 1 and 2. Managua: Casa de Arte y Cultura, 1971.

Guevara, Ernesto ("Ché"). *The Bolivian Diary of Ernesto Ché Guevara*. Edited by Mary-Alice Waters and translated by Michael Taber. New York: Pathfinder Press, 1994.

Guillen de Herrera, Celia. *Nueva Segovia*. Nueva Segovia, Nicaragua: Tipografia Telpaneca, 1945.

Gurr, Ted Robert. *Why Men Rebel*. Princeton: Princeton University Press, 1970.

Gutierrez, Pedro Rafael. *Calero, El Contra*. San José, Costa Rica: Ediciones Lena, 1987.

Gutman, Roy. *Banana Diplomacy: The Making of American Policy in Nicaragua, 1981–87*. New York: Simon and Schuster, 1988.

Handbook on Honduras: Democracy, Defense, Development, Diplomacy. Tegucigalpa, Honduras: United States Embassy, winter 1987/88.

Harris, Richard L., and Carlos M. Vilas, eds. *Nicaragua: A Revolution Under Siege*. London: Zed Books, 1985.

Helms, Mary W. *Asang: Culture Contact in a Miskito Community*. Gainesville: University of Florida Press, 1971.

————. *Middle America: A Cultural History of Heartland and Frontiers*. Englewood Cliffs, N.J.: Prentice-Hall, 1975.

Helms, Mary W., and Franklin O. Loveland. *Frontier Adaptations in Lower Central America*. Philadelphia: Institute for Study of Human Issues, 1976.

Hernández Sancho, Plutarco Elías. *El FSLN por dentro: Relato de un combatiente*. San José, Costa Rica: Trejos Hermanos, 1982.

————. "Reflections on the Past: My Journey from Revolution to Democracy." In *When the AK-47s Fall Silent: Revolutionaries, Guerrillas and the Dangers of Peace*, edited by Timothy C. Brown. Stanford: Hoover Institution Press, 2000.

Herrera Zúñiga, Norberto. "Nicaragua from Right to Left." *Causa USA Report*. September 1987.

Herrera Zúñiga, René. *Relaciones internacionales y poder politico en Nicaragua*. Mexico City: Colegio de Mexico, 1991.

Hermann, Margaret, ed. *Political Psychology*. San Francisco: Jossey-Bass, 1986.

Hersey, Paul, and Kenneth H. Blanchard. *Management of Organizational Behavior: Utilizing Human Resources*. Englewood Cliffs, N.J.: Prentice Hall, 1993.

Hodges, Donald C. *Sandino's Communism: Spiritual Politics in the Twenty-First Century*. Austin: University of Texas Press, 1992.

Horowitz, Donald L. *Ethnic Groups in Conflict*. Berkeley: University of California Press, 1985.

Houtart, Francois. *Campesinos y cultura: Analisis de los perfiles culturales de una población campesina Nicaragüense*. Louvaine-la-Neuve, Belgium: Centre Tricontinental, 1988.

Houtart, Francois, and Genevieve Lemercinier. *El campesino como actor: Sociologia de una comarca de Nicaragua*. Managua: Ediciones Nicarao, 1992.

Howell, William Hickling, ed. *Prescott: The Conquest of Peru, the Conquest of Mexico, and Other Selections*. New York: Washington Square Press, 1966.

Iams, Robert G. *Export Agriculture and the Crisis in Central America*. Chapel Hill: University of North Carolina Press, 1986.

Ibarra, Eugenia. "Los Matagalpa a principios del siglo XVI: Aproximación a los relaciones interetnicas en Nicaragua (1522–1580)." *Vinculos*, Revista de Antropologia del Museo National de Costa Rica, 18/19, no. 1/2 (1992–93), 229–43.

Incer, Jaime. *Crónicos de viajeros: Nicaragua*. San José, Costa Rica: Libro Libre, 1990.

———. *Nicaragua: Viajes, rutas y encuentros, 1502–1832*. San José, Costa Rica: Libro Libre, 1993.

———. *Nueva Geografia*. Managua: Editorial Recalde, 1970.

———. *Toponimias indigena de Nicaragua*. San José, Costa Rica: Libro Libre, 1985.

Instituto de Estudios del Sandinismo. *La insurreccion Popular Sandinista en Masaya*. Managua: Editores Nueva Nicaragua, 1982.

———. *El Sandinismo: Documentos basicos*. Managua: Editora Nueva Nicaragua, 1983.

———. *!Y se armo la runga . . . !* Managua: Editorial Nuevo Nicaragua, 1982.

Jenkins Molieri, Jorge. *El desafio indigena en Nicaragua: El caso de la Moskitia*. Managua: Editorial Vanguardia, 1986.

Jirón, Manuel. *Quien es quién en Nicaragua*. San José, Costa Rica: Editorial Radio Amor, 1986.

Jones, Jeff, ed. *Brigadista: Harvest and War in Nicaragua*. New York: Praeger, 1986.

Kagan, Robert. *A Twilight Struggle: American Power and Nicaragua, 1977–1990*. New York: The Free Press, 1996.

Karnes, Thomas. *The Failure of Union: Central America, 1824–1960*. Chapel Hill: University of North Carolina Press, 1961.

Kasten, Aleyda Veru. "Extent and Nature of the Soviet Presence in Nicaragua." Ph.D. diss., Georgetown University, 1990.

Keller, Frank Beat. *Wiwilí—1980: Monografia de un municipio Nicaraguense en cambio*. Frankfurt/Main, Germany: Vervuert, 1986.

Kinzer, Stephen. *Blood of Brothers*. New York: G.P. Putnam, 1991.

Kirkpatrick, Jeanne J. *The Kennedy-Kruschchev Pact and the Sandinistas*. Washington, D.C.: Cuban American National Foundation, 1985.

Kissinger, Henry. *Report of the President's Binational Commission on Central America*. New York: MacMillan, 1984.

Koehler, John O. *STASI: The Untold Story of the East German Secret Police*. Boulder, Colo.: Westview Press, 1999.

Kornbluh, Peter, ed. *The Secret CIA Report on the Invasion of Cuba*. New York: The New Press, 1998.

Kottack, Conrad Philip. *Anthropology: The Explanation of Human Diversity*. New York: Random House, 1974.

Lafaye, J. *Mesiás, Cruzadas, Utopias*. Mexico City: Ediciones Gallenard, 1984.

———. *Quetzalcoatl y Guadeloupe*. Mexico City: Ediciones Gallenard, 1974.

LaFeber, Walter. *Inevitable Revolutions: The United States and Central America*. New York: W.H. Norton, 1983.

Laínez, F. *Nicaragua: Colonialismo Español, Yánqui y Ruso*. Guatemala City: Serviprensa Centroamericana, 1987.

Lake, Anthony. *Somoza Falling*. Boston: Houghton Miflin, 1989.

Lancaster, Roger N. *Life is Hard: Machismo, Danger, and the Intimacy of Power in Nicaragua*. Berkeley: University of California Press, 1992.

———. "Skin Color, Race and Racism in Nicaragua." *Ethnology* [vol., issue?] 1991,[p.nos?].

Landsberger, Henry A. *Latin American Peasant Movements*. Ithaca: Cornell University Press, 1969.

Langley, Lester D. *Banana Wars: United States Intervention in the Caribbean, 1898–1934*. 2d ed. Lexington: University Press of Kentucky, 1985.

Lanuza Matamoros, Alberto. "Estructuras socioeconomicas: Poder y estado en Nicaragua, 1821–1875." Ph.D. diss., University of Costa Rica, 1986.

Le Blanc, Paul Joseph. "Workers and Revolution: A Comparative Study of Bolshevik Russia and Sandinista Nicaragua." Ph.D. diss., University of Pittsburgh, 1989.

León-Portilla, Miguel. *Religión de los Nicarao: Analisis y comparación de tradiciones culturales Nahua*. Mexico City: Universidad Nacional Autonoma de Mexico, 1972.

Leonard, Thomas M. *Central America and U.S. Policies, 1820s–1980s*. Claremont, Calif.: Regina Books, 1985.

Luciak, Ilja A. *The Sandinista Legacy: Lessons from a Political Economy in Transition*. Gainseville: University of Florida Press, 1995.

Macauley, Neill. *The Sandino Affair*. Chicago: Quadrangle, 1967.

McCarger, James. *El Salvador and Nicaragua: The AFL-CIO Views on the Controversy.* Washington, D.C.: AFL-CIO, 1985.

MacLeod, Murdo J. *Spanish Central America: A Socioeconomic History, 1520–1720.* Berkeley: University of California, 1973.

MacRenato, Ternot. "Somoza: Seizure of Power, 1926–1939." Ph.D. diss., University of California, San Diego, 1991.

Mantica, Carlos. *El habla Nicaragüense: Estudio morfologico y semantico.* San José, Costa Rica: Trejos Hermanos, 1973.

Manuales de sabotaje y guerra psicologica de la CIA para derrocar al gobierno Sandinista. Madrid: Editorial Fundamentos, 1985.

Marín, Raúl. "Los ultimos 'Paladines'." *Pensamiento Proprio* (May 1990).

Martínez, Abelino. *Las sectas en Nicaragua.* San José, Costa Rica: Editorial DEI, 1989.

Matagalpa, Juan [pseud.]. *Juan Matagalpa: Sandino, Los Somoza y Los Nueve Comandantes Sandinistas.* Tegucigalpa, Honduras: Editorial Honduras Industrial, 1984.

Maturana, Sergio. *Tenencia de la tierra en Centroamerica.* Mexico City: United Nations, UN/UNESCO/SS/SRRL/C4, 19 September 1962.

Mayorga-Cortés, Roberto. "Nicaragua pide elecciones libres, garantizadas y transparentes." *Diario Las America,* 19 October 1997, A4.

Mendieta Alfaro, Roger. *Olama y Mojellones.* Managua: Impresiones CARQUI, 1992.

Merrill, Tim L., ed. *Nicaragua: A Country Study.* Washington, D.C.: Library of Congress, 1993.

Meza, Victor, Philip Shepherd, and Medea Benjamin. *Honduras-Estados Unidos: Subordinación y crisis.* Tegucigalpa, Honduras: Centro de Documentación, 1988.

Millett, Richard Leroy. *Guardians of the Dynasty.* Introduction by Miguel d'Escoto. Maryknoll, N.Y.: Orbis Press, 1977.

Miranda, Roger, and William Ratliff. *The Civil War in Nicaragua: Inside the Sandinistas.* New Brunswick, N.J.: Transaction Publishers, 1993.

Morales Carazo, Jaime. *La Contra: Anatomia de una multiple traición: Bahia de cochinos de Reagan?* Mexico City: Editorial Planeta, 1989.

———. *!Mejor que Somoza cualquier cosa!: Revolucion Nicaragüense y Sandinismo: La otra cara de la moneda.* Mexico City: Editorial Continental, 1986.

———. *La noche del presidente.* Mexico City: Editorial Planeta, 1991.

———. "Retratos de la Contra." *Liberacion* 23/24 (November 1986).

Morales Castillo, Linda. "La Castilla" and "Asi mataron al Comandante Bravo." *Estrelle de Nicaragua,* 1–15 May 1994, 1a; 16–31 May 1994, 1a.

Musicant, Ivan. *The Banana Wars.* New York: MacMillan, 1990.

Newson, Linda. *Indian Survival in Colonial Nicaragua*. Norman: University of Oklahoma, 1987.

Nicaragua poblacion absoluta y relativa: Indicadores basicos de programación: Republicas y regiones. Managua: Ministerio de Salud, October 1989.

Nietschmann, Bernard. *Between Land and Water: The Subsistence Ecology of the Miskito Indians of Eastern Nicaragua*. New York: Seminar Press, 1973.

————. *Caribbean Edge: The Coming of Modern Times to Isolated People and Wildlife*. New York: Bobbs-Merrill, 1979.

————. "A Close Shave Sandinista Style." Occasional paper, University of California [?], Berkeley, April 1988.

Nolan, David. *FSLN: The Ideology of the Sandinistas and the Nicaraguan Revolution*. Coral Gables: University of Miami, 1981.

North, Oliver L. *Under Fire*. New York: HarperCollins, 1991.

Nosotros los Contra. Panama City: Editora Quibian, 1986.

Nuñez, Orlando, ed. *La guerra en Nicaragua*. Managua: CIPRES, 1991.

O'Brien, Connor Cruise. "God and Man in Nicaragua." *The Atlantic Monthly*, August 1986, 50–72.

Omang, Joanne. *A Historical Background to the CIA's Nicaragua Manual*. New York: Random House, 1985.

Operation Zapata: The "Ultrasensitive" Report and Testimony of the Board of Inquiry on the Bay of Pigs. Introduction by Luis Aguilar. Frederick, MD: Alethia Books, 1981.

Organization of American States (OAS). *Demobilizing and Integrating the Nicaraguan Resistance, 1990–1997*. Washington D.C.: General Secretariat of the OAS, 1998.

O'Rourke, P. J. *Holidays in Hell*. New York: The Atlantic Monthly Press, 1988.

Pardo-Maurer, Rogelio. *The Contras, 1980–89: A Special Kind of Politics*. New York: Praeger, 1990.

Parsons, J. J. "Gold Mining in the Nicaraguan Rain Forest." In *Yearbook of the Association of Pacific Coast Geographers*, Corvallis: Oregon State University Press, 1955.

Pastor, Robert A. *Condemned to Repetition: The United States and Nicaragua*. Princeton: Princeton University Press, 1988.

————. *Whirlpool: U.S. Foreign Policy towards Latin America and the Caribbean*. Princeton: Princeton University Press, 1992.

Pastora Gomez, Edén. "Nicaragua 1983–85: Two Years' Struggle Against Soviet Intervention." In *The Transition From Authoritarian Rule to Democracy in the Hispanic World*, ed. Stephen Schwartz. San Francisco: Institute for Contemporary Studies, 1986.

Pataky, Lazlo. *Nicaragua desconocida*. Managua: Editorial Universal, 1956.

Payne, Douglas W. *The Democratic Mask: The Consolidation of the Sandinista Revolution.* New York: Freedom House, 1985.

Pector, Desiré. *Indication approximative de vestiges laissez par les populations Precolombiennes du Nicaragua.* Braine-le-Compt, Belgium: Impression de Chateau Bourget, 1889.

Pellicer, Olga, and Richard M. Fagen, eds. *Centroamerica: Futuro y opciones.* Mexico City: Fondo de Cultura Economica, 1983.

Perez Brignoli, Hector. *A Brief History of Central America.* Berkeley: University of California, 1989.

Pérez Estrada, Francisco. "Breve historia de la tenencia de la tierra en Nicaragua." *Revista Conservadora del Pensamiento Centroamericano* 51 (December 1964), 15–22.

Perpina Grau, Román. *Corología de la población de Nicaragua.* Madrid: Instituto Balmes, 1959.

Pezzullo, Larry and David. *At the Fall of Somoza.* Pittsburgh: University of Pittsburgh Press, 1994.

Phelan, John L. *The Millennial Kingdom of the Franciscans of the New World.* 2d ed. Mexico City: Universidad National Autonoma de Mexico, 1972.

Pisani, Francis. *Los Muchachos.* Managua: Editorial Vanguardia, 1989.

———. *Prophets in Combat: The Nicaraguan Journal of Bishop Pedro Casaldaliga.* Managua: Editorial Vanguardia, 1983.

Pomares Ordoñez, Germán. *El Danto: Algunas correrias y andanzas.* Managua: Editorial Nueva Nicaragua, 1989.

Radell, David. *Historical Geography of Western Nicaragua: The Spheres of Influence of Leon, Granada and Managua 1515–1965.* Berkeley: Office of Naval Research/Department of Geography, University of California, n.d.

Ramírez, Sergio. *Adios muchachos.* Mexico City: Aguilar, 1999.

———. *El pensamiento vivo de Sandino.* San José, Costa Rica: EDUCA, 1974.

Ramírez A., and Julio Sergio. *Nicaragua año 2000: Es posible un acomodo con el FSLN en Nicaragua?* Alajuela, Costa Rica: INCAE Publications, 1988.

Rakowska-Harmstone, Teresa. "Chickens Coming Home to Roost." *Journal of International Affairs* 45, no. 2 (1992), 519–48.

Reimann, Elizabeth. *La historia de Moises: Yo fui un Paladin de la Libertad.* Mexico City: Ediciones El Caballito, 1986.

Robbins, Thomas, and Dick Anthony. "The Limits of 'Coercive Persuasion' as an Explanation for Conversion to Authoritarian Sects." *Political Psychology* 2, no. 2 (1980), 22–37.

Rokeach, Milton. *The Open and Closed Mind.* New York: Basic Books, 1960.

Romero Vargas, Germán. *Las estructuras sociales de Nicaragua en el siglo XVIII.* Managua: Editorial Vanguardia, 1987.

———. *Persistencia indigena en Nicaragua.* Managua: CIDCA-UCA, 1992.

Ropp, Stephen Chapman. "In Search of the New Soldier: Junior Officers and the Prospect of Social Reform in Panama, Honduras and Nicaragua." Ph.D. diss., University of California, Riverside, 1973.

Ropp, Stephen Chapman, and James A. Morris. *Central America: Crisis and Adaptation.* Albuquerque: University of New Mexico Press, 1984.

Ruchwarger, Gary. *Struggle for Survival: Workers, Women and Class on a Nicaraguan State Farm.* Boulder, Colo.: Westview Press, 1989.

Rushdie, Salman. *The Jaguar Smiles: A Nicaraguan Journey.* New York: Viking, 1987.

Ryan, Stephen. *Ethnic Conflict and International Relations.* Hanover, N.H.: Dartmouth University Press, 1990.

Sanchez Argüello, Hector. *Los Nicaragüenses en Costa Rica.* San José, Costa Rica: ITASA, 1988.

Sand, G. W. *Soviet Aims in Central America: The Case of Nicaragua.* New York: Praeger, 1989.

Schmoolker, Andrew Bard. *The Parable of the Tribes: The Problem of Power in Social Evolution.* Berkeley: University of California, 1984.

Schroeder, Michael J. "Patriots, Peasants and Process: The Denouement of the First Sandinista Revolution, 1927–1934." Occasional paper, History Department, University of Michigan, Ann Arbor, 1992.

Schwartz, Stephen. *A Strange Silence: The Emergence of Democracy in Nicaragua.* San Francisco: ICS, 1992.

Seliktar, Ofira. "Socialization of National Ideology: The Case of Zionist Attitudes among Young Israelis." *Political Psychology* 2, nos. 3–4 (1980), 66–94.

Selzer, Irene. *Cardinal Obando.* Mexico City: Centro de Estudios Ecumenicos, 1989.

Selzer, Gregorio. *El Documento de Santa Fe, Reagan y los derechos humanos.* Mexico City: Alpa Corral Editores, 1988.

———. *El pequeno ejército loco: Operación Mexico-Nicaragua.* Mexico City: Brugero Mexicana de Ediciones, 1980.

Semenario sobre la investigación sociologica y los problemas de la vida rural en America Central, Mexico y la Region del Caribe. United Nations, UNESCO (UN/UNESCO/SS/SRRL/C-4), 19 September 1962.

Serra, Luis. *El movimiento campesino: Su participación durante la Revolucion Sandinista.* Managua: Imprenta UCA, 1991.

Sheehan, Edward R. F. *Agony in the Garden: A Stranger in Central America.* Boston: Houghton Miflin, 1989.

Sherman, William L. *Forced Native Labor in Sixteenth-Century Central America.* Lincoln: University of Nebraska Press, 1979.

Sklener, L. L., and M. L. Wilson. "War Since 1945: Nicaragua, Revolution Betrayed." Quantico, Va.: Marine Corps Command and General Staff College, June 1983.

Somoza Debayle, Anastacio. *Nicaragua Betrayed.* Boston: Western Island Publishing, 1981.

Somoza Garcia, Anastacio. *El verdadero Sandino o el calvario de las Segovias.* 2d ed. Managua: Editorial y Litografia San José, 1976.

Spalding, Rose J., ed. *The Political Economy of Revolutionary Nicaragua.* Boston: Allen and Unwin, 1987.

Spoor, Max. *The State and Domestic Agricultural Markets in Nicaragua: From Intervention to Neo-Liberalism.* New York: St. Martin's Press, 1995.

Squier, Ephraim George. *Nicaragua: Its People, Scenery, and Monuments, and the Interocean Canal.* New York: D. Appleton, 1852.

————. "Observations on the Archeology and Ethnology of Nicaragua." *Transactions of the American Ethnological Society* vol. 3, pt. 1, art. 1, 1853, 85–158.

————. *Waikna, or Adventures on the Mosquito Coast.* New York: Harpers, 1855.

Stanislawski, Dan. *The Transformation of Nicaragua, 1519–1548.* Berkeley: University of California Press, 1983.

Stansifer, Charles L. *The Nicaraguan National Literacy Crusade.* Hanover, N.H.: American Universities Field Staff, 1981–86.

Steward, Julian H. "The Circum-Caribbean Tribes." In *Handbook of South American Indians.* Washington, D.C.: Smithsonian Institution, 1948.

Stone, Doris. *The Archeology of Central and Southern Honduras.* Cambridge, Mass.: Peabody Museum of Archaeology and Ethnology, 1957.

Stone, Samuel [Zemurray]. *The Heritage of the Conquistadores: Ruling Classes in Central American from the Conquistadores to the Sandinistas.* Lincoln: University of Nebraska Press, 1990.

Strachan, Harry W. *Family and Other Business Groups in Economic Development: The Case of Nicaragua.* New York: Praeger, 1976.

Suñol, Julio. *Insurrección en Nicaragua.* San José: Editorial Costa Rica, 1981.

Suri Quesada, Emilio. *Y Los Cachorros andan sueltos.* Havana, Cuba: Editora Politica, 1987.

Taylor, John Robert, Jr. *Agricultural Settlements and Development in Eastern Nicaragua.* Madison: University of Wisconsin Press, 1969.

Tinoco Zeledón, Lt. Fidel, with "Mike Lima" (Luis Moreno Payan). "Agenda Perpetua." Unpublished combat diary. Author's collection.

Tippin, G. Lee. *The Contra Connection.* Canton, Ohio.: Daring Books, 1988.

Tirado, Manlio. *La Revolucion Sandinista: La lucha por el poder.* Mexico City: Editorial Nuestro Tiempo, 1983.

Torres Espinosa, Edelberto, ed. *Sandino y sus pares.* Managua: Editorial Nueva Nicaragua, 1983.

Torres Rivas, Edelberto. *Crisis en el poder en Centroamerica.* San José, Costa Rica: EDUCA, 1989.

United Nations Development Program (UNDP). *Diagnóstico Básico de las Municipalidades.* 8 vols. Managua, July 1994.

————. *Nicaragua: Población absoluto y relativa: Indicadores básicos de programación, Republicas y Regiones.* Managua: UNDP, 1996.

Universidad Para La Paz. *Los refugiados Centroamericanos.* Heredia, Costa Rica: Universidad Nacional, 1987.

Urcuyo Maliaño, and Francisco Solís. *Las ultimas 43 horas en el Bunker de Somoza.* Guatemala City: Editorial Académico Centro Americano, 1979.

U.S. Department of Defense. *Gazetteer of Nicaragua.* Washington, D.C.: Defense Mapping Agency, 1985.

U.S. Embassy Managua. *Nicaragua Economics Fact Sheet.* Managua, March 1997.

Van Tienhoven, Nico A. *Small Holder Farming in Nicaragua.* Kiel, Germany: Wissenschaftsverlag Vauk Kiel, 1981.

Vegas Bolanos, Andres, ed. "Colección Somoza: Documentos para la historia de Nicaragua." Unpublished. Madrid, 1954.

Vilas, Carlos María. "Family Affairs: Class, Lineage and Politics in Contemporary Nicaragua." *Journal of Latin American Studies* 24, no. 2 (1992), 309–41.

————. *Perfiles de la Revolucion Sandinista: Ensayo.* Havana, Cuba: Casa de las Americas, 1984.

————. *The Sandinista Revolution: National Liberation and Social Transformation in Central America.* New York: Monthly Review Press, 1986.

————. *State, Class and Ethnicity in Nicaragua: Capitalist Modernization and Revolutionary Change on the Atlantic Coast.* Boulder, Colo.: Lynn Rienner, 1989.

Volpini, Federico. *Desde Managua.* Barcelona, Spain: Plaza y Janes Editores, 1987.

Von Houwald, Goetz. *Los Alemanes en Nicaragua.* Managua: Ediciones Banco de America, 1975.

Walker, Thomas W. *Nicaragua: The First Five Years.* New York: Praeger, 1985.

Walter, Knut. "The Regime of Anastacio Somoza Garcia and State Formation in Nicaragua, 1936–1956." Ph.D. diss., University of North Carolina, 1987.

————. *The Regime of Anastacio Somoza, 1936–1956.* Chapel Hill: University of North Carolina Press, 1993.

Wheelock Román, Jaime. *Nicaragua: El papel de la Vanguardia*. Mexico City: Editorial Diana, 1989.

――――. *Raices indigenas de la lucha anticolonialista en Nicaragua*. Mexico City: Siglo Veintiuno, 1974.

――――. *La verdad sobre la piñata*. Managua: Editorial El Amanecer, 1991.

White, Richard Alan. *The Morass: United States Intervention in Central America*. New York: Harper and Row, 1984.

Wiarda, Howard J., ed. *Rift and Revolution: The Central American Imbroglio*. Washington, D.C.: American Enterprise Institute, 1984.

Williams, Chester Y. "Presidential Leadership in Nicaragua." Ph.D. diss., Indiana University, 1977.

Williams, Robert G. *Export Agriculture and the Crisis in Central America*. Chapel Hill: University of North Carolina Press, 1986.

Wilson, John F. "Obra Morava en Nicaragua: Trasfondo y breve historia." Ph.D. diss., Semenario Biblico Latinoamericano, San José, Costa Rica, 1975.

Witness for Peace. *Nicaragua: Civilian Victims of the U.S. Contra War, July 1986–January 1987*. Washington, D.C., 1987.

Woodward, Ralph Lee, Jr. *Central America*. Oxford: Oxford University Press, 1985.

――――. *Central America: Historical Perspectives on the Contemporary Crisis*. New York: Greenwood Press, 1988.

――――. *Nicaragua*. Santa Barbara, Calif.: Clio Press, 1983.

――――, ed. *Nicaragua*. World Bibliographical Series, vol. 44. Oxford: Clio Press, 1983.

Woodward, Bob. *Veil: The Secret Wars of the CIA*. New York: Simon and Schuster, 1987.

Ycaza, Alberto. "El Güegüense: Trato y Contrato." *Pensamiento Centroamericano*, vol. LXIV, 1989, 43–50.

Zavala, Silvio. *Los Esclavos Indios en Nueva Espana*. Mexico City: El Colegio Nacional, 1967.

Zub Kurylowicz, Roberto. *Protestantismo y elecciones en Nicaragua: Estudio sobre la estratificación socio-religioso y las actitudes politico: electorales de los Protestantes en Nicaragua*. Managua: Ediciones Nicarao, 1993.

UNPUBLISHED MANUSCRIPTS

Alfaro Alvarado, Mario. "Asi Es Fuerza Democratica Nicaragüense." Hoover Institution Archives, Stanford University, n.d.

Fagoth Mueller, Stedman. "La Moskitia." N.p., n.d.

Fonseca Amador, Carlos Luís. "Historia de la Revolucion Sandinista."
Probably San José, Costa Rica, ca. 1970, author's collection.

———. "Historia de Nicaragua." With handwritten corrections by
Fonseca Amador. Probably San José, Costa Rica, ca. 1970, author's
collection.

Fuerza Democratica Nicaragüense (FDN). "Historia de Fuerza Democratica Nicaragüense." Yamales Salient, Honduras, n.d.

Junta de Reconstrucción de Matagalpa. "Las milicias en Accion." Matagalpa, Nicaragua, 1982.

Porras Mendieta, Nemesio. "Tenencia de la Tierra en Nicaragua."
Managua, 1962.

Spadafora, Hugo. "Las derrotas Somocistas y Comunistas en Nicaragua."
Panama City, Panama, 1984.

Urbiña Lara, José Manuel. "Libertad o Muerte." San José, Costa Rica, 1988.

INDEX

Detentions of highlander
peasants, 25, 32, 40, 49, 55, 193.
See also Highlander peasant
Resistance to Sandinista
Revolution, causes of
"Dimas" (Pedro Joaquín
González), 41, 45, 47, 52,
239nn.2,3, 241n.20; actions of
MILPAS group of, 26, 29, 32–35;
attack on Quilalí by, 20–21;
death of, 35–37; described,
27–31, 42; growth of Milpas
group of, 32–33; Marina
(common-law wife) on, 24–26;
operational zones of, 66–67;
takes up mantle of El Danto,
23–24
"Dimas Negro" (a.k.a. "Dimas
Sagitario") (Marcos Navarro),
20, 109, 253–54n.20
"Dimas Tigrillo" (a.k.a "Dimas de
Tigrillo") (Francisco Baldivia
Chavarria), 47–48, 67, 239n.2,
240n.13
Diriangen, Nahua chief, 150
Diriangen Regional Command,
60, 96
Disenfranchised. See Censuses;
Elections
"Doctor Javier" (name withheld),
85
"Douglas" (Anroyce Zelaya), 27,
241n.72

Echeverria Brealy, Juan José
("Johnny"), 83, 205, 251n.17
EEBI. See Escuela de Enseñanza
Basica de Infanteria
Ejército de Resistencia
Nicaragüense (ERN). See
Fuerza Democratica
Nicaragüense

Ejército Popular Sandinista (EPS),
35–37, 170, 176, 260n.32;
arsenals of, 81; arms inventory,
225–29; Nuevo Ejército,
precursor of, 16, 40, 54, 238n.16
"El Cadejo" (real name
unknown), 61
"El Chigüin." See Somoza
Portocarrero, Anastacio
El Chipote mountain, Nicaragua,
7, 14–16, 35, 38, 236n.7
"El Coyote" (real name
unknown), early MILPAS, 60
El Cuá Bocay, Nicaragua, 11, 14,
41, 155, 242n.50, 246n.33,
262n.66
"El Danto" (Germán Pomáres),
45, 47, 73, 82, 237n.11,
240nn.7,8, 241n.20; killing of
triggers Contra War, 23–24, 30,
66–67; as godfather of MILPAS,
14, 17, 19–24, 27, 29
Elections, national: of 1990, 178,
182–83; of 1996, 178–80, 182,
184, 188
Elites: 163, 206, 207, 263n.74;
described, 164–65; forced labor
of Indians by causes uprising,
158–59; Nahua, 147; post-
colonial patriarchal, 156–60,
162–63; Spanish colonial,
152–53; try to destroy identity
of Indians, 159, 162–63, 165;
vision of nation-state clashes
with peasant world view,
156–57
El Salvador, 115, 145, 151,
240–41n.18, 249n.10, 257n.4;
and anti-Indian hegemonic
discourse, 159; Comandante
Bravo flees to, 69–72; army
supports, 73